Remaking the Past

JOSEPH N. STRAUS

Remaking the Past

Musical Modernism and the Influence of the Tonal Tradition

Harvard University Press
Cambridge, Massachusetts, and London, England   1990

4p

Publication of this book has been aided by a grant from the Andrew W. Mellon Foundation.

This book is printed on acid-free paper, and its binding materials have been chosen for strength and durability.

Library of Congress Cataloging-in-Publication Data

Straus, Joseph N.
  Remaking the past : musical modernism and the influence of the tonal tradition / Joseph N. Straus.
      p.   cm.
  Includes bibliographical references.
  ISBN 0-674-75990-7 (alk. paper)
    1. Music—20th century—History and criticism.
2. Musical form.   3. Harmony.   4. Melody.
5. Neoclassicism (Music).   I. Title.
ML 197.S767   1990
780'.9'04—dc20   89-24721
                                    CIP
                                    MN

for Sally

Preface

In the first half of the twentieth century, musical life was dominated to an unprecedented degree by the music of the past. Partly as a consequence, musical compositions in that period were remarkably rich in allusions, both overt and concealed, to older music. This book develops a critical framework for interpreting these allusions in works by Stravinsky, Schoenberg, Bartók, Webern, and Berg. Exemplars of musical modernism, they were among the composers of their era best equipped to grapple successfully with a potentially overwhelming musical tradition.

This is in no sense a comprehensive study of their music. Rather, through analysis of a small number of works, I have tried to document their common strategies for coming to terms with earlier music. I have attempted to trace a variety of musical relationships, since these five composers remade their shared tradition at every level of musical structure, from the motive to the large forms.

This book is a study of musical construction, not of compositional psychology or creative process. I describe, in music-structural terms, the ways in which traditional musical elements are incorporated and reinterpreted within post-tonal musical structures. Even when traditional elements are present, it is the post-tonal structures that generally have priority. Composers use their idiomatic post-tonal procedures not only to produce musical coherence but simultaneously to comment ironically on the conventions of the past.

In a musical world as heavily dominated by older music as western Europe in the first part of this century, composers were not free to ignore their heritage. Their need to establish a position within the tradition and to assert their creative independence crucially determined the structure of their music. (Indeed, that conflict is perhaps the central feature of modernism in all of the arts.) This book reveals some of the musical results of their anxious struggle to remake the past.

––––––––––

It is a pleasure to acknowledge a research grant from the American Council of Learned Societies and the many friends and colleagues whose support, advice, and generous criticisms have helped form this book. Allen Forte's advice and guidance were indispensable to me during its long gestation. Peter Burkholder, Paul Cantor, Michael Cherlin, Stephen Dembski, James Gleick, Douglass Green, Martha Hyde, Heather Platt, Esther Schor, and Paul Wilson read part or all of the manuscript and made valuable suggestions. I am deeply grateful to them and hope they will approve a work that so clearly bears their influence. I am indebted to my editors at Harvard University Press, Margaretta Fulton and Elizabeth Hurwit, whose guidance and expert editorial work have shaped this book so much for the better. Sally Goldfarb provided her customary special assistance in matters legal, editorial, and otherwise. This book is gratefully dedicated to her.

––––––––––

Belmont Music Publishers: Little Piano Piece, Op. 19, No. 2; Piano Piece, Op. 11, No. 1; Piano Piece, Op. 33a; Pieces for Male Chorus, Op. 35; String Quartet No. 3; analytical examples from *Style and Idea;* orchestration of Bach, Chorale Prelude.

The example from Schoenberg's Concerto for String Quartet, Copyright G. Schirmer Inc., International Copyright Secured, All Rights Reserved, is reproduced by permission.

The example from Schoenberg, *Fundamentals of Musical Composition,* is reprinted by permission of Faber and Faber Ltd.

Excerpts from the following works are reprinted by permission of Boosey & Hawkes: Bartók, Concerto No. 3; Stravinsky-Bach, *Canonic Variations;* Stravinsky, *Fairy's Kiss, In Memoriam Dylan Thomas,* Octet, *Oedipus Rex, Pulcinella, The Rake's Progress,* Serenade in A, *Symphony of Psalms, Symphonies of Wind Instruments.*

Contents

Remaking the Past

CHAPTER 1

Toward a Theory of Musical Influence

Music composed in the first half of the twentieth century is permeated by the music of the past. Traditional sonorities, forms, and musical gestures pervade even works that seem stylistically most progressive. But no easy accommodation is possible across the stylistic and structural gulf that separates the traditional tonal music of the eighteenth and nineteenth centuries from the new post-tonal music of the twentieth. Sonorities like the triad, forms like the sonata, and structural motions like the descending perfect fifth are too profoundly emblematic of traditional tonal practices to meld quietly into a new musical context. Traditional elements inevitably retain their traditional associations. As a result, they become the locus of a productive musical tension. They evoke the traditional musical world in which they originated, even as they are subsumed within a new musical context. Twentieth-century composers incorporate traditional elements not out of compositional laziness and lack of imagination, and not because those elements fit so seamlessly into their post-tonal musical syntax, but precisely as a way to grapple with their musical heritage. They invoke the past in order to reinterpret it.

The eighteenth and nineteenth centuries are reasonably described as an era of musical common practice, when composers of different nationalities and temperaments nonetheless wrote music that was stylistically and structurally similar in important respects. The twentieth century, in contrast, has apparently been a period of great and increasing diversity of both style and structure. More specifically, music criticism has traditionally divided twentieth-century music into two opposing camps: the neoclassical and the progressive. This dichotomous view crystallized in the music criticism of the 1920s and has remained influential up to the present day. It depicts the neoclassicists (Stravinsky in particular) as attempting to restore and revive aspects of earlier music while the progressives (specifically Schoenberg,

Berg, and Webern) pushed music forward in a direction determined by the historical developments of late nineteenth-century chromaticism. Neoclassical music is seen as relatively simple, static, and objective—as having revived the classical ideals of balance and proportion. Progressive music is seen as relatively complex, developmental, and emotionally expressive—as having extended the tradition of romanticism.[1]

Although the neoclassical-progressive dualism has some undeniable basis in musical practice, it has tended to obscure a more fundamental unity: a common preoccupation with older music and shared musical means for expressing it. The most important and characteristic musical works of the first half of this century incorporate and reinterpret elements of earlier music. This dual process, more than any specific element of style or structure, defines the mainstream of musical modernism. Stravinsky (who had the advantage of living long enough to gain historical perspective on the first half of the century) recognized the futility of distinguishing his own music from that of his great contemporaries based on their uses of the past:

> Every age is a historical unity. It may never appear as anything but either/or to its partisan contemporaries, of course, but semblance is gradual, and in time either and or come to be components of the same thing. For instance, "neo-classic" now begins to apply to all of the between-the-war composers (not that notion of the neo-classic composer as someone who rifles his predecessors and each other and then arranges the theft in a new "style"). The music of Schoenberg, Berg, and Webern in the twenties was considered extremely iconoclastic at that time but these composers now appear to have used musical form as I did, "historically." My use of it was overt, however, and theirs elaborately disguised . . . We all explored and discovered new music in the twenties, of course, but we attached it to the very tradition we were so busily outgrowing a decade before.[2]

Stravinsky recognized that every major composer of his era used material from the past to establish a relationship with the past. He saw that Schoenberg was like him, and like all serious composers, in his need to come to terms with a powerful and living tradition.

> Was I merely trying to refit old ships while the other side—Schoenberg—sought new forms of travel? I believe that this distinction, much traded on a generation ago, has disappeared. (An era is shaped only by hindsight, of course, and hindsight reduces to convenient unities, but all artists know that they are part of the same thing.) Of course I seemed to have exploited an apparent discontinuity, to have made art of the *disjecta membra,* the quotations from other composers, the references to earlier styles ("hints of earlier and other creation"), the detritus that betokened a wreck. But I used it, and anything that came to hand, to rebuild, and I did not pretend to have invented new conveyors or new means of travel. But the true business of the artist *is* to refit old ships. He can say again, in his way, only what has already been said.[3]

REMAKING THE PAST

Stravinsky did not deny the significant stylistic differences between his music and Schoenberg's. At the same time, however, he pointed to crucial shared characteristics. Both composers were engaged in the "true business of the artist," which is to "refit old ships." This process was more overt in the music that is commonly called neoclassical, but it also shaped, in more subtle ways and despite the apparent stylistic diversity, all the most characteristic music from the first part of this century.[4]

Stylistically diverse works may share not only a preoccupation with the past but also musical strategies for its reinterpretation. Recent work in music theory has begun to reveal surprising similarities of structure between so-called neoclassical and so-called progressive music. Pitch-class set theory provides consistent ways of discussing and relating sonorities of any size or structure in any musical context.[5] This theory has spawned a large analytical literature that has grown to encompass not only the Viennese atonalists, for whose music the theory was originally designed, but Stravinsky and Bartók as well. At the same time, analysts have begun to recognize their obligation, following Heinrich Schenker, to account for the organization of the deeper structural levels of a composition and to show the relationships among all the structural levels. A concern with structural levels has been most readily apparent in studies of Bartók and Stravinsky but has begun to inform recent work on Schoenberg, Berg, and Webern.

Despite stylistic dissimilarities in this repertoire, there are shared underlying structures that are best elucidated by pitch-class set theory informed by a sense of structural levels.[6] A true unified-field theory of post-tonal music may still be a long way off; nevertheless, our halting, uncertain steps toward it have increasingly broken down what once seemed an impenetrable barrier between the music of Stravinsky and Bartók on the one hand and the music of Schoenberg, Webern, and Berg on the other. We are becoming increasingly aware of the common structures that underlie the obvious stylistic diversity of the music of these five composers.[7] They share both a preoccupation with the musical past and strategies for coming to terms with it.

Of course, the music of any era is significantly shaped by the need to come to terms with the music that came before. The evolution of musical style involves, in the most obvious sense, a series of reactions and responses to musical predecessors. Bach's sons react to their father; Haydn reacts to C. P. E. Bach; Beethoven reacts to Haydn; and so on. But the relationship between a music and its predecessors became a matter of particular urgency in the early twentieth century. Certain cultural and social developments, with roots in the late eighteenth and early nineteenth centuries, reached their culmination in that era.[8]

These developments included, first, a shift in musical taste from contemporary to older music. Before 1800 most music performed was contemporary, often composed for some specific occasion. By the middle of the nineteenth century, the works of dead composers, particularly the classical masters (Mozart, Haydn, and Beethoven) had come to dominate the concert repertoire. In the years that followed the repertoire continued to ossify and became less and less contemporaneous. In the late nineteenth and early twentieth centuries, the musical center of gravity grew more and more distant chronologically.

Before 1800 music-making revolved around the personal relationships among composer, performers, and audience. In the late eighteenth and early nineteenth centuries, a musical mass culture began to emerge in which the publishing, selling, and performing of music became an increasingly lucrative business dependent on the participation of a wide public. The burgeoning music industry and the growing mass audience contributed to a preference for the music of the old masters. As a sanctioned artistic product, older music could be more easily packaged and sold.

An important aspect of the growing musical mass culture was the increasing separation of the popular and classical traditions. Before 1800 concerts and concert repertoire tended to reflect an intermingling of tastes. During the nineteenth century, musical taste moved in two opposite directions, toward lighter entertainments to suit popular tastes and toward more serious, artistic programs for the connoisseur. The latter tendency gradually coalesced into a classical tradition oriented primarily toward the music of deceased masters. By the early twentieth century, the classical tradition had become almost entirely isolated from the popular tradition and overwhelmingly dominated by the music of the past.

In the seventeenth and eighteenth centuries, there was no central canon, no body of works or composers universally revered. The central canon developed later in music than in the other arts, but by the middle of the nineteenth century it was firmly established and centered on the classical masters. The emergence of a canon had important implications for the training of composers, who were increasingly taught through study of the masterworks of the past. When Mozart, for example, taught composition in the late eighteenth century, he taught figured bass and species counterpoint, not the works of past masters like Machaut and Landini (of whose very existence Mozart would have been unaware).[9] His orientation was practical, not historical. Figured bass and species counterpoint offered him a simple way of describing his own harmonic and voice-leading procedures. By the beginning of the twentieth century it was not surprising that Webern, in contrast, should receive a degree as a musicologist (his dissertation was on Isaac) and should have deep knowledge of the masterworks of previous centuries.

Before 1800 music publication was largely by subscription. As a result, works were published only in small quantities and not widely disseminated.

Toward the end of the eighteenth century, technological breakthroughs and increasing commercial pressures associated with the emergence of the musical mass culture made possible large-scale publication and wide distribution of musical works, including older works by dead composers. The increased availability of older music has been enormously enhanced by the technological developments of the early twentieth century, including radio and sound recording.

As a result of these developments, the early twentieth century was an era dominated by the music of the past, particularly music by a small number of classical masters. Composers in this period were more deeply immersed in the music of the past (including the distant past) than any previous generation had been. They looked back on a classical heritage grown increasingly hallowed by the passage of time, its stature enhanced by greater distance and by the deep stylistic and structural gulf between the musical periods.

In these historical circumstances it is not surprising that composers felt a deep ambivalence toward the masterworks of the past. On the one hand, those works are a source of inspiration, a touchstone of musical value; on the other, they are a source of anxiety, an inescapable burden.[10] The writings of Schoenberg and Stravinsky especially are permeated with this ambivalence. Stravinsky was quite conscious of the central significance of eighteenth-century style and structure for his own music: "I attempted to build a new music on eighteenth-century classicism using the constructive principles of that classicism."[11] As he frequently acknowledged, much of his music incorporates and reworks elements from earlier compositions: "My instinct is to recompose, and not only students' work, but old masters' as well. When composers show me their music for criticism, all I can say is that I would have written it quite differently. Whatever interests me, whatever I love, I wish to make my own."[12]

Frequently, Stravinsky himself identified the classical sources for his "re-composings"—his Violin Concerto refers to Bach's Concerto for Two Violins,[13] his Concerto for Two Pianos is related to the variation forms of Beethoven and Brahms,[14] and The Rake's Progress is "deeply involved in Così [fan tutte]"[15]—and in many cases the identification of a piece with its model is explicit, as with Pulcinella, The Fairy's Kiss, and similar pieces. It is possible to imagine Stravinsky making unconstrained choices from among the works of the past, simply choosing as models pieces that he admired. Stravinsky himself, however, suggested that the past is more than a neutral repertoire: "The artist feels his 'heritage' as the grip of a very strong pincers."[16] The artist, Stravinsky asserted, is hedged in by the past, by its powerful presence, and must struggle, at times painfully, to maintain freedom of action. The past is the source not only of inspiration but of narrow constraints.

For Stravinsky, as for all the major composers of his period, the most significant part of his heritage was the Germanic mainstream of Bach to Brahms and Wagner. Although Stravinsky was not born into and trained in that tradition as were Schoenberg, Webern, and Berg, his works frequently reach out toward it, either obliquely or overtly. Throughout his life Stravinsky was preoccupied by and deeply anxious about his relationship to what he called "the German stem." In his conversations with Robert Craft, he discussed this relationship in the characteristically flip tone of those dialogues:

Neoclassicism? A husk of style? Cultured pearls? Well, which of us today is not a highly conditioned oyster? I know that the *Oedipus* music is valued at about zero by present progressive-evolutionary standards, but I think it may last awhile in spite of that. I know, too, that I relate only from an angle to the German stem (Bach—Haydn—Mozart—Beethoven—Schubert—Brahms—Wagner—Mahler—Schoenberg), which evaluates largely in terms of where a thing comes from and where it is going. But an angle may be an advantage.[17]

There is good reason, however, to believe that Stravinsky was not always so self-assured about his relationship to that "German stem." Musicians who knew Stravinsky late in his life have reported that he was concerned about his place in the tradition and his ability to measure up to the achievements of the classical masters.[18] The same concern can be inferred from his compositions, which tend—throughout his career—to make such extensive use of the forms, sonorities, and musical gestures associated with the masterworks of the eighteenth and nineteenth centuries.

Stravinsky's relationship to the central musical tradition had two principal components. First, he frequently incorporated specific forms or structures or entire pieces from the past within his own compositions. In this way, he established a clear link with the tradition. Second, he radically revised those earlier elements, reshaping them in his own image. This dual process of incorporation and revision is the central musical expression of his underlying ambivalence toward the past, as simultaneously a model to be emulated and a challenge to be neutralized (or a "strong pincers" to be resisted).

Schoenberg was, perhaps, even more deeply ambivalent than Stravinsky toward the music of the past. It inspired his reverence but caused him pain and even anger. What Stravinsky felt as a "strong pincers," Schoenberg experienced as a sense of compulsion. In his own view he composed not from personal choice but in obedience to the dictates of history. "I have to say: 'I can do it no other way, and it does not work any other way. Only, I did not choose to write like that, I do not go out of my way to write like that, and it would be a relief to feel I might do it differently.' In the army, a superior officer once said to me: 'So you are this notorious Schoenberg, then.' 'Beg to report, sir, yes,' I replied. 'Nobody wanted to be, someone had to be, so I let it be me.'"[19]

What history requires, for Schoenberg, is progress. Music is in a continuous process of evolution. It is the composer's task to comprehend the historical trend and to keep it going in the proper direction. The musical works of the past are tyrannous; one can only choose to obey. "While composing for me had been a pleasure, now it became a duty. I knew I had to fulfill a task; I had to express what was necessary to be expressed and I knew I had the duty of developing my ideas for the sake of progress in music, whether I liked it or not." [20]

Webern spoke of a similar sense of compulsion and of the weight of the past pushing him inexorably and, at times, painfully forward: "And never in the history of music has there been such resistance as there was to [the abandonment of key]. Naturally it's nonsense to advance 'social objections.' Why don't people understand that? Our push forward *had* to be made, it was a push forward such as never was before. In fact we have to break new ground with each work: each work is something different, something new." [21] For both Schoenberg and Webern, the tradition was not a generous friend or a kind teacher; it was an intolerant despot. In their discussions of musical tradition, both composers made frequent use of the imagery of travel: they saw themselves as having left a familiar landscape and moving along new and strange paths. It is as though they had been expelled from the garden of the musical common practice and forced to earn their bread by the sweat of their brow in a much harsher land. "My destiny had forced me in this direction—I was not destined to continue in the manner of *Transfigured Night* or *Gurrelieder* or even *Pelleas and Melisande*. The Supreme Commander had ordered me on a harder road." [22] The tradition itself, by its very richness and weight, pushes the composer painfully onward. In Schoenberg's mind, the past was thus a musical Eden protected by the flaming angel who bars forever any hope of return.

The intensity of Schoenberg's ambivalence is a measure of the depth of his involvement with the music of the common-practice masters. His knowledge of earlier music was extraordinarily broad and profound. Indeed, he ranks with Schenker among the greatest tonal theorists of this century. In his teaching, and in his own music, he sought continually to establish links with the tradition. In discussing his harmony treatise, for example, he boasted of its conservatism: "My *Harmonielehre* did not speak very much about 'atonality' and other prohibited subjects but almost exclusively about the technique and harmony of our predecessors, wherein I happened to appear even stricter and more conservative than other contemporary theorists. But just because I was so true to our predecessors, I was able to show that modern harmony was not developed by an irresponsible fool, but that it was the very logical development of the harmony and technique of the masters." [23]

For Schoenberg, then, the only logical and responsible musical developments are those that grow out of the tradition. Schoenberg's discussions of his own music always related his achievement to that of the tonal masters, using their music as a touchstone of quality and value. He sought, above all, to show that his music was rooted in the past, that it embodied the structural principles of the German masters, and that it was the equal of theirs in power and coherence. These may well seem self-evident criteria of musical evaluation, but in fact they are strong evidence of the power of the musical past over Schoenberg's imagination. Musical value, for other composers, might be measured by other standards—such as how well the music expressed a program or text, or how well it pleased a patron or audience; or it might not be an issue at all if the music served the immediate need for which it was written. Certainly Bach would not have evaluated his cantatas according to how well they embodied the structural principles of, say, Machaut.

Schoenberg thus felt the past as a burden in two senses. First, he felt the need to measure up to the colossal achievements of his predecessors. He knew better than almost anyone how remarkable the music of Bach, Mozart, Beethoven, and Brahms is. Their music was constantly before him, imposing an almost impossibly high standard of musical quality against which he continually measured himself. His need to measure up to such an exalted standard and to prove himself the rightful inheritor of that overwhelming tradition were burdens indeed. Second, the vast achievements of his predecessors made it difficult for Schoenberg to compose in a way that could be simultaneously appealing and new. He recognized that he could never measure up to his predecessors by slavishly imitating them. The weight and richness of the tradition thus forced him onto that "harder road," compelling him to do what he felt as a painful duty "whether I liked it or not." The musical past, he felt, shaped his present and future. It compelled him to change and develop his musical language, to move beyond the styles he inherited, to distance himself from the past "for the sake of progress in music."

In both of these senses the burden of the past weighed heavily on Schoenberg, and in essentially contradictory ways. On the one hand, Schoenberg sought to link himself to the tradition; on the other, he sought to progress beyond it. Like Stravinsky, his dual compositional response to this double burden was to appropriate elements of earlier music and place them in the service of a new musical structure. By preventing them from functioning in their normal way, he neutralized their potential threat to the integrity of his music. By imposing a new meaning on them in a new musical context, he demonstrated his mastery of the tradition and lightened its burden on him.

The music of the first half of the twentieth century, for Bartók, Webern, and Berg no less than for Schoenberg and Stravinsky, was created, performed, and heard under the shadow of the past. This circumstance, and the ambivalence it inspired, had a profound impact on their music. Efforts to evaluate that impact have been hampered, however, by the absence of an adequate theory of influence, a theory of the relationship between a work and its predecessors.

There are three current models of artistic influence. Two of these, which I will call the "influence as immaturity" and the "influence as generosity" theories, have been with us for some time. The third, which I will call the "influence as anxiety" theory, has emerged only in recent years and is most fully expressed in the work of the literary critic Harold Bloom.[24] This last theory permits the richest interpretation of the relationships between twentieth-century works and their antecedents.

Susceptibility to influence is most commonly viewed as a concomitant of artistic immaturity. A young composer frequently uses elements of style and musical structure closely identified with a teacher or other older figure. Although tolerated in a youthful artist, being influenced is judged a sign of incapacity in a mature composer. Where it occurs, it is considered an indication of artistic weakness, a symptom of a derivative and therefore secondary work. Capable artists, in this view, are less and less susceptible to influence as they mature, until they eventually attain a unique and personal voice. Of course, during their maturity composers may refer to earlier works, but they do so only as a conscious allusion or direct homage.

Examples of this somewhat naive theory can be found in any standard biography of a composer, in the section on the composer's youth. The following description of Stravinsky's Symphony in E-flat is typical:

The Symphony in E♭, composed while [Stravinsky] was studying with Rimsky-Korsakov, and incidentally dedicated to him, shows obvious signs of the master's influence, but this influence is not really of paramount importance. In conception and in general plan, the work shows a closer kinship with Glazunov, and Stravinsky himself states that at the time he was writing the Symphony, he admired Glazunov quite as much as Rimsky-Korsakov . . . Though in his instrumental technique we recognize Rimsky-Korsakov's teaching, and other external features of his music bear the hallmark of Glazunov, the substance of the music which clothes the formal structure of his Symphony shows evidence of other influences of a most unexpected kind. The listener hearing Stravinsky's maiden effort for the first time may be astonished to find that for his opening tune he has borrowed from Richard Strauss.[25]

There is nothing wrong with this view in itself. A full appreciation of an artist must take into account the formative years and the conscious models. At the same time, our critical and analytic interest inevitably centers on the characteristic work of an artist's maturity, a subject about which the immaturity theory has little to tell us. Although this theory can trace the influence of Rimsky-Korsakov, Glazunov, or Strauss on Stravinsky's early symphony, it cannot tell us much about the Symphony in Three Movements (1945) simply because that is a mature, highly individual work without obvious antecedents. And yet the only reason we are at all interested in the early symphony is that it is by the composer of, among other masterworks, the Symphony in Three Movements. If the Symphony in Three Movements can be usefully discussed in terms of its relationship to earlier works (and I believe that it can—see Chapter 7), we will have to seek a more encompassing theory of influence.

A second theory of influence, the generosity theory, is descended most obviously from T. S. Eliot and takes a broader and more subtle view. Eliot and the critics who follow him see influences as enriching an artist, in the formative years and in the period of artistic maturity as well. Susceptibility to influence, therefore, is a sign not of incapacity but of value—the more fully the tradition is assimilated, the better the artist. Even in works that seem most individual, good artists will demonstrate consciousness of the past.

[Tradition] involves, in the first place, the historical sense, which we may call nearly indispensable to any one who would continue to be a poet beyond his twenty-fifth year; and the historical sense involves a perception, not only of the pastness of the past, but of its presence; the historical sense compels a man to write not merely with his own generation in his bones, but with a feeling that the whole of the literature of Europe from Homer and within it the whole of the literature of his own country has a simultaneous existence and composes a simultaneous order. This historical sense, which is a sense of the timeless as well as of the temporal and of the timeless and the temporal together, is what makes a writer most traditional. And it is at the same time what makes a writer most acutely conscious of his place in time, of his own contemporaneity.[26]

Here, then, is a much more comprehensive sense of what influence can mean. For Eliot, the works of the past have a decisive impact on any later work. Artists create within a tradition, and their work—including the most individual works of their maturity—reflect the shaping impact of that tradition. In Eliot's view, true artistic creativity involves self-denial, a willingness to open and subordinate oneself to the influence of the past. He disparages

our tendency to insist, when we praise a poet, upon those aspects of his work in which he least resembles any one else. In these aspects or parts of his work we pretend to find what is individual, what is the peculiar essence of the man. We dwell with satisfaction upon the poet's difference from his predecessors; we endeavour to find something that can be isolated in order to be enjoyed. Whereas if we approach a poet without this prejudice we shall often find that not only the best, but the most individual parts of his work may be those in which the dead poets, his ancestors, assert their immortality most vigorously. And I do not mean the impressionable period of adolescence, but the period of full maturity.[27]

Eliot thus characterizes the relationship between poets and their predecessors as one of mutual generosity. Earlier poets generously pass their work along as part of a shared tradition. Later poets generously receive the tradition into their own work, and its presence is beneficial to them. "What is to be insisted upon is that the poet must develop or procure the consciousness of the past and that he should continue to develop this consciousness throughout his career. What happens is a continual surrender of himself as he is at the moment to something which is more valuable. The progress of an artist is a continual self-sacrifice, a continual extinction of personality."[28]

The best recent studies of influence in music, by Leonard Meyer and Charles Rosen, are in the tradition of Eliot. According to Meyer, composers are confronted by a variety of potential influences, including not only earlier compositions but also "cultural beliefs and attitudes, the predilections of patrons, or acoustical conditions," among others, from which they choose what to incorporate into their own works.[29] Only those features that are selected are actual influences. Composers presumably choose as influences the things they find artistically congenial. The past does not impose itself upon them; they select from its offerings. Meyer recognizes a wider range of potential influences than Eliot (who focused on earlier works), and Meyer shifts the focus of the discussion from the evolving tradition to the later artists and their individual choices. Nevertheless, Meyer shares Eliot's view of influence as the free and beneficial use of the past.

For Charles Rosen, as for Eliot, influence is bound up with an evolving tradition. Rosen acknowledges influence as a subtle process by which later composers affiliate themselves with earlier ones and with the tradition as a whole. Influence can either be chosen by the later composer or accepted as "a necessary fact of creative life."[30] In either case it is something that binds composers to their predecessors in an enriching way.

For Rosen, as for Eliot, influence is too subtle a process to be measured in terms of direct allusions or quotations: "The most important form of influence is that which provokes the most original and most personal work."[31] Since this process involves the transformation of some older work, it will be harder to detect as the transformation becomes more thorough. Regardless of how it is manifested, however, influence remains for Rosen a beneficial process. An admired model can inspire composers to their best and most personal work. Influence stimulates the creative process and enriches the works that result.

Something crucial is missing from the generosity theory, however. It obscures, or ignores, the deep ambivalence felt by artists contemplating the past. It has no place for Stravinsky's concern about being crushed by a "strong pincers" or Schoenberg's distress at being forced to tread that "harder road." Furthermore, the theory impedes a full appreciation of the tension in so many twentieth-century works between traditional tonal elements and the prevailing post-tonal context in which they occur. Artistic ambivalence is often worked out compositionally through a conflict between old and new elements, and through an attempt by the new elements to subsume and revise the old ones. For a theory that pays adequate attention to artistic ambivalence, and to musical tension and conflict, we will have to turn to a third theory, that of influence as anxiety.

For Harold Bloom, the most forceful exponent of this third theory, influence is not confined to adolescent works, selected freely by the artist, or necessarily manifested in overt allusions; rather, influence—specifically, the relationship between a work and its predecessors—crucially defines every work. Furthermore, the relationship between artists and their predecessors is not one of generous and mutually beneficial borrowing, but one of anxiety, anger, and repression. Bloom's anxiety theory is relatively recent, radically different from the more familiar theories, and uniquely fruitful for understanding twentieth-century music with its rich interplay of contrasting and conflicting elements.

Bloom's complex, virtuosic prose style, his extraordinary range of references (including some unusually esoteric ones), and his unwillingness to define central terms in a clear and systematic way make it difficult to summarize his theory. Still, it is possible to distill four principal components, which I will discuss in turn.

1. A poem is not a self-contained, organic whole. Rather, it is a relational event, embodying impulses (often contradictory) from a variety of sources.

2. The poetic tradition and the history of poetry are the story of a struggle by newer poems against their predecessors, a struggle to clear creative space. The relationship between poets and their predecessors has more in common with the Oedipal struggle between son and father than with the generous relationship between disciple and teacher or between colleagues.

3. The struggle between new poems and their precursors takes the form of misreading. Later poets willfully misinterpret their predecessors in a process analogous to repression in Freudian psychoanalytic theory.

4. The anxiety of influence is a universal phenomenon in poetry; it is not confined to a single historical period. As the tradition lengthens in time, however, poets will feel an increasing sense of belatedness.

Bloom asserts that there is no such thing as a poem. What we might think of as self-contained artistic objects are in fact "relational events or dialectical entities, rather than free-standing units."[32] Specifically, a poem is "a psychic battlefield"[33] upon which poet and predecessors struggle: "Let us give up the failed enterprise of seeking to 'understand' any single poem as an entity in itself. Let us pursue instead the quest of learning to read any poem as its poet's deliberate misinterpretation, *as a poet* of a precursor poem or of poetry in general."[34] Hence, the familiar notion of poetic meaning begins to lose its significance. For Bloom, the meaning of a poem resides in its relations with other texts and, ultimately, with the entire world of literary language.

> An empirical thinker, confronted by a text, seeks a meaning. Something in him says: "If this is a complete and independent text, then it *has* a meaning." It saddens me to say that this apparently commonsensical assumption is not true. Texts don't *have* meanings, except in their relations to other texts, so that there *is* something uneasily dialectical about literary meaning. A single text has only part of a meaning; it is itself a synecdoche for a larger whole including other texts. A text is a relational event, and not a substance to be analyzed.[35]

> Unfortunately, poems are not things but only words that refer to other words, and *those* words refer to still other words, and so on, into the densely overpopulated world of literary language. Any poem is an inter-poem, and any reading of a poem is an inter-reading. A poem is not writing, but *rewriting,* and though a strong poem is a fresh start, such a start is a starting-again.[36]

Of course, traditional theories of poetry acknowledge that a poem may contain and reconcile conflicting elements. Bloom, however, goes much farther than this. In his view the poem is not necessarily concerned with achieving, or even striving toward, unity. A poem, for Bloom, is good or "strong" in proportion to the intensity of the struggle it embodies: "Poems are actually stronger when their counterintended effects battle most incessantly against their overt intentions."[37] Bloom is interested not so much in beauty as in power.

Bloom forcefully attacks Eliot and his followers, asserting that the relation between poets and their precursors is one of struggle and conflict. "Weaker talents idealize; figures of capable imagination appropriate for themselves."[38] Generosity and responsiveness are signs of weakness in the later poet: "It does happen that one poet influences another, or more precisely, that one poet's poems influence the poems of another, through generosity of the spirit, even a shared generosity. But our easy idealism is out of place here. Where generosity is involved, the poets influenced are minor or weaker; the more generosity, and the more mutual it is, the poorer the poets involved."[39]

A new poem must struggle to find a place for itself in an overcrowded literary world. To do so, it must push earlier poems aside: "Poems fight for survival in a state of poems, which by definition has been, is now, and is always going to be badly overpopulated. Any poem's initial problem is to make room for itself—it must force the previous poems to move over and so clear some space for it. A new poem is not unlike a small child placed with a lot of other small children in a small playroom, with a limited number of toys, and no adult supervision whatever." [40]

A poem is crucially defined by its relationship to its predecessors. All other relationships including, most obviously, the relationship between a poem and its readers, recede in relative importance. This view leads Bloom to question Wordsworth's characterization of a poet as "a man speaking to men": "A poet . . . is not so much a man speaking to men as a man rebelling against being spoken to by a dead man (the precursor) outrageously more alive than himself." [41] "Poetry is poems speaking to a poem, and is also that poem answering back with its own defensive discourse." [42]

Poets cannot ignore the past or evade the presence of their precursors: "Strong poets become strong by meeting the anxiety of influence, not by ignoring it. Poets adept at forgetting their ancestry write very forgettable poems." [43] Poetic strength comes not as a gift from the Muse but as the result of winning the struggle with one's great predecessors, from "a triumphant wrestling with the greatest of the dead." [44]

It is in his insistence on influence as struggle that Bloom departs most radically from Eliot and the theory of influence as generosity. Eliot speaks of influence in terms of the surrender of the later poet to the strength of the tradition and the predecessor. His language is a language of passivity. His implicit sexual metaphor for the relation between poet and predecessor is one of a forceful, if willing, seduction: the later poet surrenders to the power of the earlier one. According to Bloom, the later poet does not surrender but rather learns to struggle with and neutralize the predecessor. Bloom's sexual metaphor (explicitly acknowledged) is that of the Oedipus complex. The later poet seeks artistic freedom by symbolically killing the precursor-parent.

This symbolic murder takes the form of misreading. Bloom considers misreading a particularly powerful form of interpretation in which later poets assert artistic freedom from a precursor's domination by using the precursor's work for their own artistic ends. To read is to be dominated; to misread is to assert one's own priority, as the later poet does by making the earlier poet say what the later poet wants or needs to hear. Misreadings are *not* failed or inadequate interpretations. In fact, misreadings are usually the most interesting interpretations. A misreading is distinguished from a simple reading precisely by its power to revise. "Poetic Influence—when it involves two strong, authentic poets—always proceeds by a misreading of the prior poet, an act of creative correction that is actually and necessarily a misinterpretation. The history of fruitful poetic influence, which is to say the main tradition of Western poetry since the Renaissance, is a history of anxiety and self-serving caricature, of distortion, of perverse, wilful revisionism without which modern poetry as such could not exist." [45] Later poets misread as a way of asserting the validity of their own vision; they must, in the process, falsify the vision of their predecessors. "A poet interpreting his precursor, and any strong subsequent interpreter reading either poet, must *falsify* by his reading. Though this falsification can be quite genuinely perverse or even ill-willed, it need not be, and usually is not. But it must be a falsification, because every strong reading insists that the meaning it finds is exclusive and accurate."[46]

Power and strength are thus essential elements in the relationship between a poem and its predecessors. Bloom draws his examples from many historical periods, from the biblical to the present. At the same time, he concentrates primarily on the relationship between the romantics and Milton, and between the moderns and the romantics. In this connection Bloom observes that, particularly since Milton, English and American poets have come increasingly to experience "the exhaustion of being a latecomer."[47] Romantic poetry is characterized by an almost overwhelming sense of belatedness with respect to Milton and Shakespeare: "Romantic tradition is *consciously late* and Romantic literary psychology is therefore necessarily a *psychology of belatedness.*"[48]

As descendants of the romantics, poets of the modern period feel an even heavier burden of anxiety and belatedness. Like the romantics, they look back to Shakespeare and Milton with an anxiety intensified by added distance. In addition, modern poets feel anxiety with respect to the romantics themselves. Bloom's theory of influence thus becomes a theory of poetic history as well. The history of romantic and modern poetry is the story of successive misreadings as poets attempt, against greater and greater odds, to clear creative space for themselves.

Despite the universalist pretentions of Bloom's theory, his discussions are largely confined to works of the central canon, that is, to works by white, male poets living in England or the United States between 1550 to 1950. The centrality in Bloom's theory of the Oedipal struggle between sons and fathers suggests the extent to which it is a theory designed not for poetry in general but for a narrow slice of poetry, a single tradition within a much richer and larger poetic world than Bloom generally acknowledges.[49] At the same time, within a single, relatively self-contained tradition, Bloom's theory offers remarkable interpretive richness.

The integrity of the central musical tradition from Bach through Schoenberg, Stravinsky, Webern, Berg, and Bartók makes it equally amenable to a Bloomian approach. While some allowance will need to be made for applying a theory of poetic influence to music, most of Bloom's central ideas are not exclusively bound to language and translate easily into a musical context. In particular, Bloom's theory of influence is indispensable for music of the twentieth century. The wide array of musical structures that emerged in this period precisely to resist the pressures of the past will never be fully understood apart from a theory of influence as anxiety.

Bloom offers a useful antidote to what has become a virtual dogma in music theory: organic coherence. Musical analysis has traditionally been devoted to demonstrating that all components of a given work are integrated with one another in the service of a single generating idea.[50] But, in their combination of stylistically and structurally disparate elements, many twentieth-century works truly are relational events as much as they are self-contained organic entities. Our understanding of such pieces will be enriched if we can fully appreciate their clash of conflicting and historically distinct elements.[51]

Bloom makes possible a shift of critical focus from the demonstration of organic unity to the evaluation of elements of conflict and struggle within a work. The crucial concept here is that of *intertextuality*. No text can be truly discrete, its boundaries clearly marked and impermeable. Rather, every text is interpenetrated by others and speaks with a variety of voices. In most of the musical works discussed in this book, there is a clear delineation of new and old elements. The older elements are recognizable but placed in a new context that confers upon them a new meaning. Works containing this clash of elements may be coherent, although not in an organic sense. Rather, their coherence depends upon the ability of the new musical context to hold the older elements in its grasp. Old and new are not reconciled or synthesized but locked together in conflict. The coherence of these works is won through a struggle.

Bloom further offers a corrective to the prevailing view that composers approach their predecessors uniquely in a spirit of admiration and homage. Indeed, in both their prose and their music, twentieth-century composers express a profound ambivalence toward older music. Their admiring comments often have an ironic or angry edge. And whatever their expressed personal feelings toward their predecessors, their works often bespeak anxiety and conflict. By incorporating traditional elements, twentieth-century composers enter into dialogue with their predecessors; by radically reinterpreting those elements, they inject a spirit of anxious revisionism into the dialogue.

Bloom's concept of misreading vividly captures the revisionary spirit of both musical and written commentaries on earlier music by twentieth-century composers. Instead of passively subordinating themselves to the tradition, they willfully reinterpret traditional elements in accordance with their own musical concerns. This book provides a map of musical misreadings, a summary of strategies for remaking the past. These strategies are analogous to what Bloom calls "revisionary ratios." They are "mechanisms of defense" whereby a later work simultaneously resists and remakes its predecessors.[52] Bloom's own revisionary ratios, which have fanciful, Greek names like *clinamen, kenosis,* and *apophrades,* are general enough to have some applicability to music, and I will consider them in due course. My primary concern, however, is with specifically musical strategies of reinterpretation. Composers in the first part of the twentieth century, despite their superficial stylistic dissimilarities, share musical techniques for remaking earlier forms, style elements, sonorities, and musical works, which include the following.

Motivicization. The motivic content of the earlier work is radically intensified.

Generalization. A motive from the earlier work is generalized into the unordered pitch-class set of which it is a member. That pitch-class set is then deployed in the new work in accordance with the norms of post-tonal usage.

Marginalization. Musical elements that are central to the structure of the earlier work (such as dominant-tonic cadences and linear progressions that span triadic intervals) are relegated to the periphery of the new one.

Centralization. Musical elements that are peripheral to the structure of the earlier work (such as remote key areas and unusual combinations of notes resulting from linear embellishment) move to the structural center of the new one.

Compression. Elements that occur diachronically in the earlier work (such as two triads in a functional relationship to each other) are compressed into something synchronous in the new one.

Fragmentation. Elements that occur together in the earlier work (such as the root, third, and fifth of a triad) are separated in the new one.

Neutralization. Traditional musical elements (such as dominant-seventh chords) are stripped of their customary function, particularly of their progressional impulse. Forward progress is blocked.

Symmetricization. Traditionally goal-oriented harmonic progressions and musical forms (sonata form, for example) are made inversionally or retrograde-symmetrical, and are thus immobilized.

By using these musical revisionary ratios at all levels of structure, twentieth-century composers reinterpret earlier music in accordance with their own compositional needs. These strategies, more than any specific musical structure, define a twentieth-century common practice.

Bloom's concept of belatedness is particularly germane to the music of this century. Although a central canon emerged later in music than in poetry, the musical life of the twentieth century is even more dominated by the past than is the world of literature and is much more dominated by the past than was the musical life of earlier periods. Music is dependent upon performance (recorded or live) for dissemination, and performing repertoire has changed very slowly in this century. As a result, modern music has found itself in a losing battle for access to a public. Bloom's metaphor of an anxious struggle to clear creative space becomes almost literally true in music and is an especially pressing problem in this century. One of the most obvious signs of belatedness in the first part of this century was the new self-consciousness of composers about their own music. There is a long tradition in music of composers acting as theorists, but only in this century have composers engaged in intensive analysis of their own music, a development that bespeaks anxiety, self-consciousness, and belatedness.

It is important to distinguish, as Bloom does, between the anxiety of influence and the anxiety of style. The anxiety of style is a more general phenomenon: it refers to a feeling that some past era, as a whole, represents a never-to-be-reattained artistic pinnacle. In this century the anxiety of style appears in the constant comparisons of the new music to classic-romantic music amid defensive assertions that the new music is as rich, as expressive, as comprehensible, and as capable of producing coherence as the music that came before. When a previous musical style (in this case, common-practice tonality) seems to embody remarkable structural and expressive powers, an entire generation of composers may feel an anxiety of style with respect to it. Stravinsky's sense of the tradition as a "strong pincers" and Schoenberg's sense of the past pressing him forward are both manifestations of the anxiety of style.

This anxiety has manifested itself in the twentieth century in a number of musical ways. When twentieth-century composers use triads, the central sonority of traditional tonal music, they are responding to a widely shared musical element, not to some specific work or individual composer. Similarly, when they write in sonata form, they are responding to an icon of a previous style, not to a single predecessor. Anxiety of influence, by contrast, concerns a relationship between a piece and some earlier piece. It refers to specific structural features of the two works and specific strategies by which the later work comes to terms with the earlier.

In theory the two types of anxiety are reasonably distinct—Bloom claims not to be concerned with anxiety of style—but in practice they are closely related. Anxiety of style is the more inclusive concept. A composer can respond compositionally to generally shared attributes of an earlier style without invoking a specific earlier piece, but any attempt to misread a specific earlier piece will inevitably also involve misreading elements of an earlier style. In direct recompositions and more subtle misreadings of specific earlier works, twentieth-century composers work out an anxiety of influence. At the same time, they reveal a more general anxiety of style with respect to the tonal language of the common-practice era. Bloom's own work focuses on the anxiety of influence but is rich in implications for the anxiety of style as well.

Given more conventional models of influence, it is reasonably clear how one would go about showing the influence of one work upon another. Affinities of style, form, motivic or harmonic content, direct quotation, and strong resemblances in any musical domain can all be evidence of the influence of one work upon another or of one composer upon another. Given Bloom's model, however, this process is more difficult to discern, since influence is manifested in anxious struggle with the predecessor and may thus be somewhat concealed.

Bloom himself is quite specific about what sorts of things do not constitute evidence of influence. He is not interested in source study ("The profundities of poetic influence cannot be reduced to source study, to the history of ideas, to the patterning of images"),[53] and he is not interested in the presence in later works of specific ideas or images from earlier ones, except insofar as they have a new, revised appearance.[54] If influence involves misreading, the later work might have little superficially in common with its influential predecessor. "Poetic influence, in the sense I give to it, has almost nothing to do with the verbal resemblances between one poet and another . . . Poets need not *look* like their fathers, and the anxiety of influence more frequently than not is quite distinct from the anxiety of style. Since poetic influence is necessarily misprision, a taking or doing amiss of one's burden, it is to be expected that such a process of malformation and misinterpretation will, at the very least, produce deviations in style between strong poets."[55]

Nevertheless, even in the absence of obvious stylistic affinities the later work usually bears at least a subtle trace of its influential predecessor. In a variety of more or less explicit ways, Bartók, Stravinsky, Schoenberg, Berg, and Webern incorporate and reinterpret elements of their musical past, thereby creating compositions that are often radically unlike those of their influential predecessors. Chapters 2 through 4 of this book concentrate on compositions that make explicit and unambiguous reference to elements of earlier music. Here, the influence relation, significant in all pieces, is most central and most easily discussed. Chapter 2 considers the analytical and theoretical prose of these five composers. The pitch structure of much early twentieth-century music is based to a significant degree on contextually established associations of pitch–class sets. In their analytical and theoretical writings, composers frequently misread structures of this kind back into the works of their predecessors. Chapter 3 analyzes works that are recompositions of earlier ones. Through reorchestration and other subtle alterations, the structure of an earlier work may be entirely reshaped. In such works the conflict between the traditional (a virtually intact tonal composition) and the new is overt and easily documented. Chapter 4 considers a variety of twentieth-century uses of the triad. Twentieth-century composers confront traditional harmony by enmeshing its most salient sonority within characteristic types of post-tonal harmonic organization. The triad becomes the locus of the struggle between present and past.

Chapters 5 through 7 deal with larger musical units and discuss works in which the influence relationship has begun to move underground, leaving few immediately evident traces on the surface. The subject of Chapter 5 is sonata form. Using a new musical language, twentieth-century composers remake the emblematic form of the common-practice era. Chapter 6 is devoted to the anxiety of influence and to works that misread a single influential predecessor. Here, the influence relation is at its subtlest and most profound. Finally, Chapter 7 considers large-scale structural motions that mimic a traditional tonal appearance, such as a descending perfect fifth. In such cases a misreading takes place at the deepest levels of musical structure.

CHAPTER 2

Analytical Misreadings

Twentieth-century composers have produced an unusual amount of prose devoted to theory and analysis, including analysis of their own works. In earlier periods composers generally wrote about music in a practical vein, when they did so at all. The history of music theory, from the middle ages through the classic-romantic period, is full of "how-to" books by composers. In this century, however, two new trends become apparent. Composers begin for the first time to write knowledgeably and analytically about music of the past, including the distant past. This development is clear evidence of their preoccupation with their predecessors. And they engage, also for the first time, in intensive self-analysis. This change suggests a high degree of historical self-consciousness and bespeaks their anxiety about their place within the tradition.

When twentieth-century composers write about their own music, they generally do so in a competitive way, comparing themselves, often favorably, to their predecessors. Their self-analysis tends to have a self-aggrandizing character. When they analyze the music of their predecessors, they generally do so in light of their own compositional concerns, specifically their interest in motivic relations. Such relations crucially determine musical structure in the first part of this century, most obviously in the "free atonal" works of Schoenberg, Berg, and Webern, but also in their twelve-tone works and in the works of Stravinsky and Bartók. These composers depict their predecessors as similarly preoccupied. Their central misreading is that of motivicization.

Motivic design is, of course, a rich part of musical construction before the twentieth century. The music of the sixteenth century and earlier contains subtle motivic interconnections within a prevailing modal organization.[1] In the period of common-practice tonality (eighteenth and nineteenth centuries), motivic design played an increasingly important role,[2] if we understand a motive as any intensively used diminution or embellishment.[3] The possibility that a single diminution or embellishment might occur at different levels of structure is the essence of *concealed repetition*. According to this concept, a motive may be stated directly at the surface level and later (or concurrently) repeated at a deeper structural level. This latter, large-scale statement of the motive is a concealed repetition of the explicit foreground statement. Concealed repetitions may significantly contribute to the unity and coherence of a composition, providing all of the structural levels with the same motivic content.[4]

Despite their intrinsic interest, however, concealed repetitions and other motivic relations are neither necessary nor sufficient for tonal coherence, which is assured by the relations among the structural levels, by the systematic prolongation at each level of events at the higher levels, and by the composing-out of the tonic triad, the ultimate structural determinant. The composing-out may follow a motivic path, but it need not do so. Motivic association is thus only a secondary determinant of structure in tonal music. Furthermore, what motivic relations there are always have a tonal function to fulfill. They not only are less important structurally than the tonal relations but also function primarily to express and elaborate those relations. They are constrained by what Milton Babbitt calls "the boundary conditions of tonality."[5] While these boundary conditions—shared norms of harmonic progression and voice leading—remain in force, motivic relations must be secondary to and dependent upon the underlying tonal syntax. When these boundary conditions are removed, however, as they were in the late nineteenth and early twentieth centuries, motivic relations come to dominate the structure.

Accounts of musical structure in the late nineteenth and early twentieth centuries have generally focused on the decline and fall of traditional tonal relations. Music of this period is thus most often discussed in terms of what it does not do, namely, conform to earlier norms of tonal organization. Recent studies have begun to balance this essentially negative view by shifting critical focus from the decline of traditional tonal relations to the compensating rise of motivic relations.[6] The late nineteenth century now appears as a period in which motivic association, a secondary and dependent determinant of structure in the classical and early romantic eras, was elevated into a central and independent organizing principle. Recent scholarship on late romantic music (particularly that of Wagner, Brahms, Liszt, and Mahler) has concentrated more and more on what Allen Forte calls "the primal importance of the motive."[7] In the music of this period, motivic structure waxes as tonal structure wanes.

This development has had crucial consequences for the nature of musical structure in the first part of this century. To compensate for the loss of tonality as an organizing principle, composers in this century seek, above all, to enhance the motivic content of their music. They begin increasingly to see themselves, and each other, as motivic composers and to take pride in that. When Webern praises the early work of Schoenberg, he praises most of all its coherence with respect to its themes and motives. "Like the consciousness of his sense of form, Schoenberg's art of thematic writing is immensely enhanced in [String Quartet No. 1] Op. 7. It is marvellous to observe how Schoenberg creates an accompaniment figure from a motivic particle, how he introduces themes, how he brings about interconnections between the principal sections. And everything is thematic! There is, one can say, not a single note in this work that does not have a thematic basis. This is unparalleled."[8] Berg's comment on the same work is remarkably similar in its emphasis on thematicism (that is, motivic coherence).

These first ten bars [of String Quartet No. 1, Op. 7] and their varied repeats represent a very, very small fraction of the work, which lasts about an hour. They can only give a hint of an idea of the harmonic, polyphonic and contrapuntal occurrences (in an excess unheard-of since Bach) that flourish so luxuriantly in the thousands of bars of this music. One can assert this without being guilty of any exaggeration: Every smallest turn of phrase, even accompanimental figuration is significant for the melodic development of the four voices and their constantly changing rhythm—is, to put it in one word, thematic.[9]

In the "free atonal" music written by Schoenberg, Webern, and Berg during the second decade of the century, the last vestiges of tonal harmony fall away, leaving the structure resting entirely on a foundation of contextually established motivic associations. Schoenberg disliked the designation "atonal" for the music of this period and preferred to think of it as "working with tones of the motif."[10] In analyses of his own work from this period Schoenberg emphasizes motivic interconnections. His discussion of the Four Orchestral Songs, Op. 22, traces the motivic major and minor second and their use in conjunction to form a "fixed motivic unit" that is "varied and developed in manifold ways."[11] "In these songs," he explains, "I am in the preliminary stages of a procedure which is essentially different both from the Italians and from Wagner. I am myself not yet quite able to say how far this may apply to my most recent works. At any rate, I am aware that it is mainly a concern with the art of variation, which allows for a motif to be a constant basis while, at the same time, doing justice to the subtlest nuance in the text."[12]

In response to its motivic density, a number of theorists have begun to reject the negative label "atonal" for this music and instead refer to it as "motivic" music.[13] This designation also applies, although in a modified way, to twelve-tone music generally and to the most characteristic works by

Stravinsky and Bartók as well. Our best analytical tool for this entire repertory—pitch-class set theory—reflects a motivic orientation. A pitch-class set involves generalizing and extending the traditional concept of motive. Set theory views an ordered, pitch-specific pattern (the traditional idea of a motive) as one of many possible representations of an unordered pitch-class set. A pitch-class set is a motive from which many of the identifying characteristics—register, rhythm, order—have been boiled away. What remains is simply the basic pitch-class and intervallic identity of a musical idea. In this more general sense pitch-class set analysis *is* motivic analysis. A set-theory analysis shows that the coherence of a pitch structure derives from its use of a small number of closely related harmonic or melodic ideas.

There is now a large analytical literature documenting the motivic richness of early twentieth-century music. The first phrase of Schoenberg's Piano Piece Op. 11, No. 1, gives a hint of this richness, and of the ability of set theory to describe it. Example 2-1 shows this phrase and identifies occurrences of a single musical idea: set-class 3-3 (014).[14] Beneath a surface suggestive of traditional procedures, coherence is assured by motivic development. As with any occurrences of set-class 3-3, those circled on the example have the same interval content—each contains a 1, a 3, a 4, and no other intervals—and hence sound similar. The first three notes in the melody thus present one of the basic musical ideas for the piece, an idea that is repeated and developed in the music that follows. The sustained chord in measures 4–5 contains the same pitch-classes, now heard simultaneously instead of melodically. The chord in measure 3 is another form of the same set-class, related to the opening melodic fragment by transposition. The middle three notes in the moving tenor part in measures 4–5 are related to the opening melodic fragment by inversion.[15] The circled sets are different from one another in their manner of presentation, but they all have the same total interval content, and they all represent the same set-class. Schoenberg presents a musical idea, then develops it throughout the passage. In this way the music is made motivically coherent.

EXAMPLE 2-1   Occurrences of set-class 3-3 (014) in Schoenberg, Piano Piece Op. 11, No. 1

REMAKING THE PAST

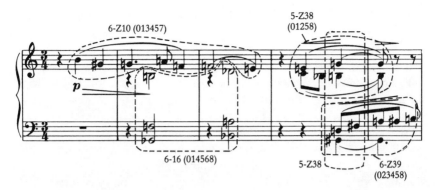

EXAMPLE 2-2 Additional motivic shapes

Actually, the music is motivically much more dense than the development of a single set-class. Example 2-2 suggests the extraordinary motivic saturation of this music by identifying a number of additional pitch-class sets, including some of the hexachords that are the building blocks of the piece as a whole.[16] The melody in measures 1–3 and the left-hand accompaniment in measures 4–5, although not members of the same set-class, do share the same interval content.[17] Furthermore, two statements of set-class 5-Z38 (01258) occur in measures 4–5, one formed by the two lines in the right hand and the other by all the notes sounding on the last beat of measure 4. These relationships suggest Schoenberg's expanded understanding of motives and motivic development. The other sets identified here are developed later in the piece; they are part of its large-scale motivic organization. Examples 2-1 and 2-2 together hint at the motivic richness and density of this music.

It is striking that these motivic riches unfold beneath a musical surface so evocative of traditional tonality. The texture of upper-voice melody with chordal accompaniment, the phrasing and contour of the melody, and the rhythmic relationship between the parts are all reminiscent of an earlier style. But analysis based on tonal assumptions produces dismal results. One analyst has tried to read the phrase in G major, identifying the harmony in measure 2 as the tonic and that in measure 3 as the dominant of the dominant.[18] The inadequacies of this approach are all too painfully evident.[19] It is hard to see how the sonority in measure 2 could reasonably be called a G-major chord much less a tonic chord. A tonic, if the term is to mean anything at all, must be the referential sonority for a composition, a source of musical stability and repose. In this passage and in the rest of the composition, neither this sonority, nor the G-major triad, nor even the pitch-class G, functions as a tonic. The music seems to invite, and then frustrate, a tonal analysis.

The same frustration awaits the analyst who looks in this passage for traditional tonal voice leading. The rhythmic disposition of the melody in relation to the chords suggests the traditional pattern of suspension and resolution. In measure 2, for example, the rhythmic organization implies that a dissonant G resolves (after a brief embellishing upper neighbor note) to F over the sustained chord. But, even though F is a member of the chord, the sonority formed on the least beat of the measure is no more stable, consonant, or referential for this piece than the sonority formed on the first beat of the measure. The sense of dissonance and resolution, created rhythmically, thus has no harmonic foundation. In measure 3, similarly, neither the melodic F nor the E to which it apparently resolves creates with the accompanying chord a sonority that can in any sense be considered consonant or referential for this piece.

The rhythmic organization of these measures is thus belied by the pitch organization. The tonal expectations aroused by the seeming suspensions are denied by a harmonic organization that expresses not traditional harmony but the integration of musical space with respect to a small number of motives. The F in measure 3, for example, is not an upper neighbor to the E but a structurally equal member of various motivic sets. Behind a facade of antiquated stylistic mannerisms, Schoenberg erects a musical structure based on new musical relationships. He thus undercuts and comments ironically on the conventions he invokes. Whatever the allusions on the musical surface, this is profoundly motivic music.

If a dense web of motivic associations defines the pitch structure of "free atonal" music, then the same principle achieves a kind of apotheosis in the twelve-tone system. This idea is expressed succinctly by Ernst Křenek:

When key consciousness vanished completely and music became "atonal," technical unity could no longer emerge from a solid harmonic groundwork. Quite logically, the attention was focused on the motif-relationships. Whereas they had formerly been a superstructure erected above the harmonic groundwork, they now became responsible for the consistency of the whole edifice . . . Thus the primary function of the series is that of a sort of "store of motifs" out of which all the individual elements of the composition are to be developed.[20]

A series is a matrix of motivic relations; embedded within it are the structures that will largely determine the pitch organization of the work.

Through the twelve-tone system, Schoenberg attempts to ensure the motivic unity of his compositions. More specifically, he seeks a means for equaling or surpassing what he considers the greatest achievement of his predecessors, the concentration and coherence of their motivic structure. "For the sake of a more profound logic, the Method of Composing with Twelve Tones derives all configurations [elements of a work] from a basic set (Grundgestalt) [tone-row or note-series]. The order in this basic set and its three derivatives—contrary motion [inversion], retrograde, and retrograde inversion respectively—is, like the motive [in classical music], obligatory for a whole piece."[21]

For Webern, similarly, the great virtue of the twelve-tone system is the assurance it offers of a unified set structure. He singles out its ability "to develop everything from *one* principal idea!"[22] and explains, "Composers tried to create unity in the accompaniment, to work thematically, to derive everything from one thing, and so to produce the tightest—maximum—unity. And now everything is derived from this chosen succession of twelve notes, and thematic technique works as before, on this basis. But—the great advantage is that I can treat thematic technique much more freely. For unity is completely ensured by the underlying series."[23]

For Schoenberg, like Webern, the motivic relations established by the ordering of the series largely determine the pitch structure. "In twelve-tone composition one need not ask after the more or less dissonant character of a sound-combination, since the combination as such (ignoring whether its effect creates a mood or not) is entirely outside the discussion as an element in the process of composition. This combination will not develop, or, better, it is not *it* that develops, but the relationship of the twelve tones to each other develops, on the basis of a particular prescribed order (motive), determined by the inspiration (the idea!)."[24]

Motivic saturation is an organizational principle most closely associated with Schoenberg, Webern, and Berg, yet an overwhelming preoccupation with motivic coherence characterizes a whole range of early twentieth-century music, including much of the work of Stravinsky and Bartók.[25] Furthermore, a pitch organization based on the kinds of motivic associations best described using the powerful tools of pitch-class set theory is uniquely characteristic of twentieth-century music and is precisely what distinguishes this repertoire from the music of earlier periods.

This preoccupation with motivic relations profoundly shapes the twentieth century's view of earlier music. In published studies and remarks, Schoenberg, Webern, Berg, Bartók, and (to a lesser extent) Stravinsky, look in earlier music for the same kinds of complex motivic relations that they compose and identify in their own works. Like their compositions, but in a more literal sense, their analyses of earlier music are strong misreadings. They assert that earlier music is most interesting and valuable precisely in those places where it anticipates the structural concerns of the twentieth century.

We are accustomed to thinking chronologically and are comfortable with the notion that an earlier composer may influence a later one. But the reverse is also possible. Composers' interpretations of their predecessors, in words or in notes, may strongly shape our experience of earlier works and thus their meaning. Schoenberg's analyses attempt this reversal with particular force and clarity. His analyses of his own music and of earlier music are founded on two central principles: the *Grundgestalt* (basic shape) and the developing variation.[26] These are both fundamentally motivic conceptions. The *Grundgestalt* is the basic musical idea of the piece, from which every aspect of the musical structure derives. Developing variation is the process of evolving the diverse structures of a composition from a basic shape.

The *Grundgestalt* is the referential source of musical structure. It has the status in Schoenberg's analytical outlook that the tonic triad does in Schenker's: the irreducible core of musical coherence. "Whatever happens in a piece of music is nothing but the endless reshaping of a basic shape. Or, in other words, there is nothing in a piece of music but what comes from the theme, springs from it and can be traced back to it; to put it still more severely, nothing but the theme itself. Or, all the shapes appearing in a piece of music are *foreseen* in the 'theme.'"[27] The term *Grundgestalt* is not precisely synonymous with motive but is rather to be understood as a kind of Ur-shape that spawns motives. "*Grundgestalten* are those gestalten that (if possible) occur repeatedly within a whole piece and to which derived gestalten are traceable. [Formerly, this was called the motive; but that is a very superficial designation, for gestalten and Grundgestalten are usually comprised of several motive-forms; the motive is *at any one time the smallest part*.]"[28] The motivic component thus looms large in Schoenberg's discussions of the concept and dominates his apparent analytical applications of it.

In Schoenberg's view a single *Grundgestalt* underlies the structure of any piece of music (either tonal or post-tonal) and all the particularities of the surface are derived from it. This is a strikingly contextual view of musical structure. Instead of emphasizing shared musical syntax as the source of musical coherence (as Schenker does), Schoenberg emphasizes piece-specific elements like motives. This contextual orientation is particularly well suited to twentieth-century music, which has no evident common practice. Its retroactive application to classic-romantic music is evidence, as we shall see, of Schoenberg's desire to remake his predecessors in his own image.

Similarly, the concept of developing variation is one with roots in Schoenberg's own compositional process. Developing variation is the "reshaping of a basic shape." Its essence is repetition, but not literal or sequential repetition. Rather, developing variation involves continual alteration of the basic shape, although never so much as to render it unrecognizable. "Variation, it must be remembered, is repetition in which some features are changed and the rest preserved. All the features of rhythm, interval, harmony and contour are subject to various alterations . . . but such changes must not produce a motive-form too foreign to the basic motive."[29] The principle of developing variation finds its fullest expression in Schoenberg's own music.

The previous brief discussion of the first phrase of his Piano Piece Op. 11, No. 1, gives a hint of the elaborate reshaping of basic shapes that takes place throughout his music. When Schoenberg applies this principle to earlier music, he is misreading via the revisionary ratio of motivicization.

In his most famous and profound analytical essay, "Brahms the Progressive," Schoenberg sets himself the task of identifying the progressive features in Brahms's music as a way of rescuing Brahms from charges of academicism and conservatism.[30] He identifies many progressive features of Brahms's harmony and rhythm; still, for Schoenberg, Brahms's music is progressive primarily because of the richness and subtlety of its motivic structure. Schoenberg's most extended analyses—of the main theme of the second movement from the String Quartet in A Minor, Op. 51, No. 2, and the third of the Four Serious Songs, Op. 121—are overwhelmingly focused on motivic content. He praises their "unique artistic quality, as regards their motival elaboration and internal organization."[31] His analysis of the quartet theme, reproduced in Example 2-3, shows that it "contains exclusively motive forms which can be explained as derivatives of the interval of a second."[32] Each of the bracketed successions in the example is explained by Schoenberg as a direct, transposed, inverted, or expanded statement of the basic motive of the passage, marked 'a'. Even a brief glance at the analysis shows a motivic density approaching that of Schoenberg's own music.

Let us look in some detail at the first eleven notes of the melody, labeled by Schoenberg as "1st phrase" and "2nd phrase." The first two notes introduce the principal motive ('a'), the ascending step. All else in the passage, Schoenberg claims, is derived from this. The third and fourth notes ('b') are the inversion of 'a'. Motives 'a' and 'b' together comprise 'c', which spans the first four notes of the melody. The neighbor-note figure, motive 'd', is formed by the second, third, and fourth notes of the melody. Motive 'e', a descending scalar tetrachord, results from a combination of two descending seconds, that is, two consecutive statements of 'b'. That descending fourth, inverted and with the inner notes omitted, becomes motive 'f', an ascending leap of a fourth.

In the first eleven notes of the melody, Schoenberg identifies no fewer than twelve motive statements that inevitably overlap to a large extent. It is this motivic overlap that causes Schoenberg to use extra staves above and below the melody. The second D in measure 2, for example, is part of four motive statements: 'b', 'd', 'e', and a slightly enlarged statement of 'c'. The rest of the analysis proceeds in similar fashion. The density of motives and the intensity of their development over the course of this brief passage are remarkable.

But the analysis is as revealing in what it ignores as in what it includes. There is no mention of harmony or voice leading, the principal focus of

EXAMPLE 2-3 Schoenberg's motivic analysis of a melody from Brahms, String
Quartet in A Minor, Op. 51, No. 2 (second movement)

most tonal theory and analysis. If we look again at the first eleven notes, we
can easily discern a gradual ascent from C-sharp through D to E, spanning
an interval within the tonic triad. This voice-leading motion certainly plays
a role in unifying the passage but plays no role in Schoenberg's analysis. He
not only ignores voice leading but actually contradicts it in places. The E in
measure 2, for example, is clearly a neighbor note. As a result, the descending
fourth (motive 'e') is not a meaningful voice-leading unit. Schoenberg is apparently interested not in voice leading but in establishing the richest possible network of motivic associations. In terms of our revisionary ratios,
Schoenberg marginalizes the voice leading, relegating it to the periphery of
his analysis, and centralizes the motivic structure, taking a secondary and
dependent aspect of the music and making it the essential core of his analysis.

I point this out not in the spirit of correcting errors—Schoenberg's analysis is extraordinarily interesting and reasonably convincing as far as it goes—but simply to suggest an analytical approach that he might have taken instead. His willful ignorance of harmony and voice leading and the intensity of the motivic saturation give the analysis an obsessive, forced quality. It is easy enough to hear the voice-leading motions, easier perhaps than to hear the scores of motives. Why, then, is Schoenberg so intent on asserting the primacy of the motive?

The answer has to do with Schoenberg's concerns as a composer. Like his analysis, his own music derives its coherence primarily from the density and richness of its motivic structure, not from any common practice of harmony and voice leading. By analyzing Brahms in this way, by motivicizing him, Schoenberg accomplishes two related aims. First, he establishes a link between his music and Brahms's. He thus justifies his own music by showing that its structural principles are not revolutionary but are hallowed by tradition. Second, he attempts to neutralize Brahms as a threat to his compositional autonomy. It is difficult to compose under the shadow of giant predecessors, to escape the shackles of permanent apprenticeship to earlier masters. One way to achieve artistic freedom is to try to bring about the kind of reversal of priority described earlier. Instead of seeing himself as the weak descendant of Brahms, Schoenberg tries to depict Brahms as a prototypical Schoenberg. When Schoenberg analyzes Brahms, he is not dispassionately and neutrally revealing musical structure; rather, he is passionately struggling with the tradition, simultaneously to establish links with it and domination of it, to see himself not as the latest and least in a dwindling line, but as the culmination of all that has come before.

The same struggle is evident in his second extended analysis, of a passage from the song "O Tod." His analysis, reproduced in Example 2-4, again shows an extraordinary motivic saturation, this time by motive forms derived from the interval of a third. Again, Schoenberg has motivicized a work by Brahms, marginalizing the harmony and voice leading while centralizing the motivic structure. In measures 1–5 Schoenberg accounts for every note in the melody (and many in the accompaniment) in terms of motive 'a' (a descending third), motive 'b' (the inversion of 'a'), and motive 'c' ('a' filled in with a passing note). The additional staves below the music introduce a chain of descending thirds (called motive 'e'), an idea that becomes important later in the piece.

As before, the intensity of the analysis is striking. Schoenberg's motivic preoccupations override all other concerns. In his analysis of the melody in measure 5, for example, Schoenberg identifies an occurrence of 'b' followed by 'a'. But neither of these statements is a structural unit in any voice-leading sense. The B is not related to the G; rather, the B is an upper neighbor to the A, itself an upper neighbor to the G. At moments like this, where other interpretations easily suggest themselves, the depth of Schoenberg's

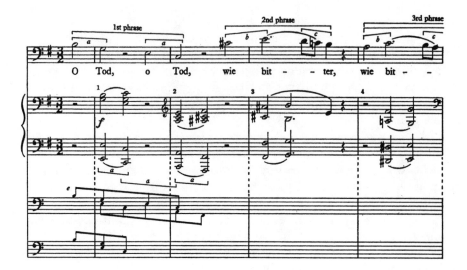

EXAMPLE 2-4   Schoenberg's motivic analysis of Brahms, "O Tod," from *Four Serious Songs,* Op. 121

EXAMPLE 2-4 (*Continued*)

commitment to his motivic orientation becomes clear. One does not have to analyze in that way—one can search for other sources of coherence—but Schoenberg has his own artistic reasons for his insistence on the primacy of the motive.

The active, assertive nature of the analysis is apparent throughout. The statements of motive 'e' in measures 8, 9, and 10 are particularly notable, since each involves an obvious musical distortion. The statements in measures 8 and 9 require reversing two notes written by Brahms (that is the meaning of the ** at the beginning of these measures). The statement of motive 'e' in the melody in measure 10 involves an even more radical interpretation. To construct this motive Schoenberg plucks notes from the chain of descending thirds that concludes the measure—the second note from D–B, no notes from A–F-sharp, and both notes from G–E. The analysis at this point has a particularly forced quality. Schoenberg is not so much revealing a statement of 'e' as he is imposing it as an affirmative, assertive act. He is trying to bend the piece to his will, to force it to behave in a certain way, a Schoenbergian way. The analysis reveals much about Brahms, but even more about Schoenberg.

Speaking of "O Tod," Schoenberg says, "The sense of logic and economy and the power of inventiveness which builds melodies of so much natural fluency deserve the admiration of every music lover who expects more than sweetness and beauty from music."[33] These words, particularly since they refer directly to Brahms's motivic organization, could apply equally well to Schoenberg's own music, so often praised for the density of its structure and criticized for its lack of sweetness. In other words, Schoenberg values Brahms to the extent to which Brahms emulates Schoenberg. This is putting it a bit starkly, but it is important to acknowledge openly the self-aggrandizing nature of Schoenberg's analytical work. Schoenberg seems to praise Brahms, but in fact depicts Brahms as one who does partially what Schoenberg does better than anyone else, namely "working with the tones of the motif."

Schoenberg's *Fundamentals of Musical Composition,* a textbook in musical composition for young composers, contains many illustrative examples. All are drawn, as was Schoenberg's usual procedure, from the masterworks of the eighteenth and nineteenth centuries, and most reflect Schoenberg's motivic orientation. Even his discussion of a seemingly unrelated topic such as phrase structure is permeated by motivic thinking. For example, he identifies four aspects of constructing simple themes (of approximately eight measures), and each of the four is characterized by its motivic role:

Beginning of the sentence. "The construction of the beginning determines the construction of the continuation. In its opening segment a theme must clearly present (in addition to tonality, tempo and metre) its basic motive."[34]

Antecedent of the period. "The first phrase is not repeated immediately, but united with more remote (contrasting) motive-forms, to constitute the first half of the period, the *antecedent*." [35]

Consequent of the period. "The consequent is a modified repetition of the antecedent, made necessary by the remote motive-forms in mm. 3–4." [36]

Completion of the sentence. "Development implies not only growth, augmentation, extension, and expansion, but also reduction, condensation and intensification. The purpose of liquidation is to counteract the tendency toward unlimited extension . . . In conjunction with a cadence or half cadence, this process can be used to provide adequate delimitation for a sentence." [37]

This motivic orientation is reflected in most of the brief analyses that accompany the text. His analysis of the opening of Mozart's Piano Sonata K. 331 (first movement), is typical (see Example 2-5). [38] Schoenberg uses this example to demonstrate various aspects of antecedent-consequent theme construction, including the possibility that "a coherent contrast can also be produced through a decrease of smaller notes, in which case the motive-form appears to be a reduction." [39] The "motive-form" he traces is the interval of a third. As with his analyses of Brahms's music, Schoenberg's concern with the motivic third seems, at times, to override Mozart's apparent voice leading. The melodic leap from C-sharp to E in measure 4, for example, is not obviously a structural unit. The E has only the most local kind of voice-leading significance—it is an accented upper neighbor to the D that immediately follows it. The voice-leading motion in this half of the measure is from C-sharp to D, not from C-sharp to E. Schoenberg's insistence on the third is evidence of his commitment to motivic structure as the principal determinant of musical coherence. He thus misreads into Mozart the kind of

EXAMPLE 2-5 Schoenberg's motivic analysis of Mozart, Piano Sonata K. 331 (first movement)

motivic coherence that he values in his own music. As with his analyses of Brahms and other tonal masters, this analysis reveals as much about Schoenberg as about his ostensible subject.

A similar kind of misreading is involved in Schoenberg's discussion of nonharmonic tones in his *Theory of Harmony*. There, he considers sonorities formed by what traditional tonal theory would term "nonharmonic tones," purely linear events without harmonic significance. Schoenberg argues that, in a tightly constructed piece, no sonority can be irrelevant to the structure and, therefore, that sonorities formed by nonharmonic tones must be taken seriously as harmonic events.

The historical evolution, after all, tells only in what order and by what route those harmonies broke into music, but not how they relate to the principal aim of our activity. Thus, whereas these harmonies may of course have arisen as accidental harmonic structures, they could be, nevertheless, just as legitimate and basic as the others, whose fundamental character we have already recognized.[40]

I believe now I have shown that these combinations are neither any more accidental nor necessarily any less influential than the chords of the system, that neither the historical evolution nor the treatment observable in the literature determines their harmonic significance. I have also shown that they would not belong in the study of harmony if they were non-harmonic, and I can now surely come to the conclusion that: *There are no non-harmonic tones, for harmony means tones sounding together* . . . Non-harmonic tones are merely those that the theorists could not fit into their systems of harmony.[41]

This attitude leads Schoenberg to analyses of Mozart's Symphony in G Minor and a motet by Bach in which he "discovers" harmonies and harmonic relations that traditional tonal theory would explain away as incidental linear events. In Mozart's G-Minor Symphony, for example, Schoenberg calls attention to a single chord type—set-class 4-19 (0148)—that occurs in two different dispositions within a short span of music but which would be unclassifiable by traditional labels. Schoenberg suggests that there is a direct sonic connection between these two occurrences, a connection not mediated by functional harmony. Schoenberg thus "discovers" in Mozart one of his own characteristic harmonies used in his own characteristic way. This is the mark of a strong misreading: Schoenberg makes Mozart look like Schoenberg.[42] Thus, even in the common-practice works of the eighteenth and nineteenth centuries, he finds that the motivic relations as much as the tonal relations determine the musical construction. "We shall find in the classics, besides the unity of tonal relations, that at least the same end of coherence is attained with at least the same amount of carefulness, through the unity of configurations, the unity of ideas. Tonality is thus seen to be not the only means of producing the unity of a piece."[43] Schoenberg has expressed the same idea in even stronger terms: "Coherence in music can only depend on motifs and their metamorphoses and developments."[44]

Schoenberg's best-known analysis of a tonal work concerns the fourth movement of Beethoven's String Quartet in F Major, Op. 135. The context of this analysis, in the essay "Composition with Twelve Tones," makes clear its self-justifying nature. Schoenberg asserts the validity of his own compositional procedures by finding precedents for them in universally acknowledged masterworks. "The basic set is used [in twelve-tone works] in diverse mirror forms. The composers of the last century had not employed such mirror forms as much as the masters of contrapuntal times; at least, they seldom did so consciously. Nevertheless, there exist examples, of which I want to mention only one from Beethoven's last String Quartet, Op. 135, in F major." Schoenberg's analytical example is reproduced here as Example 2-6. "The original form, *a*, 'Muss es sein', appears in *b* inverted and in the major; *c* shows the retrograde form of this inversion, which, now reinverted in *d* and filled out with passing notes in *e*, results in the second phrase of the main theme."[45]

Schoenberg makes a valiant effort here to equate his own motivic usage with Beethoven's. In doing so, he necessarily obscures crucial differences between tonal and twelve-tone composition. In tonal music the motivic manipulations are constrained by the norms of tonal syntax. In twelve-tone music the motives themselves determine the progression and structure of the music.[46] Yet it is not difficult to imagine why Schoenberg did not want to dwell on such distinctions. He wanted to present himself as the rightful heir to the classical tradition by emphasizing his continuity and connection with his predecessors. At the same time, he sought to prove his own originality and independence, by depicting his predecessors as nascent Schoenbergs. They work with tones of the motif in a relatively rudimentary way; he does so with unprecedented abundance and intensity.

Of course, motivic relations are not the exclusive focus of Schoenberg's theoretical studies. He devotes considerable attention to harmonic function, which is the subject of two of his most important published works— *Theory of Harmony* (1911) and *Structural Functions of Harmony* (1954). But in most of his specifically analytical work he centralizes motivic structure and marginalizes harmony and voice leading.

Like Schoenberg, Webern also discusses the evolution of Western music primarily from the point of view of motivic relations. In *The Path to the New Music* Webern outlines a teleological view of history, tracing musical developments that culminate in his own music. In his discussions of early music (from Gregorian chants through the late sixteenth century), Webern says,

EXAMPLE 2-6   Schoenberg's interpretation of motivic development in Beethoven, String Quartet in F Major, Op. 135 (fourth movement)

"We must look at all this from two standpoints; on the one hand, that of comprehensibility and unity, on the other that of the conquest of the tonal field."[47] The phrase "conquest of the tonal field" refers to the evolution of functional harmonic relations and major-minor tonality. His discussion focuses much more on questions of "comprehensibility," by which he means motivic structure. The earliest source of unity in music, for Webern, was direct repetition and, in polyphonic music, direct imitation. Later,

REMAKING THE PAST

composers became more resourceful in varying and developing the original motivic ideas: "Resourcefulness soon went further; something can be the same but under slightly altered conditions, as when the line is turned backwards (cancrizan). But then the following also happened—the series of notes was repeated but altering the direction of the intervals (inversion). What can we conclude from this? What are we to make of it? We already see in this epoch that composers' every effort went to produce unity among the various parts, in the interests of comprehensibility."[48]

From these historical roots, Webern traces the rise of the motive ("the smallest independent particle of a musical idea") with varied or unvaried repetition as the basic principle. Webern's analytical standpoint, then, is very similar to Schoenberg's. Both see the universal source of musical coherence as stemming from a *Grundgestalt* composed-out via developing variation. "An ash-tray, seen from all sides, is always the same, and yet different. So an idea should be presented in the most multifarious way possible. One such way is backwards movement—cancrizan; another is mirroring—inversion. The development of tonality meant that these old methods of presentation were pushed into the background, but they still make themselves felt in a way, even in classical times, in 'thematic development.' This path led to ever-increasing refinement of the thematic network."[49]

According to Webern, this "ever-increasing refinement" reaches its culmination in Schoenberg's music and in Webern's own. Motivic unity and concentration are the standards by which earlier music is judged and the goal toward which composition must always strive.

So the style Schoenberg and his school are seeking is a new inter-penetration of music's material in the horizontal and vertical: polyphony, which has so far reached its climaxes in the Netherlanders and Bach, then later in the classical composers. There's this constant effort to derive as much as possible from one principal idea.

To develop everything else from one principal idea! That's the strongest unity— when everybody does the same, as with the Netherlanders, where the theme was introduced by each individual part, varied in every possible way, with different entries and in different registers. But in what form? That's where art comes in! But the watchword must always be "Thematicism, thematicism, thematicism!"[50]

Webern did not publish any analyses of individual earlier works, but his general remarks on tonal and pre-tonal music make his analytical bias unmistakable. Like Schoenberg, he motivicizes his predecessors, valuing in them their application of his own structural credo: "Thematicism, thematicism, thematicism!"

Berg shows a similar motivic orientation in his discussions of earlier music. His only sustained analysis of a tonal piece comes in his response to an essay

EXAMPLE 2-7 Berg's motivic analysis of "Traümerei," from *Kinderszenen,* Op. 15

by the composer Hans Pfitzner, in which Pfitzner had argued that melodic beauty is ineffable, beyond the reach of analysis or explanation.[51] Pfitzner effusively praised Schumann's "Traümerei," for example, but proclaimed the impossibility of ever understanding the sources of its beauty. As a rebuttal, Berg offers a motivic analysis of "Traümerei," one strikingly similar, both in its appearance and in its orientation, to Schoenberg's analyses discussed earlier. Berg demonstrates the beauty of Schumann's music in the same way that Schoenberg demonstrates the progressiveness of Brahms's. The first part of Berg's analysis, with the various motivic segments he marked, is shown in Example 2-7. Berg comments on this passage,

My feeling is—to take only this recurrent rising phrase (see the motif marked *a*)— that the auxiliary note E, dissonant with respect to the F major triad disposed as a succession of notes, is the characteristic and charming element. And we must not forget that this whole turn of phrase is felt immediately as a variation (and what a variation!) of the initial leap of a fourth. This leap also survives in the motif of the descending phrase (b, c, d) constantly changing into different intervals (m) by taking advantage of every opportunity provided by the harmony.[52]

For Berg, the beauty of Schumann's melody *can* be explained—it resides in the melody's motivic richness and coherence. "The beauty of this melody does not actually lie so much in the large number of motivic ideas, but in the three other characteristic features of beautiful melodies. Namely: the exceptional pregnancy of the individual motifs; their profuse relations with one another; and the manifold application of the given motivic material."[53] Like Schoenberg and Webern, then, Berg misreads his predecessors by motivicizing their music. I do not mean to suggest that these composers are in any sense falsifying the "facts" about earlier music, except insofar as any analysis must be partial and must reflect the biases and interests of the analyst. Rather, we must recognize that their passionate interest in earlier music is simultaneously a passionate commitment to their own compositional interests.

Bartók published no analyses of earlier Western art music and virtually ignored the classical mainstream in his writings generally. It might thus be argued that his true predecessors were Hungarian and Rumanian folk musicians, not the classical masters. Many studies of Bartók have adopted this point of view and have focused on his relation to the folk tradition. Certainly with regard to the written evidence, the contrast to Schoenberg could hardly be more stark. Where Schoenberg wrote traditional harmony treatises stocked with examples from the Western canon, Bartók published transcriptions and recordings of folk music. Bartók explicitly claimed Hungarian and Rumanian peasant music, not Beethoven or Brahms, as his principal influence.

It would be a mistake, however, to take Bartók's writings at face value. To a large extent, Bartók used folk materials precisely as a way of avoiding the anxiety of influence of the mainstream art tradition. He used folk materials not because he was unaffected by the overwhelming legacy of the Western classical tradition, but because he hoped to circumvent that tradition. The intensity of his interest in Eastern European folk music is, to a significant degree, a measure of the burden on him of the classical tradition.

Although the folk materials do not render him immune to the weight of tradition, they do assist him in coming to terms with it. What Bartók "finds" in the folk tradition is just what Schoenberg "finds" in Brahms, Mozart, and Bach—namely, an affirmation of a type of musical structure based on the integration of musical space with respect to the motive. Only in this way, both composers apparently concluded, could there emerge a new type of musical structure powerful enough to resist the pull of the past.

In his discussion of his Suite No. 2 for Orchestra, Op. 4, Bartók traces the source of its structure to pentatonic folk melodies: "A principal motive in my [Suite for Orchestra] is as follows" (see Example 2-8A). "The final chord of the movement," shown in Example 2-8B, "is a simultaneous resonance of all four (or five) tones of the motive: a condensed form of the same, to a certain extent, a vertical projection of the previous horizontal form. This result is obtained by a logical process, and not, as many objectors believed, through sheer whimsicality. The incentive to do this was given by these pentatonic melodies."[54] Bartók claims that pentatonic melodies were the source of this procedure, but he still arrives at the Schoenbergian structural principle of a motivically determined integration of musical space.

Bartók acknowledges this seeming coincidence without, however, offering a convincing explanation for it: "Rumanian and Slovak folk songs show a highly interesting treatment of the tritone . . . as may be seen in the

EXAMPLE 2-8A

EXAMPLE 2-8B

EXAMPLE 2-9A   EXAMPLE 2-9B

following examples." Four folk tunes follow that are not reprinted here. "These forms brought about the free use of the augmented fourth, the diminished fifth, and of chords such as [those shown in Examples 2-9A and 2-9B]. Through inversion, and by placing these chords in juxtapositions one above the other, many different chords are obtained and with them the freest melodic as well as harmonic treatment of the twelve tones of our present-day harmonic system. Of course, many other (foreign) composers, who do not lean upon folk music, have met with similar results at about the same time—only in an intuitive or speculative way, which, evidently, is a procedure equally justifiable. The difference is that we created through Nature, for: the peasant's art is a phenomenon of Nature."[55]

Bartok's attribution of causality—that certain melodic patterns "brought about" certain kinds of harmonic usages—is not convincing. The folk music that Bartók so assiduously collected can be interpreted in a variety of ways and can thus "bring about" many different kinds of usages. What it "brought about" for Bartók was a new structural principle that permitted him to come to terms with the Western art tradition. Bartók's misreadings of the folk tradition permitted his even stronger misreadings of his Germanic predecessors. He found in the folk tradition what he needed to find— a way of organizing music through motivically controlled integration of musical space. He then used this principle to resist and remake the central classical canon.

It is virtually impossible to discuss Stravinsky as an analyst. He never gave sustained attention to a specific passage of earlier music, and there is not a single remark—in the *Autobiography,* the *Poetics,* or the dialogues with Robert Craft—that could reasonably be called analytical. Stravinsky simply had an aversion to theory and analysis: "Analysis as little explains a masterpiece or calls it into being as an ontological proof explains or causes the existence of God."[56]

It is easy, however, to glean Stravinsky's general aesthetic and philosophical principles from a variety of sources. He frequently expresses his tastes in earlier music, identifying his favorite or least favorite passages. Although he never gives specific reasons for his preferences, it is possible to get a sense, in general terms, of the kinds of things he admires in earlier music. For example, he tends to praise structural surprises, intrusions, and seeming discontinuities. Thus he cites a certain C-natural from Bach's Cantata "Ich bin vergnügt" as an example of "the wonderful jolts, the sudden modulations, the unexpected harmonic changes, the deceptive cadences that are the joy of every Bach cantata."[57] Similarly, his favorite passage in Beethoven's Eighth Symphony is "the entrance of the trumpets and drum in F major in the last movement, after the F-sharp minor episode."[58] The kind of seeming discontinuity he praises in earlier music is clearly a reflection of what Pieter van den Toorn calls "block juxtaposition" in Stravinsky's own music: "a permanent and evidently indispensable part of his musical thought (of whatever orientation or 'stylistic' persuasion)."[59] In terms of our revisionary ratios, Stravinsky shows a preference for fragmentation and neutralization.

Stravinsky also admires the structural economy of certain earlier works. His praise for Beethoven's Great Fugue—"It is pure interval music, this fugue, and I love it beyond any other"—[60] strikingly recalls his comment on his own music, made during the same period: "I have always composed with intervals."[61] Like Schoenberg, although with incomparably less intensity and depth, Stravinsky tends to praise in earlier music the qualities that most characterize his own. Given the dearth of written evidence, however, one cannot go beyond this very general observation. As we will see in subsequent chapters, he worked out his relationship to the past primarily in notes, not in words.

CHAPTER 3

Recompositions

In notes as in words, twentieth-century composers misread their predecessors in accordance with their own conceptions of musical structure. As their written analyses show, Schoenberg and other composers assert the centrality of motivic relations for earlier music. Their recompositions of earlier pieces make the same assertion in musical terms. In arranging or otherwise subtly modifying tonal works, these composers radically enhance their motivic content and thus create new works by recomposing older ones.

Recomposition is a genre with a long history. The fifteenth century saw arrangements of songs for instruments, the adding of voices to preexistent compositions, the revision of earlier works, and the structural modeling of one piece upon another.[1] In the later Renaissance the use of parody was widespread, most obviously in masses based upon preexistent polyphonic compositions.[2] More recent examples include Bach's arrangements of Vivaldi, Liszt's settings of Beethoven, and Mahler's orchestrations of Schumann's symphonies, among many others.[3] The desire to recompose the works of one's predecessors seems to be almost as old as Western music itself.

In the twentieth century, however, that predilection has reached a peak of intensity and, for several reasons, produces unprecedented kinds of recompositions. First, the historical distance between the recomposition and the original work has lengthened considerably and spans a deep stylistic gulf. Bach's recompositions of Vivaldi and, to a lesser but still significant extent, Liszt's of Beethoven take place within a common musical language. This is far less true of Stravinsky's recompositions of Pergolesi or Schoenberg's of Handel. As a result, twentieth-century recompositions project a particularly striking stylistic clash; the two layers of such works—the original material and the recomposed elements—remain distinct.

Furthermore, a different artistic impulse gives rise to the twentieth-century recompositions. Bach arranged Vivaldi's music to make it playable on the organ. In the process he may have altered it somewhat, but his practical intentions limited the extent of the alterations. When Schoenberg, in contrast, arranged a Bach organ work for large symphony orchestra, his intention was clearly not a practical one. Rather, he attempted to create a new, autonomous work with the same artistic integrity as the original one. Recompositions of this kind do not so much serve an earlier work as transform it.

Most important, twentieth-century recompositions reveal the greater sense of anxiety and belatedness felt by twentieth-century composers toward their predecessors. As with their analyses of earlier music, they recompose older music as a way simultaneously of establishing a link to the tradition and of lightening its burden on them. Recompositions have been largely ignored in the analytical literature, in part because they have been considered atypical of their composers and of the musical mainstream generally. But in their anxious misreading of earlier music, recompositions lie much closer to the mainstream of early twentieth-century music than has generally been acknowledged.

Schoenberg frequently recomposed earlier works, including those of tonal masters such as Bach, Handel, and Brahms.[4] His orchestrations of organ works by Bach are extraordinarily similar in effect to the analytical studies discussed in Chapter 2, in focusing on motivic relations to the virtual exclusion of other structural considerations. His orchestration of Bach's Chorale Prelude "Schmücke dich" (BWV 654) is typical. In this work Schoenberg reveals, and to some extent creates, a musical coherence based upon the motive of a major or minor third. The first six measures, for example, are rich in timbrally isolated third-progressions, as Example 3-1 shows. In measure 1, for instance, the principal melody is in the first English horn and the first E-flat clarinet. The three structural tones in that melody—G, F, and E-flat—are isolated, an octave higher, in the harp. The harp part thus presents a structural, motivic analysis of the principal melody. The other descending thirds identified in Example 3-1 work in the same way, by doubling selected notes from the florid melody. Most of the thirds projected by Schoenberg in this way would be recognized by a voice-leading analysis. The harp's descending third in measure 1, for example, clearly projects the structural framework of Bach's melody.

In some cases, however, Schoenberg isolates a third that has no structural integrity in the Bach, as in the first cello part in measures 2–4. In these measures the melody in the first violin moves from E-flat down to C (by way of D-flat) and then back up to E-flat (by way of D-natural). The structural motions are E-flat–D-flat–C and C–D–E-flat. But the line in the first cello cuts across these motions by moving from D-flat through C down to B-flat.

EXAMPLE 3-1 Motivic thirds in Schoenberg's orchestration of Bach, Chorale Prelude, BWV 654

Although those notes are consonant with the harmonies, they do not constitute a viable voice-leading strand. This tendency for motivic considerations to override voice leading is one familiar from our discussion of Schoenberg's analyses in the preceding chapter. In cases like these Schoenberg is not so much revealing a motivic structure as imposing one, in reflection of his own compositional interest in motivic saturation. Perhaps the most extreme example of motivicization via instrumentation in "Schmücke dich" is Schoenberg's use of the glockenspiel. This instrument plays its only three notes of the entire piece in measures 78–79, where it states the structural descending third of the opening theme: G–F–E-flat.

In addition to instrumentation, Schoenberg employs articulation, register, and even added notes to reinforce the motivic third. For the most part Schoenberg only adds notes for the sake of instrumental doubling or filling out the harmony. The few melodic fragments he adds, however, always have motivic significance. For example, the lines played by the piccolo in measures 57–58 and 59–60 and the horn in measure 65, not contained in Bach's original music, all involve descending thirds. Frequently, Schoenberg uses phrasing marks to break up and articulate what was, in the Bach, an undifferentiated flow of eighth notes. Frequently, as in measures 7–9 and 19–21, the articulation reflects the motivic third. Manipulation of register also plays a role in the projection of the motive. In the final measures of the piece, the flute and piccolo transfer what was originally an inner part into the highest register in order to present a concluding descent from B-flat to G.[5]

Through instrumentation, register transfer, articulation, and an occasional added melodic fragment, Schoenberg has made "Schmücke dich" into a paradigm of the kind of motivic coherence that typifies his own compositions. When he analyzes earlier music (as shown in Chapter 2), he identifies the motivic units with brackets and letters. When he recomposes earlier music, he identifies the motivic units with timbre, register, and articulation. Schoenberg claims that he learned motivic saturation from Bach: "From Bach I learned . . . the art of developing everything from one basic germ-motif and leading smoothly from one figure into another."[6] But influence is a two-way street. Certainly Schoenberg learned from Bach, whose music is often extraordinarily dense motivically. At the same time, however, Schoenberg uses analyses and recompositions to impose motivic organization upon Bach. In this way, he ceases to be Bach's student and becomes his teacher.

In his own comments on his Bach orchestrations Schoenberg comes close to capturing the forceful nature of his interpretations:

Our modern conception of music demanded clarification of the *motivic* procedures in both horizontal and vertical dimensions. That is, we do not find it sufficient to rely on the immanent effect of a contrapuntal structure that is taken for granted, but we want to be aware of this counterpoint in the form of motivic relationships. Homophony has taught us to follow these in the top voice; the intermediate phase of the "polyphonic homophony" of Mendelssohn, Wagner and Brahms has taught us to follow several voices in this manner. Our powers of comprehension will not be satisfied today if we do not apply the same yardstick to Bach.[7]

When Schoenberg speaks of applying the motivic yardstick to Bach, he acknowledges misreading Bach by motivicizing his music. There are many ways to hear Bach's music. Schoenberg, because of his own compositional commitments, encourages us to hear it motivically. In this way, he asserts his position as the culmination of a long historical line of motivic composers.

Schoenberg's Concerto for String Quartet is an orchestration and recomposition of the Concerto Grosso Op. 6, No. 7, by Handel. His misreading of Handel is a bit more elaborate than his misreading of Bach. It not only centers on a somewhat more complex motivic shape, a trichord instead of a single interval, but also involves generalizing that motive into the set-class of which it is a member. The last three movements of Schoenberg's concerto are really fantasias on material derived from Handel's concerto grosso, but the first movement is a direct recomposition, corresponding almost measure for measure with the model. Example 3-2 contains the slow introduction to

EXAMPLE 3-2A   Handel, Concerto Grosso Op. 6, No. 7 (introduction)

REMAKING THE PAST

EXAMPLE 3-2B Schoenberg's recomposition (Concerto for String Quartet)

EXAMPLE 3-2B (*Continued*)

the first movement both in Handel's original and in Schoenberg's recomposition.

Schoenberg has taken the relatively spare Handel composition and projected it onto the rich canvas of the modern symphony orchestra. The pro-
fusion of orchestral colors fragments the lines into small timbral units and
undermines any sense of directed, forward movement. The integrity and

EXAMPLE 3-2B (*Continued*)

strength of the harmonies are subverted as each harmony dissolves into a sea of constantly shifting timbres. The music seems to move more from color to color than from harmony to harmony. In the last measure, for example, the structural arrival on the dominant harmony seems almost incidental to the rapidly changing orchestration: each eighth note in the measure has a distinctive and unique timbre. Schoenberg uses orchestration to neutralize the forward thrust of the harmonic progression.

Even as he undermines the functional harmony of the passage, Schoenberg enhances its motivic structure. A recurring neighbor-note figure in the Handel is indicated with asterisks in Example 3-2A. Schoenberg dramatizes and develops this motive in his recomposition of the passage. In measures 1 and 2 the motive is intensified dynamically, by the sudden crescendo in clarinets and bassoons. In measure 3 the motive is reinforced orchestrationally, by its isolated statement in the lower strings. Beginning in measure 7 the same figure is picked up in the solo instruments, first in the first violin and cello, then in measure 9 by all four solo instruments. Measure 10, where the only moving line is this figure in the solo instruments, represents the culmination of the motivic development in the passage. At the beginning of the passage Schoenberg uses dynamics and instrumentation to reinforce motivic shapes composed by Handel. Toward the end of the passage he adds figures of his own, thus greatly enhancing the music's motivic content.

This added material reinforces the traditional contrast in a concerto between orchestra and soloists. The orchestra plays a substantially unaltered version of the original work, while the solo string quartet introduces new material. In the slow introduction the new material is closely related to the old. In the fugal portion of the movement the solo parts and their more modern style of writing assert themselves more and more, culminating in a wild Schoenbergian cadenza. Some of the music in the solo quartet is foreign both to Handel's concerto grosso and to eighteenth-century musical style in general.

The short passage in example 3-3 contains one of Schoenberg's interpolations of new material in the solo quartet. In texture and musical content this material is clearly differentiated from the accompanying parts, written by Handel. As the example indicates, the solo parts make systematic use of a single trichord, 3-8 (026). The transpositional levels are also indicated, with the second occurrence designated T_o, for reasons that will soon become apparent. While the accompanying parts continue within the constraints of tonality, the solo quartet music is made coherent by the motivic development of this small cell of notes.

Where did Schoenberg get the idea for this particular trichord? Is its selection arbitrary or does it have some explicit connection to Handel's tonal accompaniment, with which it occurs? The accompaniment includes a

EXAMPLE 3-3   Handel's motive generalized in Schoenberg's setting

three-note melodic figure that pervades all of the fugal episodes. In traditional tonal theory this figure, with its prominent tritone, would be understood as part of an embellished arpeggiation of a dominant-seventh or leading-tone chord, leading here toward C minor. But by presenting it in conjunction with the free, atonal development of set-class 3-8 (026) in the solo instruments, Schoenberg invites us to hear it differently. Handel's three-note melodic figure is a member of the same set-class, and Schoenberg suggests musically the possibility of hearing it in that way. He has generalized it into the set-class of which it is a member.

Within measure 58 there are three members of set-class 3-8 (026). Two of them, at T_2 and T_0, were written by Schoenberg. The third, at T_6, was written by Handel. Together, these three transposition levels—T_0, T_2, and T_6—replicate the content of the motive itself (026). In this way, Handel's three-note figure, both in its content and its pitch level, is deeply embedded in the set structure of the music.

There are thus three types of pitch relations operating here and throughout the movement. First, there are the relationships within Handel's original music, relationships defined by traditional tonal harmony and voice leading. Second, there are the motivic or set-class relations within Schoenberg's interpolations, independent of traditional tonal procedures. Third, there is a profound mutual influence between these two networks of relations. Handel's music provides the material for Schoenberg's recomposition. At the same time, Schoenberg suggests new ways of hearing Handel's music, based not on traditional tonal relations but on motivic manipulation.

Schoenberg considered his Concerto for String Quartet an important work, one on which he lavished considerable time and attention: "Whereas it took me only six weeks, respectively, for my 1,100-measure opera [*Von heute auf morgen*] and for the [third] quartet, I spent a good three months on the no more than 400 measures of [the Handel] arrangement—in other words, twice as long."[8] In its revisionary attitude toward the past, and in its thorough motivic structuring, Schoenberg's Concerto for String Quartet is not an anomalous work but one that lies right in the mainstream of his normal compositional practice.

The belief that Stravinsky and Schoenberg were compositionally antithetical, so prevalent among critics during the earlier part of this century, diminished rapidly after Stravinsky adopted the serial approach and has diminished further as our understanding of his pre-serial music has deepened. Stravinsky's recompositions, generally considered the epitome of his neoclassicism (and thus of his dissimilarity to the progressive Schoenberg), reveal a Schoenbergian concern with motivic structure. Like Schoenberg, Stravinsky motivicizes (and generalizes) as he recomposes.

Stravinsky's treatment of Tchaikovsky's song "Lullaby in a Storm," Op. 54, No. 10, in *The Fairy's Kiss* is freer than his other recompositions but gives a good idea of his approach. The melody makes its first complete appearance at Rehearsal 4 (see Example 3-4). The melody is Tchaikovsky's, but the accompaniment is pure Stravinsky in its static, nonprogressional diatonicism and in its lack of traditional harmonic coordination between melody and accompaniment. By setting the melody in this way, Stravinsky has already begun to transform it. He neutralizes the forward progression of its implied tonal harmonies and drains it of its normal expressiveness. The transformation extends even further, however.

The head motive of the melody consists of three notes—C, E, and F— which would be understood as representing scale degrees $\hat{5}$, $\hat{7}$, and $\hat{8}$ in a normal tonal context. But that motive can also be understood in another way, as a member of set-class 3-4 (015). The varied repeat of the motive in measures 3 and 4 can be understood in the same way. This rehearing, which involves generalizing a motive into a pitch-class set, is Stravinsky's central misreading. In the extended coda of the work, reminiscent stylistically of the rapturous endings of *Les Noces, Symphony of Psalms,* and *Symphonies of Wind Instruments,* that process of generalization comes to full flower.

EXAMPLE 3-4 Stravinsky's setting of a melody by Tchaikovsky ("Lullaby in a Storm," Op. 54, No. 10)

Toward the conclusion of the coda Tchaikovsky's melody dissolves and fragments amid sustained notes in the outer voices and an ostinato-like inner voice. The last six measures of the piece are shown in Example 3-5. The moving part (upper strings) states another member of set-class 3-4 (015), now containing the pitch-classes G, A-flat, and C. This repeating fragment arises from inverting Tchaikovsky's motive around pitch-class C, retaining C as a common tone. It also involves registrally expanding Tchaikovsky's motive to span a major tenth instead of the original perfect fourth. Through registral expansion and pitch-class inversion, the motive is radically transformed. Even more striking, the vertical sonority formed in two places (indicated by arrows in Example 3-5) is produced by the same process of pitch-class inversion. The sounding notes are E-flat, G, and A-flat. This new form of 3-4 is related to the simultaneous melodic statement by inversion around G and A-flat, retaining those pitch-classes as common tones.

An extended network of transformations thus leads from Tchaikovsky's motive to Stravinsky's coda. The motive, understood as a pitch-class set, is inverted and expanded into a new melodic fragment; that fragment is then

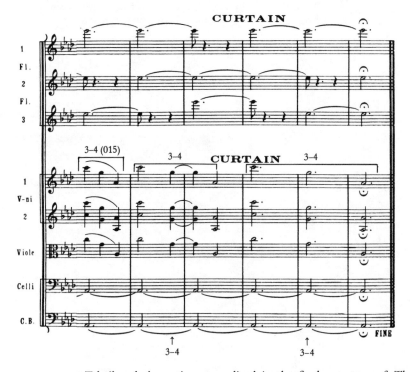

EXAMPLE 3-5 Tchaikovsky's motive generalized in the final measures of *The Fairy's Kiss*

itself inverted into the penultimate chord of the work. That chord harmonizes the fragment, thus creating the integration of musical space so characteristic of post-tonal music. Stravinsky takes a motive from Tchaikovsky and generalizes it into a pitch-class set. He then manipulates that set in characteristically post-tonal fashion. From these manipulations a new musical structure emerges, one that incorporates Tchaikovsky's music and simultaneously transforms it.

The transformation reveals Stravinsky's deep ambivalence toward his model. Stravinsky seems initially to have turned to Tchaikovsky out of admiration, but the radical nature of his recomposing expresses a more critical attitude.[9] This ambivalence is evident in Stravinsky's own comments on *The Fairy's Kiss*. In his *Autobiography* Stravinsky claims to have recomposed Tchaikovsky as an homage. "The idea was that I should compose something inspired by the music of Tchaikovsky. My well-known fondness for this composer, and, still more, the fact that November, the time fixed for the performance, would mark the thirty-fifth anniversary of his death, induced me to accept the offer. It would give me an opportunity of paying my heartfelt homage to Tchaikovsky's wonderful talent."[10]

Yet, the work is perhaps less an homage than a clash of competing musical styles. By recomposing Tchaikovsky, and by subjecting his music to a full range of post-tonal transformations, Stravinsky asserts his independence from his traditional Russian tonal roots. That Stravinsky was not motivated exclusively by admiration for the earlier composer was something he acknowledged later in his life: "Listening the other day to a concert of the saccharine source material for [*The Fairy's Kiss*], I almost succumbed to diabetes."[11] Much of Stravinsky's recomposition, in fact, tends to alter the "saccharine" quality of Tchaikovsky's music by disrupting the square regularity of its phrase structure and infusing its accompanimental figures with greater rhythmic energy. The romantic expressiveness of Tchaikovsky's music is even more profoundly disrupted by the generalization of his motives into pitch-class sets and by the post-tonal manipulation of those sets. Stravinsky recomposes Tchaikovsky in part as a commentary on romanticism in music, a familiar Stravinskian bête noire.

This process is closely related to the revisionary ratio that Bloom calls *kenosis*. A kenosis occurs in poetry when the later poet takes images from a predecessor and empties them of all excess: "The later poet, apparently emptying himself of his own afflatus, his imaginative godhood, seems to humble himself as though he were ceasing to be a poet."[12] In certain cases, elements that in an earlier work were charged with heightened emotion are treated in a dry or austere way in a later one. As a result, the precursor work is made to seem overinflated and self-indulgent by comparison. This is a common strategy among twentieth-century artists who seek forcefully to resist the excesses of romanticism. Stravinsky's recomposition of Tchaikovsky by generalizing his motives into pitch-class sets involves a kenosis in this sense.

––––––––––

Pulcinella is probably the best known twentieth-century recomposition and, like *The Fairy's Kiss,* it reveals a deep ambivalence on the part of Stravinsky toward his source pieces, by Pergolesi and others.[13] This ambivalence is perfectly captured by Stravinsky's own comment on the piece, in which his claim of love for his models is couched in aggressive metaphors of force, penetration, and possession: "Should my line of action with regard to Pergolesi be dominated by my love or by my respect for his music? Is it love or respect that urges us to possess a woman? Is it not by love alone that we succeed in penetrating to the very essence of a being? But, then, does love diminish respect? Respect alone remains barren, and can never be seen as a productive or creative factor. In order to create there must be a dynamic force, and what force is more potent than love?"[14]

Stravinsky's love is thus not a generous one but one that involves asserting his power over the love object. As with *The Fairy's Kiss,* Stravinsky's "possession" of the eighteenth-century source pieces of *Pulcinella* involves the radical revision of their pitch structure through motivicization and generalization. In much of *Pulcinella* the original scores are either left substantially intact or are altered only by rhythmic or timbral means. In certain movements and at certain key moments, however, Stravinsky significantly alters the pitch structure. The alterations are never so extreme as to obscure the underlying source piece; the eighteenth-century models are always easy to discern beneath the surface. At the same time, the alterations are so consistent that a new source of unification emerges superimposed on the old one. By subtly modifying his models, Stravinsky creates a small number of new, nontriadic harmonies that permeate the entire suite.

The music of the andantino section (shown in Example 3-6) is typical of Stravinsky's procedure. The melody in the first violin is precisely as it occurs in the Trio Sonata No. 8, once attributed to Pergolesi but now known to be by one Domenico Gallo. The line in the second violin is a truncated but otherwise virtually unaltered statement of the second melodic voice of the original trio sonata. The accompaniment, however, shows Stravinsky at work. Instead of moving flexibly to support the melody, the accompaniment is an ostinato. This ostinato neutralizes the customary forward flow of traditional tonal harmony. It makes the music static rather than progressive. The ostinato sometimes coincides with the implied harmonization of the melody and sometimes does not, thus undermining the sense of functional movement from tonic to dominant and back. It stratifies the texture into relatively autonomous layers; the melody and accompaniment are not integrated with each other. Finally, it makes of these measures a self-

EXAMPLE 3-6 Motivic tetrachords in *Pulcinella*

contained, insulated musical block. The cessation of the ostinato at Rehearsal 43 becomes a point of abrupt change rather than gentle articulation. In each of these respects—static diatonicism, layered texture, and block juxtaposition—the piece recalls other works by Stravinsky rather than classical tonality.

A significant transformation takes place in the pitch organization as well. Stravinsky's entire new accompaniment consists of four notes—B-flat, C, D, and F—that form a member of set-class 4-22 (0247). Sometimes these notes coincide with the implied tonal harmonization (or with Gallo's figured bass) and sometimes they do not. The "wrong notes" (circled in Example 3-6) generally form either 4-22 (0247) or 4-23 (0257), two tetrachords that could occur in tonal music only as a by-product of certain kinds of embellishments. The simultaneity on the downbeat of the fourth measure of Rehearsal 42, containing two notes from the original music and two notes added by Stravinsky, replicates the pitch-class content of Stravinsky's accompaniment. In this way, the musical space is integrated with regard to Stravinsky's tetrachords. The tetrachords are formed by taking away or adding notes to a triadic original, and it is easy enough to hear these sets as deformed or altered triads.[15] But this interpretation would lose what is most exciting about the music, the clash of two fully developed conceptions of musical structure—the tonal and the post-tonal—and the reinterpretation of the tonal elements that this clash brings about. These two tetrachords, 4-22 and 4-23, are virtual signature sonorities of Stravinsky, occurring in a variety of contexts throughout his oeuvre. Their pervasiveness in *Pulcinella* is the essence of Stravinsky's transformation of his tonal models.

Their usage in the andantino movement of *Pulcinella* culminates in the

EXAMPLE 3-7   Motivic tetrachords in *Pulcinella*

music shown in Example 3-7. The accompaniment is again an ostinato, this time comprising the collection C, D, F, and G, a member of set-class 4-23 (0257). Why did Stravinsky choose this particular collection in this context? I believe the imitative entrances of the principal melody in the flutes hold the answer. As Example 3-7 shows, the first two notes of the melody (C, D) and the first two notes of its imitation (F, G), taken together, form the same set-class. This is an instance of the revisionary ratio of compression. Musical elements that are independent in a tonal context are compressed into a single entity. The result of that compression here is a member of set-class 4-23 that is simultaneously heard as a single musical unit in the accompaniment.

In a similar vein, the first four measures of each of Gallo's melodies comprise set-class 4-22 (0247), recalling the accompaniment from the beginning of the movement (see Example 3-6). A typically post-tonal pitch organization, derived from elements in the source piece, is imposed upon the source piece. A radical transformation is thus achieved through the most economical means. Not only do we hear the links among the statements of 4-22 and 4-23 created by Stravinsky's alterations, but more radically, we begin to hear occurrences of those sets within the tonal model itself. By placing a tonal melody in a new musical context, Stravinsky invites us to hear it in a new way.

In the serenata movement from *Pulcinella,* Stravinsky's alterations of his original (an aria from *Il Flaminio* by Pergolesi) are subtle and not very

numerous. Still, as in the andantino, they have the effect of superimposing a
new dimension of musical organization upon the old one. The traditional
tonal relations remain intact, but they now operate side by side with an
organization based on recurring pitch-class sets. The first phrase of the movement is shown in Example 3-8. In this passage the oboe and violas play unaltered the upper voice and bass line from Pergolesi's aria. The remaining
parts, Stravinsky's addition to the passage, project an ostinato. Stravinsky's
most significant alterations of his models usually involve ostinati, and they
usually have the kinds of effects discussed above: they undermine the sense
of progression, they stratify the texture, and they create insulated sonorous
blocks. In addition, the transformation reaches into the pitch relationships.
Specifically, the interaction of Stravinsky's ostinato with Pergolesi's melody
and bass line creates nontriadic harmonies and not in a random fashion but
in a way that lends consistency and coherence to the music. The harmony
formed on the third beat of the first measure, for example, is a member
of set-class 3-4 (015). Needless to say, this is not a triad and was not part of
the original music. It consists of the C–G of Stravinsky's ostinato together
with Pergolesi's A-flat. The harmony formed at the end of the second beat

EXAMPLE 3-8   Motivic trichords in *Pulcinella*

of the second measure is an inverted form of the same set-class, now formed by Stravinsky's C–G combined with Pergolesi's B. It is followed, on beat three of the second measure, by a repeat of the original trichord. Stravinsky has thus set up an aural link between the two measures, unifying them through motivic association.

A similar association is created through a second trichord, 3-9 (027). The occurrences of this trichord (both in its original and inverted forms) are also indicated in Example 3-8. Interestingly, the first occurrence of this chord (at the end of the first beat of the first measure) is found in Pergolesi's music, a by-product of an accented passing note within the tonic harmony. Stravinsky, however, exploits the sonority in a more systematic way, as an integral musical unit. Again we see the familiar process of transformation: a sonority is taken from the tonal model, generalized into a pitch-class set, then developed following post-tonal norms.

The most striking passage in this movement occurs in the cadence at its midpoint (see Example 3-9). This moment is pure Stravinsky: a static, diatonic block. The five notes sounding here (C, E-flat, F, G, and B-flat) form the pentachord 5-35 (02479), which is a superset of most of the other important nontriadic harmonies of the movement. The cadential pentachord is partitioned into two smaller sets, clearly articulated by instrumentation and rhythm. The concertino parts have set-class 4-22 (0247) and the ripieno have 3-9 (027). Both of these sets play an important role in shaping this movement and, indeed, in shaping *Pulcinella* as a whole.

As in the andantino movement, the sets used by Stravinsky are derived

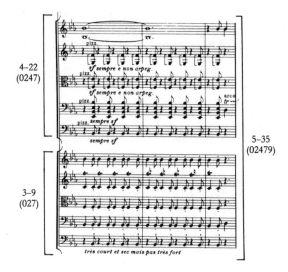

EXAMPLE 3-9   Cadence in *Pulcinella*

REMAKING THE PAST

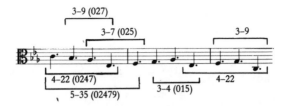

EXAMPLE 3-10   Subset structure of Pergolesi's bass line

from elements in the source piece. Example 3-10 contains Pergolesi's bass line for the first few measures (assigned to the viola in Stravinsky's orchestration). As the example shows, virtually all of the sets I have been discussing, including those from the andantino movement, are linear subsets. The sets are thus stated horizontally at the beginning and vertically elsewhere, the kind of multidimensional presentation that is characteristic of post-tonal works. Obviously, Pergolesi and his contemporaries would not have conceived a musical line in these terms. Yet it seems that Stravinsky did conceive it in this way and, through his recomposition, leads us to conceive it that way also.

Stravinsky's procedure is consistent throughout *Pulcinella*. His ostinati transform not only the texture of the music but its pitch organization as well. They contain a small number of closely related pitch-class sets, giving them a reasonably uniform sound. The interaction between the added music and the original lines creates additional forms of the same sets. Most radically, the presence of these sets in the music added by Stravinsky brings about a rehearing of the tonal models. Stravinsky's additions teach us to listen for his favorite pitch-class sets in music by Pergolesi, Gallo, and others.

It is no coincidence that Stravinsky's favorite sets tend to be subsets of the diatonic collection: 5-35 (02479), 4-22 (0247), 4-23 (0257), 3-7 (025), and 3-9 (027) are all diatonic, but none would be the principal harmony or motive of a traditional tonal piece. In recomposing his eighteenth-century models, Stravinsky takes certain incidental sonorities and makes them the central structures in a new type of pitch organization. He creates a new kind of diatonicism, one based not on traditional harmony and voice leading, but on characteristically post-tonal manipulations of diatonic subsets. This new diatonicism is apparent in *Pulcinella* and throughout Stravinsky's oeuvre, from the beginning of *Petrushka* to the last scene of *The Rake's Progress*.

Just as Schoenberg depicted Bach and Handel as prototypical Schoenbergs, Stravinsky has turned his eighteenth-century models into prototypical Stravinskys. This is perhaps what he means when he calls *Pulcinella* "a look in the mirror." "*Pulcinella* was my discovery of the past, the epiphany through which the whole of my late work became possible. It was a backward look, of course—the first of many love affairs in that direction—but it was a look in the mirror, too."[16] A strong composer like Stravinsky chooses to see himself not as the progeny of past masters but as the creator of himself and his past. When Stravinsky looks at earlier composers, he insists upon seeing a reflection of himself.

Of course, original works are not effaced by the procedures of recomposition. They may be subverted and covered over, but they continue to exert a structural pull. As a result, recompositions are riven by tension. The source piece tries to speak in its customary way, through its tonal harmony and voice leading, while the added material tries to put new words in its mouth. This struggle for priority between post-tonal and tonal, and between twentieth-century composers and their eighteenth-century models, is waged continuously in these recompositions.

The struggle begins with the selection of a well-crafted piece of traditional music. Then, certain sonorities or motivic structures that might lend themselves to subsequent transformations are identified in the source piece. Finally, the original piece is recomposed in such a way as to produce these sonorities, or their transpositionally or inversionally equivalent forms, throughout the music. The struggle produces a composition with two layers of structure, one based on traditional tonal relations and one based on recurring motivic structures or pitch-class sets. The tonal layer influences the motivic layer by providing material for it. At the same time, the presence of the motivic layer forces a reinterpretation of the tonal layer, and traditional formations come to be heard in a novel way.

Bach's *Canonic Variations* on the chorale melody "Vom Himmel hoch" represent a pinnacle of his canonic craft. Using the melody as a cantus firmus (in the manner of a chorale prelude), Bach adds a series of canons at different intervals (including one by augmentation) and, sometimes, a florid free part as well. The material for the canons is always drawn from the chorale melody, and the counterpoint can become remarkably complex. In the fifth and final variation, for example, there are canons in inversion—at the sixth, third, second, and ninth—culminating, in the final measures of the piece, in an extraordinary stretto where the different phrases of the chorale are sounded at various intervals, directions, and rates of speed.

By contrast (and with some notable exceptions), Stravinsky did not generally make extensive use of contrapuntal devices. Yet, in his recomposition of the *Canonic Variations,* his most significant alterations involve the addition of contrapuntal lines to an already rich fabric. Stravinsky undertook this recomposition during his last compositional period and, without question, his interest in Bach's canonic procedures is related to his serial concerns.[17] In addition to the implicit relationship of canon to serialism, Stravinsky's later works include many explicit contrapuntal and canonic devices. Stravinsky thus confronted in his later works not only the contrapuntal tradition epitomized by Bach but also the more recent generation of predecessors, the classical twelve-tone composers.

By the time he recomposed the *Canonic Variations,* Stravinsky's musical style had changed dramatically since *Pulcinella.* Yet his procedure in both instances is remarkably similar, as are the musical and aesthetic results. He does not add or elide any measures of the original work (as he did in *Pulcinella*), but through a series of subtle alterations and modifications he entirely transforms the original.

Among his most subtle changes are those involving articulation. The dry, staccato articulations so characteristic of his own music are used extensively in his orchestration of the *Canonic Variations.* Similarly, he tends to emphasize syncopations where they occur in the *Canonic Variations* by doubling them or preceding them with a rest, evoking his own stylistic predispositions. He thus imposes on the *Canonic Variations* a performance practice and compositional outlook associated with his own music.

The stylistic performance problem in my music is one of articulation and rhythmic diction. Nuance depends on these. Articulation is mainly separation . . . For fifty years I have endeavoured to teach musicians to play

$$sf\ \text{(dotted eighth note + three eighth rests, with accent)} \quad \text{instead of} \quad \text{(quarter note)}$$

in certain cases, depending on the style. I have also laboured to teach them to accent syncopated notes and to phrase before them in order to do so . . . In the performance of my music, simple questions like this consume half of my rehearsals.[18]

The recomposition also penetrates to the pitch organization. As he did in *Pulcinella,* Stravinsky constructs a new post-tonal layer that comments ironically on the tonal original. Example 3-11 contains a characteristic passage from the first variation. The chorale melody is stated in the violas and double basses, at the bottom of the score. With the exception of the circled material in measures 7–8, the oboes, English horn, and bassoons share the two lines of Bach's canon at the octave. The remaining music, including the circled material, was added by Stravinsky. The descending arpeggios in the flutes and harp in measure 7 do not contradict Bach's harmony, but they are interesting nonetheless. Their 6/4 meter clashes with the prevailing 12/8. This kind of layered texture with each layer rhythmically distinct is characteristic of Stravinsky's own music. Also characteristic is the dry, staccato articulation in the first flute. In these subtle rhythmic, textural, and articulative ways, Stravinsky already begins to leave his mark on the piece.

EXAMPLE 3-11 Stravinsky's recomposition of Bach, *Canonic Variations* (first variation)

Stravinsky also works with pitches, as in the brief canon he inserts in measures 7–8. A more striking contrapuntal development immediately follows. The harp presents an ascending, then a descending, stack of perfect fifths that as a unit make up set-class 4-23 (0257). The last part of the descent is doubled by the contrabasses. The descending fifths are imitated, in inversion, by the violas in measure 9. At the same moment, the flute presents a new descending figure, a stack of fourths, that is imitated in diminution by the harp. These stacks of fourths, like the original stacks of fifths, constitute set-class 4-23. As observed earlier, 4-23 is one of Stravinsky's signature sonorities and is particularly prominent in *Pulcinella*. This same set is also formed vertically in this passage, on the third beat of measure 8 (where its pitch-class content—D, E, G, and A—replicates that of the harp's descending fifths and the first stack of descending fourths in flute and harp) and the third beat of measure 9 (where its pitch-class content—G, A, C, and D—replicates that of the viola's ascending fifths and the second stack of descending fourths in flute and harp). A subset, 3-7 (025), is the harmony on the downbeat of measure 10. The musical space is thus integrated, in normal post-tonal fashion.

Bach's music and Stravinsky's interpenetrate each other in complex and mutually influential ways. Their interaction becomes particularly intense in the third variation, a brief passage from which is shown in Example 3-12. The bassoon, harp, and contrabasses share a canon at the seventh written by Bach to accompany the chorale melody in the chorus and violas. A florid additional melody by Bach begins in the first flute in measure 10, then moves to the first oboe in the middle of measure 12. To these preexisting four parts, Stravinsky has added two more: a line in the trombone that imitates the chorale melody a seventh below and, in the oboe, a line that imitates the flute part a seventh below. Then, in the second half of measure 12, where Bach's melody moves from flute to oboe, a new line in the flutes imitates it in augmentation. The result is a triple canon with each of the following voices a seventh or a ninth away from its leader.

In a sense Stravinsky has simply tried to go Bach one better here, topping Bach's technical achievement with one even more ingenious. Of course, Stravinsky's added lines do not conform to the prevailing harmonic logic of Bach's original. The departures from normal triadic harmony are striking and persistent. It would be trivial to add canonic lines to any contrapuntal piece, or to write any kind of canon, by disregarding the ways in which the lines interact, but Stravinsky's alterations are anything but trivial. The harmonies formed by the lines are no longer triadic; instead, they consistently create a small number of nontriadic sets, particularly the tetrachords 4-22 (0247) and 4-23 (0257) and their subsets 3-7 (025) and 3-9 (027), which are the principal motives from *Pulcinella* as well. The lines thus *are* regulated to each other, but on Stravinsky's terms, not Bach's. Even the final chord of this variation (not shown in the example) bears Stravinsky's stamp: it is also a form of 4-22.

In addition to adding contrapuntal lines, Stravinsky also transposes the middle movements away from the tonic, C. Figure 3-1 compares the key schemes of the Bach and Stravinsky versions. Stravinsky has created a symmetrical layout with D-flat at the center. The reason for this arrangement, as for so many of Stravinsky's alterations, has to do with increasing motivic content. Stravinsky's layout consists of two overlapping statements of set-class 3-5 (016). At the exact midpoint of the entire piece (measures 13–14 of the middle movement), the point of particularly intensive contrapuntal treatment discussed above, this motive occurs twice as a vertical sonority, as indicated in Example 3-12. The first of the occurrences (in measure 13) results from an event virtually unique in the piece: the alteration by Stravinsky of a note written by Bach. Here, on the third beat of the measure, the bassoon and contrabasses should have a B-flat, not a tied C. The changed note creates a vertical statement of 3-5, repeating at the midpoint of the

EXAMPLE 3-12 Stravinsky's recomposition of Bach, *Canonic Variations* (third variation)

piece its large-scale harmonic plan. The recomposition thus involves every aspect of the piece, from its articulations to the highest levels of its structure. At each level Stravinsky imposes his own musical sensibility.

Stravinsky's recomposition of Bach's *Canonic Variations* is symptomatic of his increasing preoccupation, late in his life, with the mainstream of the classical tradition in music. His last published piece was a recomposition of two songs by Hugo Wolf and virtually the last piece he worked on was a setting of selected preludes and fugues from *The Well-Tempered Clavier*. Recomposition was for Stravinsky, as for Schoenberg, a way of coming to terms with

EXAMPLE 3-12 (*Continued*)

movement:	1	2	3	4	5
Bach:	C	C	C	C	C
Stravinsky:	C	G	Db	G	C

3-5
(016)

3-5

FIGURE 3-1

his predecessors. For most of his life, however, Stravinsky avoided a direct confrontation with the classical mainstream, preferring instead to focus on weaker, more susceptible predecessors like Pergolesi and Tchaikovsky. Through them he would comment on common-practice styles without dealing directly with the true giants of those styles. His turn to serialism, however, marks a new willingness to enter into direct dialogue with the inheritors of the tradition and, through them, with their great contrapuntal predecessors, especially Bach. Stravinsky's turn toward serialism and his late recompositions of Bach and Wolf thus have a common source. In both, Stravinsky confronts the musical mainstream and shows remarkable ability to remake his predecessors in his own image.

––––––––––

Webern's orchestration of the ricercare from Bach's *Musical Offering* is at once the most radical and the most economical of recompositions. The subject alone reveals the network of motivic relationships Webern creates through timbral means. Webern's recomposition begins with fragmentation. He slices up Bach's continuous melody into distinct timbral bits, thus undercutting its sense of seamless coherence.[19] But why does Webern fragment it in this particular way? More specifically, why does he assign certain pitches to certain instruments? The answer lies in the implicit set structure of Bach's melody. Example 3-13 shows the melody with an ordinal number assigned to each note and identifies a certain number of pitch-class sets, formed by groups of adjacent notes.

Webern's instrumentation, shown in Example 3-14, projects an additional dimension of set structure. The trumpet, for example, is assigned four notes (F, E, E-flat, and D) occupying order positions 8–9 and 18–19. These four

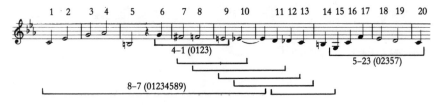

EXAMPLE 3-13   Subset structure of Bach's melody

EXAMPLE 3-14   Webern's instrumentation of Bach's melody

REMAKING THE PAST

TABLE 3-1

Instrument	Order positions	Pitch content	Set-class	Location of set-class in subject
Trumpet	8–9, 18–19	F, E, E♭, D	4-1 (0123)	6–9, 7–10, 8–11, 9–12, 10–13, 11–14
Horn	10–11, 15–17	E♭, D, G, C, F	5-23 (02357)	15–20
Horn	6–7, 10–11	G, F♯, E♭, D	4-7 (0145)	1–10 (complement)

notes constitute the chromatic tetrachord 4-1 (0123), which is formed in many places by adjacent notes of the subject. Similar considerations determine the other instrumental assignments. The last five notes played by the horn (E-flat, D, G, C, and F), occupying order positions 10–11 and 15–17, create a form of the same set-class, 5-23 (02357), as that found in order positions 15–20. Similarly, the first four notes assigned to the horn constitute 4-7 (0145), which is the nonliteral complement of the set formed by the first eight pitches of the subject.[20] These relationships are summarized in Table 3-1.

There is one additional important set-class relationship, somewhat more abstract than the others. The trombone part as a whole states set-class 7-6 (0123478). The first four notes of the horn part and the last four notes of the trombone part, linked by the shared pitch in order position 11, constitute a different form of the same set. What is more, the shared six-note subset of these two forms of 7-6, namely set 6-Z37 (012348), is found twice in the adjacent pitches of the subject (order positions 5–10 and 10–15).

Webern has used timbre to isolate noncontiguous collections of pitches in the subject. Those timbrally isolated collections share set-class membership with linear segments of Bach's melody. Webern's instrumentation thus results not in arbitrary fragmentation, but in a rich network of set-class relationships.[21] He has imposed a post-tonal set structure onto Bach's tonal pitch organization without, remarkably, altering any of Bach's notes.

Given this network of motivic associations, Webern's own comments on this piece seem understated, if not actually misleading. "My instrumentation attempts to reveal the motivic coherence. This was not always easy. Beyond that, of course, it is supposed to indicate the character of the piece as I feel it. What music it is! To make it accessible at long last, by trying through my orchestration to express my view of it, was the ultimate object of my bold undertaking."[22] Like Schoenberg, Webern says that his orchestration merely "reveals" relationships already present in Bach's music. Instead, as we have seen, the process is not nearly as neutral and passive as this makes it sound. In one sense, of course, the relationships Webern "reveals" *are* present in Bach's music, if deeply latent, since Webern does not actually add or change any notes. At the same time, the relationships discussed above are much more characteristic of Webern's pitch organization than of Bach's. Webern thus attempts to define Bach as a prototypical Webern rather than seeing himself as the weak descendant of Bach.

Webern's remarks on his orchestration of dances by Schubert come closer to capturing this attempted reversal of priority, even though his recomposition of Schubert is much less radical than his recomposition of Bach. He says in a letter to Schoenberg, "I took pains to remain on the solid ground of classical ideas of instrumentation, yet to place them into the service of *our* idea, i.e. as a means toward the greatest possible clarification of thought and context."[23] "Our idea" is a conception of musical structure based on motivic saturation and integration. Webern's words describe the subordination of an earlier composer to the structural ideals of a later time.

––––––––––

Despite the obvious stylistic differences among the works discussed here and despite the span of years involved—from *Pulcinella* in 1919, through the Bach recompositions by Schoenberg and Webern of the twenties and thirties, up to Stravinsky's *Canonic Variations* in 1956—there are profound similarities among these recompositions. First, each recomposer attempts to neutralize a source piece by undermining its tonal harmony and voice leading. In the process, our normal, customary ways of apprehending these familiar objects are subverted. Second, each recomposer urges us to rehear older pieces in light of post-tonal concern with motivic saturation and pitch-class set manipulation. The motivic structures may be quite simple—a single interval in the case of Schoenberg's "Schmücke dich"—or quite complex, involving sets of four or more pitch-classes and relatively complicated manipulations. Of course, the imposition of a new source of musical coherence does not eradicate the old one. Each recomposition is stratified into two distinct layers—one governed by traditional tonal relations and one by the logic of recurring motives (or pitch-class sets)—without any larger resolution or synthesis. In each piece the contrasting styles and structures are locked in a continuous conflict. The power of these pieces resides not so much in their integration of competing elements into an organic whole as in the very intensity of the conflict they embody.

These recompositions are thus the scene of a struggle between styles and between types of pitch organization. I have emphasized the sense of struggle within these pieces in order to counteract the traditional view, fostered by the composers themselves, that these recompositions were undertaken in the spirit of homage, the generous recognition by one master of the greatness of some earlier master. The internal evidence of the pieces, on the contrary, suggests a vigorous and self-aggrandizing struggle on the part of the later composer to assert his priority over his predecessor, to prove himself the stronger. Bach is the towering genius of the contrapuntal art, and everyone who comes later is Bach's artistic child. The strongest of the children, however, may not be content with this subordinate relationship. By rehearing and recomposing Bach, by misreading him, the children foster the illusion of having fathered their father. In listening to the *Canonic Variations,* "Schmücke dich," or the ricercare from the *Musical Offering* in Bach's original instrumentation, one cannot help recalling those 4-22's, those motivic thirds, those timbrally defined associations. Bach now sounds as though he is imitating Stravinsky, or Schoenberg, or Webern, attempting to project the motivic density so characteristic of them.

Harold Bloom refers to this reversal as an *apophrades,* which means "the return of the dead." In such situations, Bloom says, "the uncanny effect is that the new poem's achievement makes it seem to us, not as though the precursor were writing it, but as though the later poet himself had written the precursor's characteristic work."[24] The effect is that "the tyranny of time almost is overturned, and one can believe, for startled moments, that [the later poets] are being *imitated by their ancestors.*"[25] Only the strongest misreadings can bring about an apophrades. Through recomposition, Schoenberg, Stravinsky, and Webern transform not only their source pieces, but our entire understanding of traditional music.

CHAPTER 4

Triads

The triad is the central harmony of traditional tonal music. It is both the prevailing sonority of the musical surface and the background generator of the entire pitch structure. Tonal pitch organization is characterized by the direct or indirect relationship of every tone, via voice leading and harmony, to a central triad. The triads on the surface of a tonal piece compose-out the triads of the structural middleground and background. Tonal music is, in this sense, profoundly triadic music.[1]

When triads occur in contexts other than the traditionally tonal one, careful critical attention must be paid. The presence of triads on the musical surface need not imply a triadic middleground and background as well. Many observers naively transfer the theoretical categories of tonal music to a post-tonal context. To some extent, of course, the amount of tonality one hears will depend upon the amount of tonality one brings to one's hearings. It is possible, even in the remotest of contexts, to insist on a tonal hearing.[2] To do so, however, is to impoverish the musical experience. Our experience as listeners will be richer if we can simultaneously sense the triad's tonal implications and the countervailing urge toward redefinition provided by the post-tonal context. Like the recompositions discussed in Chapter 3, post-tonal works that contain triads are stratified into two layers. The triads become the locus of a conflict between old and new. Twentieth-century composers enmesh the most characteristic and fundamental sonority of common-practice music in a new network of structural relations. They mis-read the triad, striving to neutralize its tonal implications and to redefine it within a post-tonal context.

Perhaps the most famous triad in the post-tonal literature occurs in Act 2, Scene 1, of Berg's *Wozzeck*. In that scene a C-major triad plays a striking dual role. It is used for symbolic effect and is simultaneously integrated into the pitch-class set structure of the opera. Within the drama the triad symbolizes the banality of Wozzeck's role as financial provider for Marie. In Berg's words, "How could the objectivity of money be more relevantly expressed than by this chord!"[3] (see Example 4-1). But the C-major triad, and triads generally, are not significant structural determinants in *Wozzeck*. The dramatic impact of the C-major triad here depends precisely upon its estrangement from the prevailing musical context. It is an echo of a different musical world, a world that Berg suggests is so commonplace as to be banal. It is not only money but the entire edifice of traditional tonality that seems hackneyed and "prosy" at this moment. Berg thus subverts the traditional function of the triad. Instead of taking pride of place at the center of a structure, the triad in *Wozzeck* is isolated and out of place, a gently ironic reflection of an outdated musical tradition.

The triad retains its sonorous identity but not its structural power. Instead, it is itself defined by the larger harmonies of which it is a part. While it is sustained in the orchestral strings, Wozzeck sings a recitative-like vocal line comprising six brief utterances, each followed by a rest. Each utterance ends with a note that is not a member of the C-major triad. The four-note harmonies that result, except for 4-26 (0358), are all important pitch-class sets throughout the opera. In measure 120, for example, Wozzeck's A-flat, together with the sustained C-major triad, forms a member of set-class 4-19

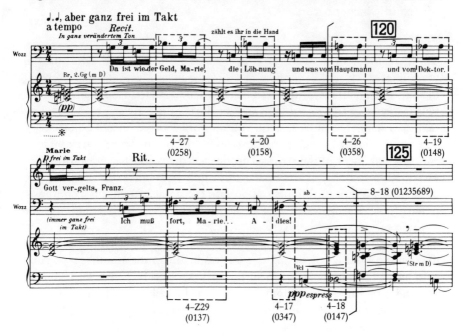

EXAMPLE 4-1   C-major chord in *Wozzeck*. *Wozzeck* Copyright 1931 by Universal Edition A.G., Wien, Copyright Renewed

(0148). This is the principal harmony associated with the character Wozzeck, the set-class of his famous declamation: "Wir arme leut!"[4] In this way, the C-major triad, while retaining symbolic force, is reduced in structural status.

The appearance of D-flat in the bass in measure 124 signals the end of this brief dramatic episode. Together with the final sounding of the C-major triad, this note creates set-class 4-18 (0147). Just as 4-19 (0148) is the principal harmony associated with Wozzeck, 4-18 is the principal harmony associated with Marie.[5] This musical shift thus expresses Wozzeck's departure from the scene and the return of the dramatic focus to Marie. That same shift is confirmed by the larger harmonies. The arrival of D-flat in measure 124 not only creates a local statement of 4-18 but also completes a statement of 8-18 (01235689), the complement of 4-18. That large set is formed by the orchestral D-flat and C-major chord together with all of Wozzeck's notes beginning with his A in measure 119.

The C-major triad in *Wozzeck* is thus subsumed by various larger harmonies. It is not a living, structure-generating force but a dead artifact. It has been reduced to nothing more than an ironic commentary on the banality of material things and, by implication, the banality of traditional tonality. Its meaning is constrained by the harmonic logic of the musical context in which it occurs.

The C-major triad in *Wozzeck* is first stated plainly, then drawn into the prevailing set structure. Stravinsky's *In Memoriam Dylan Thomas* presents the opposite possibility—the gradual emergence of a triad from a post–tonal field. Stravinsky completed *In Memoriam* during the early stages of his interest in serialism. The pitch structure of the work is based on a five-note series and, as Stravinsky himself generously indicated on the score, every pitch is part of a statement of the series. Throughout the work the series forms are presented melodically. The simultaneities are by-products of the serial voice leading. Their lack of full integration into the serial structure is a compositional problem in this work, one for which Stravinsky sought solutions over a period of years.[6]

The simultaneity that concludes the first phrase of the instrumental introduction is a triad (see Example 4-2). It results from the simultaneous conclusions of four different forms of the basic series—E, E-flat, C, C-sharp, D—and forms an F-flat–major triad.[7] Stravinsky calls upon this triad to play a traditional role, at least in part. First, it functions as a point of repose and relative stability, although many phrases in the work, and the work as a whole, do not end with a triad. Second, it acts as a sonorous reinforcement for its lowest note, F-flat, as though that note were a functional harmonic

EXAMPLE 4-2   F-flat–major chord emerging from a serial texture (Stravinsky, *In Memoriam Dylan Thomas,* Prelude)

root. Pitch–class F-flat (or E) is also stressed in other ways throughout the phrase and throughout the work.

Despite these traditional associations, this triad is held inextricably in the grip of the serial structure from which it emerges. Over the course of the work, many different simultaneities result from the serial melodic structure. The triad is only one of these. It retains its sense of stability and rootedness but is otherwise stripped of its traditional function. It is not a triad among triads in a network of tonal relations, but a simultaneity among simultaneities in a network of serial relations. Whatever traditional associations it suggests are undermined by the musical context in which it occurs, a context in which triads occurs as anomalies—enfeebled, constrained, and reinterpreted.

Triads that occur in a twelve-tone context are often particularly striking. One of Schoenberg's explicit goals in evolving the twelve-tone system was the avoidance of the kinds of tonal resonances that are created by octave doubling and triads. "To double is to emphasize, and an emphasized tone could be interpreted as a root, or even as a tonic; the consequences of such an interpretation must be avoided. Even a slight reminiscence of the former tonal harmony would be disturbing, because it would create false expectations of consequences and continuations. The use of a tonic is deceiving if it is not based on *all* the relationships of tonality."[8]

Most classical twelve-tone music does, in fact, avoid triads, but where they do occur, they need not be considered a concession to traditional tonal constraints. The source of musical coherence remains the twelve-tone system, not the tonal system. Schoenberg himself has made this point: "As regards hints of a tonality and intermixing of consonant triads one must remember that the main purpose of 12-tone composition is: production of coherence through the use of a unifying succession of tones which should function at least like a motive. Thus the organizatorial efficiency of the harmony should be replaced. It was not my purpose to write dissonant music, but to include dissonance in a logical manner without reference to the treatment of the classics."[9] The twelve-tone system is a powerful means of musical organization that can produce extremely varied musical surfaces. When a triad occurs in a twelve-tone context, what is usually most striking is not the modifications of the twelve-tone procedures but rather their complete integrity. The twelve-tone system is not altered to accommodate tonal formations; rather, their meaning is altered to accommodate the twelve-tone context.

Berg's Violin Concerto is a twelve-tone work that frequently presents a triadic surface. Although this has led some to adduce the work as an instance of Berg's willingness to compromise twelve-tone procedures, the accommodation usually works the other way.[10] The triads emerge from, and are most richly interpreted within, a twelve-tone framework. Berg marvelously mimics the harmonic processes of tonal music in a demonstration of the power of the twelve-tone system to encompass salient features of traditional tonality.

After a ten-measure introduction, the Violin Concerto begins with the passage shown in Example 4-3. In isolation from its musical surroundings,

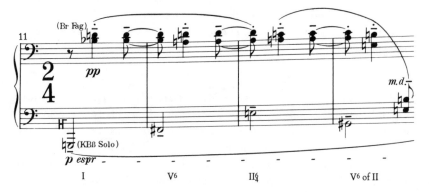

EXAMPLE 4-3   Tonal interpretation of a triadic passage from Berg, Violin Concerto. Violin Concerto Copyright 1938 by Universal Edition, Copyright Renewed

REMAKING THE PAST

EXAMPLE 4-4   Registral lines in Berg, Violin Concerto (solo violin part, pitches only, measures 1–10)

this passage has a very traditional feel. It can be understood harmonically as a succession of triads, one per measure: G minor, D major, A minor, and E major. This succession even lends itself to a functional interpretation: I–V–II–V/II in G minor. Furthermore, the progression is apparently elaborated by 4–3 and 7–6 suspensions, traditional embellishment types. This tonal interpretation does not make the passage seem particularly interesting, but it does make it reasonably intelligible.

A more potent meaning is imposed on the passage by the musical context in which it occurs. In the ten-measure introduction that precedes it, the solo violin traces the arpeggiated figures shown in Example 4-4. In four statements the solo violin alternates a stack of fifths, set-class 4-23 (0257), with a stack of whole tones, set-class 4-21 (0246), as it gradually unfolds the entire chromatic. The twelfth pitch-class, F, is reached in measure 8 as the highest pitch in the passage. A twelve-tone series emerges gradually from the arpeggiating figures, which present segments, usually consisting of alternating pitch-classes, from what is later revealed as the prime ordering of the series. Four distinct registral lines are presented in the violin figures. Each registral line begins by outlining a triad. In ascending registral order, these are G minor, D major, A minor, and E major. The temporal order of these four triads in measures 11–14 thus recapitulates their registral order in measures 1–7. That relationship places the triads of measures 11–14 in a very different perspective. Instead of referring to common-practice norms of harmonic progression, they now sound like verticalized statements of previously heard registral lines.

Still richer meanings are imposed on the triads by the music that immediately follows them, in measures 15–20 (see Example 4-5). In these measures the solo violin gives the first clear statement of the twelve-tone series for the concerto, concluding with a restatement of its seventh and eleventh tones (order positions within the series are indicated on Example 4-5). The accompaniment also presents P_0, although somewhat more freely. As in any twelve-tone composition, the segmental subsets of the series are primary harmonic building blocks. The G-minor, D-major, A-minor, and E-major triads occur, overlapping one another, as segmental subsets. This immediately suggests a rehearing of the triads in measures 11–14 in twelve-tone terms. The triads now seem to relate to each other not as functional harmonies within a traditional progression, but rather through their intervallic as-

EXAMPLE 4-5   Twelve-tone interpretation of a triadic passage

sociations—all are members of a single set-class, 3-11 (037)—constrained by twelve-tone relations.

The segmental subsets of the series suggest another, even more radical rehearing of the triads in measures 11–14. In the traditional, tonal interpretation of these measures, the nontriadic tones were explained away as nonharmonic suspensions. In light of the structure of the series, however, those tones can be heard to combine with the tones of the triads to form set-classes that are also formed as segmental subsets of the series (see Example 4-6). In measures 12–13, for example, two forms of set-class 4-22 (0247) are indicated. The first of these (D, E, F-sharp, A) is formed by the pitches in order positions 3, 4, 5, and 7 of P_o. The second (A, C, D, E), inversionally related to the first, is formed by the pitches in order positions 3, 5, 6, and 7 of P_o. Neither is a segmental subset of P_o, but both represent a set-class that is formed as a segmental subset of the series, in order positions 8–11. The remaining set-classes marked in Example 4-6 are also segmental subsets of the series. Set-class 4-19 (0148) occurs four times in the series (in order positions 1–4, 2–5, 5–8, and 6–9) and set-class 5-Z17 (01348) occurs twice (in order positions 1–5 and 5–9). This twelve-tone construction reshapes the meaning of the passage. Instead of hearing triads and nonharmonic tones, one hears set-class associations within which the triads function as subsets. In this way, the triads are denied their traditional primacy.

In the passage beginning in measure 21, the triadic music from measures 11–14 is heard in pitch-class inversion. The ordering is somewhat free, but the music is clearly derived from I$_o$, a linear statement of which is heard in the solo violin beginning in measure 24 (see Example 4-7). The rhythms and textures of measures 11–14 are preserved, as is much of the set structure, since these elements can remain invariant under inversion. But the incipient functional relationships among the triads have been entirely overthrown. The changes in serial ordering also contribute to obliterating any sense of functionality. In measures 11–12 it sounds as though a tonic is moving to a dominant. When those measures are inverted and altered into measures 21–22, no functional relationship can be inferred. This is an example of the revisionary ratio of symmetricization. By imposing inversional symmetry on the chord succession, Berg neutralizes its tonal functionality.

The triads from measures 11–14 are thus drawn into a twelve-tone network that redefines them. Set structure and serial procedures govern the musical relations at every level, even when the surface of the music is triadic. For Berg, then, this passage is not so much an homage to the norms of the past as a demonstration of the power of the new syntax to encompass and redefine earlier elements. The triads accommodate themselves to the prevailing twelve-tone logic and exist as a self-conscious artifact within the constraining frame of twelve-tone relations. Their presence simultaneously

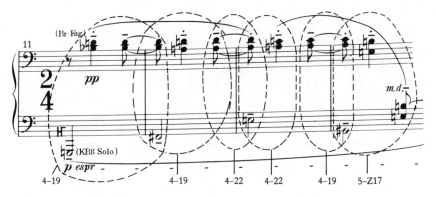

EXAMPLE 4-6 Triadic passage interpreted in terms of the segmental subsets of a twelve-tone series

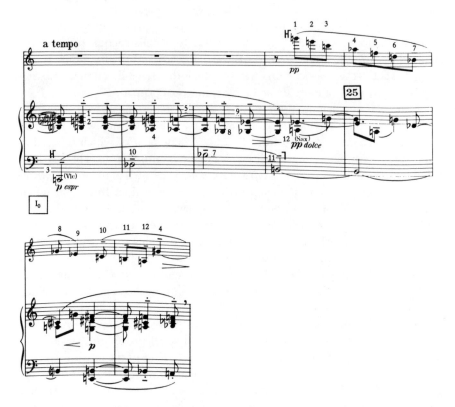

EXAMPLE 4-7   Free inversion of a triadic passage

establishes a link to the past and proclaims the subsumption and domination of that past.

———————

Schoenberg was explicitly aware of the potential danger of introducing triads into his music and of the need for undermining or, as he says, "paralyzing" their tonal implications.

My formal sense (and I am immodest enough to hand over to this the exclusive rights of distribution when I compose) tells me that to introduce even a single tonal triad would lead to consequences, and would demand space which is not available within my form. A tonal triad makes claims on what follows, and, retrospectively, on all that has gone before; nobody can ask me to overthrow everything that has gone before, just because a triad has happened by accident and has to be given its due. On this point I prefer if possible to start right and continue in the same way, so far as error is avoidable . . . But even standing where I do at the present time, I believe that to use the consonant chords, too, is not out of the question, as soon as someone has found a technical means of either satisfying or paralysing their formal claims.[11]

Like Berg in his Violin Concerto, Schoenberg uses pitch-class inversion to deflate the sense of tonal expectation aroused by a triadic surface in "Verbundenheit," the sixth of his Pieces for Male Chorus, Op. 35. Four of the other five pieces in this group (the exception is "Glück") are typical of Schoenberg's mature, richly allusive serialism. "Verbundenheit," however, begins with a triadic passage easily susceptible to a functional harmonic interpretation (see Example 4-8). As with a tonal analysis of the triadic passage in Berg's Violin Concerto, this analysis does not make the passage seem particularly interesting, but it does make it comprehensible. The entire first half of the piece proceeds in a similar way and concludes with a D-major triad.

In the second half of the piece, however, the intimations of tonal functionality are rudely overthrown as the entire first half is simply inverted. The inversion takes place around a B/C–F/F-sharp axis and brings about the mappings shown on the "inversional clock" in Figure 4-1. Simultaneously, bass 1 and tenor 1 exchange parts. Example 4-9 contains the beginning of the second half of the piece. This is a pitch-class inversion of the first phrase, not the step-class inversion of traditional tonal practice. The root position chords of the opening are now in 6/4 position; all the major chords have inverted to minor and vice versa. The original succession of triads—

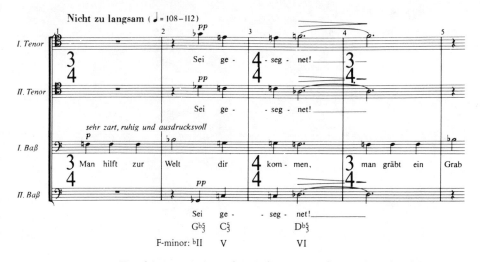

EXAMPLE 4-8 Tonal interpretation of a triadic passage from Schoenberg, "Verbundenheit," Six Pieces for Male Chorus, Op. 35

G-flat major, C major, D-flat major, all in root position—could be interpreted as ♭II–V–♭VI in F minor. The succession of triads in its inverted consequent—B-flat minor, E minor, E-flat minor, all in 6/4 position—makes any tonal analysis inconceivable.

This places us in an interpretive bind. Our tonal analysis was initially attractive, but if we cling to it, we will be unable to perceive "Verbundenheit" as a coherent whole. The first phrase will stand out as an anomaly, isolated from the rest of the piece and from the other pieces in the opus. The two passages are clearly related, but we will be forced to explain them in entirely different ways. Our only alternative is to rehear the first phrase, listening this time for sources of unity that remain invariant under inversion. Our desire to relate the two passages to each other and to hear the work as co-

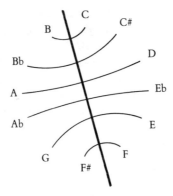

FIGURE 4-1

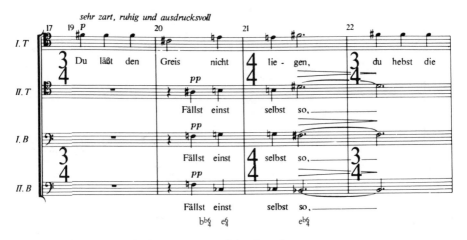

EXAMPLE 4-9 Pitch-class inversion of the first phrase

REMAKING THE PAST

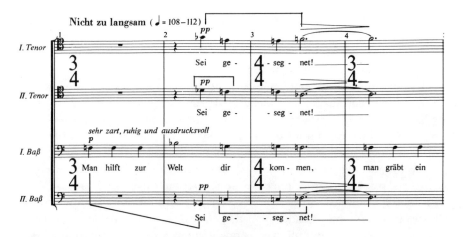

EXAMPLE 4-10 Motivic interpretation of the first phrase

herently as possible requires us to relinquish our tonal understanding of the first passage. The inverted second phrase thus necessitates a reinterpretation of the first phrase.

The first phrase can be understood in terms of its motivic and set-class organization (see Example 4-10). The initial dyad in tenor 2, D-flat–C, is repeated in inversion as the final dyad in bass 2. Similarly, the dyad formed by the first note in bass 1 and the first note in bass 2, F–G-flat, is repeated in inversion as the highest notes in tenor 1. The combination of these motives into set-class 4-8 (0156) has further consequences for the organization of the passage. The lowest four notes in the passage are G-flat2, C2, D-flat2, and F2,* another member of the same set-class, now articulated by register. Each of these notes is doubled in the upper parts, and they are the only ones in the passage to be emphasized in that way. All of these relationships are preserved when the passage is inverted, except that, because of the inversional plan, D-flat–C is replaced by B-flat–B. The dyad F–G-flat retains its importance and combines with the new dyad, B-flat–B, to create another form of 4-8, related by inversion to the one in the first phrase.

This set-class perspective, imposed by the juxtaposition of the two phrases, brings about a reinterpretation of the triads themselves.[12] Initially, we hear the triads as representatives of harmonic function-classes: G-flat represents ♭II, C represents V, and D-flat represents VI. Now we come to

---

*In this book the octave placement of notes is indicated by a number following the note name, according to the notation system used by the Acoustical Society of America. The C three octaves below middle C is C1. An octave number refers to pitches from a given C through the B above.

hear them instead as representatives of set-classes. All three triads are members of set-class 3-11 (037), as, of course, are the three triads in the inverted passage. This common set-class membership reinforces the motivic relationships in linking the two passages.

By inverting the first phrase (and, in fact, the entire first half of the piece), Schoenberg neutralizes its incipient tonal progressions. He causes us to hear what had seemed a progression of triads in terms of motivic and set-class relations, which remain invariant under inversion. He thus asserts the priority of a new musical syntax over the old formations.

"Verbundenheit" and other late pieces of Schoenberg's have been severely criticized by composers of the postwar generation, especially Pierre Boulez, for their "outmoded" usages. "All severity in composition is thrown overboard from now on. Pseudo-thematic octaves, pseudo-cadences, strict canons at the octave return all over again; as though we had arrived at a new method merely in order to recompose the music of the past."[13] In fact, the new method, for Schoenberg, *did* have the crucial function of enabling him to recompose the music of the past. His doing so in work after work, either explicitly or implicitly, does not testify to his compositional weakness, as Boulez suggests. Rather, it signifies his courageous struggle with his predecessors. Schoenberg turns to the past not because he is too weak or unimaginative to avoid doing so but in order to demonstrate the power of his new methods to encompass and redefine the music of his predecessors.

A triad may occur as a subset of a number of larger collections. In tonal music, of course, the triad occurs as a subset of the diatonic collection. One other large collection in which it occurs, one that has been widely used in this century, is the octatonic collection. This collection, formed by alternating half and whole steps, is particularly prominent in the music of Stravinsky and Bartók.[14] Although both collections have triads as subsets, they have radically different structural properties. Briefly, the octatonic collection has a much higher degree of internal symmetry, both transpositional and inversional, and, as a result, it has a much more restricted subset and

EXAMPLE 4-11 The "Psalms chord" (Stravinsky, *Symphony of Psalms,* first movement)

REMAKING THE PAST

EXAMPLE 4-12 Psalms chord in an octatonic setting

intervallic content. The diatonic collection's unique multiplicity of interval-class makes it highly susceptible to transpositional hierarchization, whereas the octatonic collection has only three distinct forms and is thus one of Olivier Messiaen's "modes of limited transposition."[15] These differences ensure that triads in a diatonic context and in an octatonic context will have very different musical meanings.

The first movement of Stravinsky's *Symphony of Psalms* is largely an octatonic piece with a surface rich in triads. The piece begins with the striking sonority shown in Example 4-11. Both the internal construction of the sonority and the surrounding musical context make it clear that this is not an ordinary E-minor triad. By virtue of doubling (the G occurs in four different octaves) and spacing (the G occurs alone in the two central octaves), the chord asserts G as a potential counterweight to its bass-note, E. In fact, the entire movement is concerned with the harmonic conflict between E and G, finally resolved in favor of the G. The movement begins with a sonority built on E but weighted toward G; it ends by moving strongly from E to G. Stravinsky has thus forced the triad to bear the weight of a structure-generating harmonic polarity. The triad is not, as in a traditional tonal context, a single, unitary sonority; rather, it is riven by a powerful harmonic polarity.

In its first occurrences, and in many of those that follow, this "Psalms chord" is heard in an octatonic context that paralyzes the triad's traditional function. The apparent dominant-seventh chords that follow it flesh out the collection and provide a context for interpreting the initial chord—not a tonic in the key of E minor but an octatonic subset (see Example 4-12). The dominant-seventh chords, like the triad itself, have been stripped of their normal function. They partition the octatonic collection and, at the registral extremes of the arpeggiations, present two important voice-leading motives, A-flat–G and B-flat–B, which embellish tones of the E-minor triad. The Psalms chord is thus embedded in an octatonic framework.

EXAMPLE 4-13 Psalms chord in a diatonic setting

REMAKING THE PAST

At other points in the movement, however, the Psalms chord is heard in a diatonic context (see Example 4-13). The prevailing collection in these measures is the white-note collection on E. Neither the harmony nor the voice leading is traditionally tonal, but the referential collection is diatonic. This diatonic collection and the prevailing octatonic collection share the Psalms chord as a common subset. The Psalms chord is thus a mediating element between two contrasting collections.[16] In this collectional sense, as in the centric polarity of E and G, the Psalms chord is the fulcrum upon which conflicting elements balance.

Throughout almost the entire movement, the harmonic focus is on E, kept there by frequent use of the neighbor note F. At the final cadence of the movement, the firm relationship between the E and F is disrupted: the F passes upward to G rather than moving back down to E, while the harmonic movement from E to G is simultaneously confirmed in the bass (see Example 4-14). Of course, the concluding G triad is also a subset of the prevailing octatonic collection. The arrival on this triad is in no sense a modulation from E minor to G major. Traditional tonal relations are not used either to establish a tonal center or to move from center to center. Rather, the harmonic movement in this piece is from one trichordal partitioning of the octatonic collection (E–G–B) to a contrasting partitioning (G–B–D). Stravinsky has thus taken the most basic formation of tonal music, the triad,

EXAMPLE 4-14   Motion from E to G in the final measures

and radically reinterpreted it. He liberates the triad from its usual context, paralyzes its tonal implications, and redefines it in new musical terms.[17]

Like *Symphony of Psalms,* Stravinsky's *Oedipus Rex* is a work with a triadic surface constrained by a post-tonal substructure. Example 4-15 shows the central moment of the opera, when Oedipus realizes who he is and what he has done. The concluding sonority, D–F-sharp, gives the superficial impression of an arrival in D major.[18] But the surrounding music belies a traditionally tonal interpretation. There is no V–I cadence in D major, and

EXAMPLE 4-15 Oedipus's moment of enlightenment (Stravinsky, *Oedipus Rex*)

nothing anywhere in the passage can be construed as a functional harmonic progression. Triads are much in evidence, but the music is not tonal. The concluding D–F-sharp is the culmination of a number of characteristically Stravinskian processes.

Prior to Oedipus's climactic utterance, the Shepherd and Messenger confirm his identity with repetitive short declamations that center on a D-minor triad, frequently supporting an upper-voice tone F. As the Shepherd and Messenger depart (and Example 4-15 begins), a B-minor triad, with an F-sharp on top, is presented in flutes and tympani. The resulting juxtaposition of a D-minor triad with a B-minor triad creates a clash from which the concluding D–F-sharp sonority will ultimately emerge. This clash has two related aspects. The first is the centric conflict between D and B, a conflict with clear dramatic reference in this work. D is generally associated with moments of revelation. When the Shepherd and Messenger reveal the truth about Oedipus, they do so with an orientation toward D. The B, in contrast, seems to be associated with Oedipus's blindness. Related to this centric conflict is an upper-voice conflict between F-natural (associated with the D-minor triad) and F-sharp (associated with the B-minor triad). Oedipus's music moves toward the resolution through synthesis of these conflicts.

When Oedipus sings, he arpeggiates a B-minor triad. The harmonization of his melody, however, is ambiguous. Moments of seeming cross-relation between F and F-sharp and competition between B and D occur throughout. The first two times Oedipus concludes a vocal phrase on F-sharp, the note is harmonized by set-class 3-3 (014), including both F and F-sharp. The conflicts are not resolved until the five measures beginning at Rehearsal 169. Oedipus concludes this vocal phrase, as he did the others, on F-sharp, only now the harmony is clarified, even as the symbolic light breaks in on Oedipus. The bass descends from B to D, resolving the centric conflict in favor of D. In an inner voice, F-natural, spelled as E-sharp, trills with F-sharp before definitively resolving to it. The F (previously associated with D) thus moves to F-sharp (previously associated with B) just at the moment the bass moves definitively from B to D. The final sonority, D–F-sharp, thus represents a synthesis of the competing elements. The F-sharp from the B-oriented music is now heard in the context of D. At the moment of Oedipus's enlightenment, the musical ambiguities are crystallized through the revisionary strategy of fragmentation. The concluding D–F-sharp dyad is simultaneously a fragment of the D-major and B-minor triads. From a dramatic point of view, Oedipus's knowledge (symbolized by the D in the bass) still bears the trace of his former spiritual blindness (symbolized by the F-sharp, previously linked to B).[19]

The final sonority is further defined by the large-scale motivic processes of the work. The final three notes of the passage (E-sharp, F-sharp, and D) constitute set-class 3-3 (014), which also occurs elsewhere in the passage. This set-class is central to the work as a whole. It pervades the surface of the music throughout and is also composed-out at both middleground and background levels. The central musical figure of the piece is the so-called Fate Motive in repeated thirds, which was the first musical notation Stravinsky made in composing *Oedipus Rex*.[20] In its first occurrence (Rehearsal 2), B-flat is in the bass. The motive comes back toward the middle of the piece (Rehearsal 61), transposed so that B-natural is in the bass. The large-scale dyad, B-flat–B, formed by these bass notes would, with the addition of either D or G, create a statement of set-class 3-3. The G arrives at the end of the work, when the Fate Motive makes its final appearance. There is also an arrival on D, in precisely the passage we have been discussing, an arrival that features (as we have seen) small-scale statements of the same set-class. The background structure of the piece thus consists of two overlapping large-scale statements of set-class 3-3 (see Example 4-16).

From this broader perspective it is clear that the D–F-sharp sonority after Rehearsal 169 is thoroughly defined by processes typical of Stravinsky and deeply rooted in the particularities of this composition. It is not a tonic triad in D major. Rather, it is the synthesis of competing tonal centers and the conclusion of a large-scale composing-out of set-class 3-3. Stravinsky's compositional achievement, here and elsewhere, is not the discovery of a new sonority (something that has been greatly overemphasized in accounts of musical evolution in any case) but rather his insistence that an old sonority function in a new way. Walter Piston describes Stravinsky's own account of this process: "I recall an enlightening incident during his discussion of *Oedipus Rex* when he stopped playing and observed, 'How happy I was when I discovered this chord!' We were mystified because the chord in question was just a D-major triad."[21]

Stravinsky's compositional strength lies not in stylistic originality but in an ability to transmute the meaning of received materials. He insists on reinterpreting the triad in a way that affirms his own structural procedures. He neutralizes the tonal implications of the triad. Although triads may appear on the surface of his music, they do not penetrate to the remoter structural levels. Rather, they are constrained by an underlying syntax of octatonic-diatonic interaction, motivic composing-out, and centric conflict. In a pro-

EXAMPLE 4-16 Two overlapping large-scale statements of set-class 3-3 (014) (rehearsal numbers shown)

EXAMPLE 4-17 A-minor triad embedded within the prevailing tetrachordal set structure (Webern, Five Movements for String Quartet, Op. 5, No. 2); a = 4-18 (0147), b = 4-Z29 (0137), c = 4-17 (0347). Movements for String Quartet, Op. 5, Copyright 1922 by Universal Edition, Copyright Renewed

found act of misreading, Stravinsky appropriates the central sonority of the tonal language and imposes a new meaning on it.

The occurrence of tonal formations is all the more striking in music that generally avoids them. In the music of Webern it is difficult to discover a single obvious use of a triad. With the significant exception of his orchestrations of Bach and Schubert, Webern makes little attempt to come to terms with his musical past in the overt manner of his contemporaries. In the second of his Movements for String Quartet, Op. 5, however, the notes A, C, and E are sustained in the viola and cello for most of the last three and one-half measures (see Example 4-17). The emergence of a triad is a striking event in this piece and demands analytical attention. But it would be a mistake to assume that a triad, however striking, can be explained only within the framework of traditional tonal theory. There are no other obvious triads in this piece and no hint of traditional harmony and voice leading. It is thus destructive of musical coherence to take this triad as an analytical point of departure and force this piece onto the procrustean bed of tonal theory.[22] These sustained pitches have apparently attracted analytical attention not because of their function in context, but simply because traditional tonal theory has a way of naming them. The categories of tonal theory are worse than worthless here since they focus attention on a demonstrably secondary element while ignoring the central structural issues of the piece.

An appreciation of the final measures of the piece can only come from knowledge of the specific musical context Webern has established. In con-

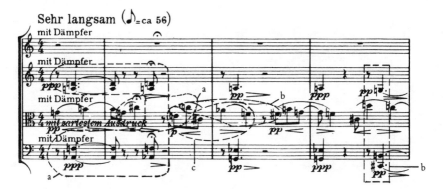

EXAMPLE 4-18 Tetrachordal set structure of the opening phrase; a = 4-18 (0147), b = 4-Z29 (0137), c = 4-17 (0347)

junction with the melodic tones in the first and second violins, the sustained A–C–E forms a number of tetrachords, the most important of which are 4-18 (0147), formed by the addition of E-flat, 4-Z29 (0137), formed by the addition of B-flat, and 4-17 (0347) formed by the addition of D-flat. These set-classes, not the triad, are the structural building blocks of this composition.

Example 4-18 identifies occurrences of these three pitch-class sets in the opening measures. The first chord, in the second violin and cello, forms set-class 4-18 (0147) with pitch-class content D, F, A-flat, and A. The forms of 4-18 in the final measures are transpositions of this form at T_7. Like the concluding statements of 4-18, this initial statement also contains a triad as a subset, in this case, a D-minor triad. But with A-flat in the bass and with a contrasting melody moving above, the D-minor triad is entirely suppressed. It plays no structural role at all. When this set-class returns in the closing measures, the triadic subset emerges to a position of prominence. At the same time, the triad retains its primary identity as a subset of a subsuming 4-18, an identity established for it in the opening measures.

The treatment of 4-Z29 (0137) and 4-17 (0347) is similar. In the opening measures these set-classes are deployed in such a way that their triadic subsets play a negligible role. When these sets return in the closing measures, a triadic subset, the A-minor triad, is prominently featured. The musical context, however, determines that the tetrachords, not the triad, are structurally primary. The context defines the triad as what Forte would call a "nonset," a formation that is not a true structural determinant.[23] The triad is embedded, as one subset among many, within the principal harmonies.

Of course it is significant that Webern has chosen to feature this particular subset at this particular point in the piece. These triads are, in a sense, latent in the opening music. They are present within the basic set-class structures of the piece but, at first, are unemphasized musically. When they finally emerge from a post-tonal framework, their meaning is predetermined. It is too late for them to assert structural independence. The triad is not, as in earlier music, the central generating structure. Rather, in this piece, it is the by-product of other more fundamental processes. Webern wrests it from its usual function and, by embedding it in a new context, forces it to function in a new way. The triad has no independent existence here; it is trapped within Webern's motivic matrix.

Webern is like other twentieth-century composers in using triads simultaneously to establish a link to the past and to demonstrate their power over it. This demonstration has two parts. First, the triad is neutralized, its normal tendencies paralyzed. Its traditional roles as a consonance, a functional harmony, and a structural generator are all stripped away. Second, a new meaning is imposed, a meaning that varies from context to context. In Berg's Violin Concerto it is defined as a segmental subset of a twelve-tone series. In *Symphony of Psalms* and *Oedipus Rex,* it is defined in terms of harmonic polarity. In Berg's *Wozzeck,* Schoenberg's "Verbundenheit," and Webern's Five Movements for String Quartet, Op. 5, No. 2, it is a subordinate set-class amid a network of motives and pitch-class sets. In each of these contexts the traditional sonority is defamiliarized. It is subverted, subsumed, reinterpreted, and made anew.

CHAPTER 5

Sonata Forms

The paradigmatic form of tonal music is the sonata. Used in the symphonies, quartets, and sonatas of Haydn, Mozart, Beethoven, Schubert,
Schumann, and Brahms, the sonata form epitomizes common-practice tonality and, to the twentieth-century mind, seems laden with the tremendous
weight and prestige of that repertoire. It has been a magnet of attention for
twentieth-century composers who attempt, by using this form in their own
music, to come to terms with their musical heritage. The twentieth-century
sonata form is thus the scene of an artistic struggle in which later composers
attempt to appropriate for themselves an exemplary element of an earlier
style, to confront and master their predecessors on the predecessors' home
ground.

There have been two principal ways of interpreting and writing sonata
forms, which can be loosely termed the eighteenth- and nineteenth-century
approaches, although the chronological boundaries are somewhat blurred.[1]
For eighteenth-century theorists, the sonata form, which had not yet taken
on that name, was essentially a two-part structure shaped by contrasting
harmonic areas. In this view the first large section of the form contains two
subsections, the first of which begins in the tonic key and either remains
there or moves to another key (usually the dominant if the tonic is major or
the mediant if the tonic is minor), and the second of which confirms and
remains in the new key. The second large section begins with rapid digres-
sions or modulations through a variety of keys and concludes with a return
to the tonic, which then prevails until the end of the piece.

By focusing on harmonic contrast rather than thematic recurrence as
the principal determinant of form, this approach accounts for the most
profound and widely shared attribute of musical structure in the classical
period: the polarity of contrasting harmonic areas as the essential form-
generating element. The section of the piece that later comes to be called the

exposition polarizes two contrasting tonal areas, usually the tonic and the dominant; the concluding section (recapitulation) resolves this polarity in favor of the tonic, usually by restating in the tonic material that had formerly been stated in another key. The eighteenth-century sonata form is, in a sense, the outward expression of an underlying tonal polarity.

In the nineteenth century the sonata form changed as the nature of the musical language changed. With the rise of a less sharply focused tonal language and the abandonment of the sharp textural contrasts that reinforced the harmonic polarization, the generating force of the harmony became dulled. As boundaries between tonal areas blurred, they grew less effective in delimiting the formal sections. At the same time, and partially in compensation, thematic contrast increased in importance.

For nineteenth-century theorists, the essence of the form was its themes; the form was determined by thematic contrast and thematic repetition. This view, still enshrined in many modern textbooks on form, considers the sonata a three-part form defined by thematic contrast and repetition. The first section (exposition) has two contrasting themes; the second section (development) varies and develops the themes; the third section (recapitulation) restates the two themes from the exposition. Thematic contrast, which functioned originally as reinforcement for the underlying harmonic polarity, thus survived the demise of that polarity to become, in the nineteenth century, the principal determinant of sonata form. Of course, thematic disposition is not as profound an element of musical structure as harmonic polarity. The sonata was therefore not as deeply a part of musical style in the nineteenth century as it had been in the eighteenth.

Twentieth-century composers have thus had two distinct analytical and compositional traditions to draw upon. Composers who have understood the sonata in a nineteenth-century sense have tended to write uninteresting sonatas. In such works the sonata form floats upon the musical surface, a mere arrangement of themes lacking in real connection to the harmonic structure beneath. There are, however, twentieth-century sonatas that grapple in a profound way with the structural issues raised by the eighteenth-century view of the form. In these works, five of which are discussed in this chapter, the sonata is recreated in something approaching its eighteenth-century fullness, where the thematic organization deeply implicates the underlying harmonic organization.

The sonata, however, has not been easy to recreate in the absence of the tonal relations that originally engendered it. Even in the strongest and most interesting twentieth-century sonatas, the fit between the form and the deeper levels of harmonic structure is never seamless. In the common-practice period one can speak of the form arising organically from the interplay of structural elements. In the twentieth century such organicism, and the compositional unself-consciousness it implies, are no longer possible. For a twentieth-century composer, the sonata form is a historical artifact, a predetermined mold refined by extensive practice and contemplation. Inevitably, then, there is a dichotomy between form and content in twentieth-century sonatas. The underlying musical organization exists in an uneasy relationship with the traditional form. A sense of tension is always present.

In the works to be discussed here the traditional form is clearly evoked by the thematic organization, which always includes an exposition with two contrasting thematic areas, a development, and a recapitulation. This form is then challenged, undermined, and held in tension with new kinds of musical organization. In some cases powerful polarities resist the propensity of the recapitulation for resolution and reconciliation. In others the developmental, dynamic nature of the form is immobilized by the imposition of larger symmetries. In all instances the form emerges from new, idiomatically post-tonal musical imperatives. The form is not revived but created anew.

The first movement of the Symphony in C is Stravinsky's most profound attempt to grapple with the sonata form. Stravinsky recreates the form even as he calls into question some of its most basic attributes. A polarity of two pitch centers, C and E, and of two triads, C–E–G and E–G–B, plays the central form-generating role in this work.

A three-note motive that permeates the movement is shown in Example 5-1 as it appears, in octaves, in the opening measures. The implied harmonic context is ambiguous. It might be C–E–G, with the B acting as a leading tone to the C. Yet, the B is much more heavily stressed than the C, by duration and instrumental reinforcement. The winds and brass, not shown in Example 5-1, double the B throughout its durational span but drop out just as the strings move up to C. Perhaps, then, it is the C that embellishes the B, implying a harmonic context of E–G–B.[2] The ambiguity implicit in this three-note motive evolves into a harmonic polarity powerful enough to generate a sonata form.

A similar ambiguity, although with clearer emphasis on C–E–G, pervades the first theme (see Example 5-2). The melody itself, though not devoid of ambiguity, seems to be centered on C. The harmonization, however, does nothing to confirm this interpretation since it consists of only two notes, E and G, which lend as much support to an E-centered interpretation as to a C-centered one. The theme as a whole establishes C as the pitch-class of priority, but the E is simultaneously suggested as a potential countervailing force. This C-centered area implies E; the rest of the exposition serves to realize that implication.

The recurring figure shown in Example 5-3 pervades the bridge section that leads to the second theme. The reiterated D's in this passage have the sound of a dominant pedal. In a traditional context this pedal would be

EXAMPLE 5-1 Principal motive in Stravinsky, Symphony in C (first movement, strings only). Symphony in C © Schott & Co. Ltd., London, 1948, © Renewed

EXAMPLE 5-2 Three-note motive (M) and set-class 4-11 (0135) in the first theme

EXAMPLE 5-3 Bridge between the first and second themes

understood as the dominant of the dominant, directing motion toward the dominant (G) for the second theme area. Here the D leads not to G but to F, the tonal center of the second theme area. The harmonic motion up to and including the second theme is summarized in Example 5-4.

These three structural tones are part of a large-scale composing-out of a central motive of this work. The motive in question is set-class 4-11 (0135). This motive permeates the surface of the work, most obviously in the first theme itself, where it represents a filling in of the basic three-note motto (see Example 5-2). The completion of the large-scale statement of 4-11 requires a structural E, the ultimate goal of the exposition.[3] The final measures of the exposition, with their strong cadence on E, are shown in Example 5-5. The resulting centric structure of the exposition is shown in Example 5-6. The structural tones representing the first theme, bridge, and second theme, push the exposition toward its concluding E.

The exposition as a whole thus poises the initial C against the concluding E. C and E balance each other at opposite ends of a large-scale motivic statement. In his use of an underlying polarity to generate a sonata exposition, Stravinsky is following the general outlines of traditional practice. At the same time, he subverts and comments ironically on that practice. His principal revision of the traditional form concerns his treatment of the second theme area. Traditionally, the tonal area of the second theme is balanced against that of the first theme. In this work, however, the tonal center of the second theme, F, is merely an agent that directs the motion toward E. The central polarity is not that of C–F but of C–E. Stravinsky thus undercuts the traditional structural role of the second theme, even while preserving the traditional thematic outline.

EXAMPLE 5-4   Structural outline through the second theme

EXAMPLE 5-5   Conclusion of the exposition on E

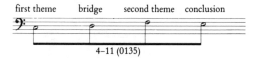

first theme   bridge   second theme   conclusion

4-11 (0135)

EXAMPLE 5-6 Structural outline of the exposition

This revision has dramatic consequences for the recapitulation and coda. The traditional sonata exposition is tonally open and requires resolution by a balancing section that closes on the tonic. In Symphony in C the exposition is also tonally incomplete, but it contains two nontonic areas—F, the pitch center of the second theme, and E, the pitch center of the concluding phrase. Therefore, merely transposing the second theme to the tonic in the recapitulation (the traditional procedure) will not suffice to resolve the tension. Just as the polarity of the exposition is not fully set forth until after the second theme, the reconciliation of the polarity in the recapitulation does not take place until the coda.

The recapitulation is thus denied its traditional function. It has been supplanted by the coda, and the reconciliation of the polarity is deferred until the last moment. (We will see a similar procedure in the sonata forms of Bartók discussed below.) The polarity underlying the structure is so powerful that the recapitulation alone cannot resolve it. The coda is called upon to play the crucial reconciliatory role, but even there, the polarity may be powerful enough to resist any ultimate reconciliation, powerful enough almost to burst through the boundaries of the form.

In the Symphony in C the coda makes an attempt to resolve the polarity in favor of the C. Beneath the repeated, ambiguous accompanying E–G's in the inner strings, the cellos and bassoon establish a final-sounding C, as the movement draws to its close (see Example 5-7). The polarity seems at this moment to have been resolved in favor of the C, and the ambiguous accompanying figure seems to be definitively interpreted as part of a C-major triad.

But the movement does not end at that point; it ends with the explosive alternation of the two chords shown in Example 5-8. The underlying polarity, with its strong E component, reasserts itself dramatically in these chords. These chords intrude almost brutally on the tranquillity of what appeared to be a definitive close on C. The final chord, C–E–G–B, dramatically crystallizes the polarity of the movement as a whole. The lowest notes, E and G, recall that ambiguous accompanying figure. E and G are the common tones between the competing harmonies C–E–G and E–G–B, and the common tones between the alternating chords. In the upper voices of the final chord, B is heard against C. In the motto with which the movement began, the B and C were heard in an ambiguous linear relationship: the B seemed to embellish the C in an implied context of C–E–G; simultaneously, the C seemed to

EXAMPLE 5-7   Seemingly definitive ending on C

EXAMPLE 5-8   Final chords

embellish the B in an implied context of E–G–B. Now, at the end of the
movement, B and C are heard as a simultaneity, precluding forever any
chance of resolving that ambiguity. The final chord thus compresses, in a
single sonority, the duality of C and E and of C–E–G and E–G–B. The
promise of reconciliation held out by the traditional form is thus rudely denied at the last moment.

Although the traditional formal outline remains intact in Symphony in C,
beneath it Stravinsky explores new musical imperatives. He retains contrasting first and second themes within an exposition but gives them new
meaning. The second theme does not create a polarity; it merely directs the
music along a large-scale motivic path that leads to the polarizing E. He retains a tonic-level recapitulation of the two themes but denies it the possibility of reconciling the underlying polarity. He retains a coda, and even holds
out the promise of a last-minute reconciliation, only to dash that hope in the
final chords. It is here, at the end of the movement, that the tension between

the traditional form and Stravinsky's musical syntax is felt most acutely. Stravinsky's tonal polarity is powerful enough to endow the traditional form with new meaning. Indeed, it is powerful enough to thwart the fundamentally closed nature of the form. The movement is not so much an example of sonata form as an ironic commentary on that form.

In the first movement of the Octet, Stravinsky has again clearly invoked the traditional sonata as his formal model, although with some important revisions. After a slow introduction the movement has the customary exposition with two contrasting thematic areas, a development, and a recapitulation in which the first theme comes after the second theme (a departure from the traditional practice). Example 5-9 summarizes the formal plan of the movement and also shows the principal pitch-class for each formal area. The first theme is centered on E-flat, and the second theme is a half-step lower, on D. In the recapitulation the second theme is on E, and the first theme is a half-step lower, at its original level of E-flat. The tonal motion in both cases is down by half-step, departing from E-flat in the exposition and returning to E-flat in the recapitulation. Thus, the motion that brought about harmonic openness in the exposition brings about harmonic closure in the recapitulation.[4] Taken together, this pair of motions embellishes a central tone with chromatic upper and lower neighbors. This chromatic neighboring motion is the central middleground motive of the piece, appearing particularly at important cadential points. Its use as the fundamental structure (Example 5-9) reflects these middleground usages.

The approach to the recapitulation, the scene of one such middleground statement, is shown in Example 5-10.[5] The pitch center at the beginning of the recapitulation, E, is approached from F and E-flat, that is, from pitches a half-step above and a half-step below. This approach reflects the structure of the background and has the force of a strong arrival.

A second moment of crucial structural importance is the return of the first theme in the second half of the recapitulation, shown in Example 5-11. At the end of a long linear descent, the E-flat is approached from a half-step above (E) and from a half-step below (D). As in Example 5-10, this double-

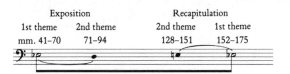

EXAMPLE 5-9   Formal outline of Stravinsky, Octet (first movement)

EXAMPLE 5-10   Approaching the recapitulation of the second theme

EXAMPLE 5-11   Approaching the recapitulation of the first theme

neighbor idea has strong cadential force. And, what is more, the melodic motion at this point nearly recapitulates the background tonal structure of the entire movement. That is, this passage, like the structural background, presents the dyads E-flat–D and E–E-flat but in reverse order.

The same chromatic double-neighbor idea is the first voice-leading gesture of the entire movement (see Example 5-12). The opening B-flat progresses first to B-natural at the end of measure 2, then to A-natural in measure 4, and finally again to B-flat at the end of measure 4. The instrumentation very closely reflects this underlying voice leading. The first significant voice-leading gesture establishes a tone, embellishes it with chromatic upper and lower neighbors, then returns to the initial tone. The background tonal structure of the movement is thus presaged in the opening measures of its introduction.

By using the upper-lower neighbor idea to motivate the most significant arrivals in the movement as well as to describe the background tonal structure, Stravinsky lends the work a remarkable coherence. In tonal music the use of tonic and dominant at the local level to form cadences corresponds to the use of tonic and dominant at the highest level as tonal areas and structural goals. In the Octet Stravinsky creates a compelling analogy to this relationship by using the chromatic neighbor idea both at the local level to create a sense of cadential arrival and at the highest level as the structural background.

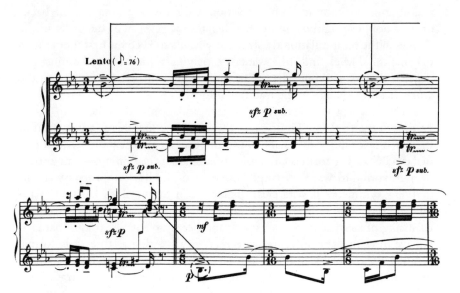

EXAMPLE 5-12   The first voice-leading gesture

FIGURE 5-I

Chromatic neighbor notes cannot be used in place of tonic-dominant relations, however, without a profound effect on the sonata form. The most obvious effect is a reversal of the order of first and second themes in the recapitulation. This procedure is rare in traditional sonata forms and virtually unknown after about 1780.[6] The traditional form requires the presentation of second-theme material in the tonality of the tonic. This represents the resolution of what Rosen calls the "structural dissonance" resulting from its original presentation at some other tonal level.[7] It would be dramatically unsatisfying, in the traditional conception, to have this resolution occur at the beginning of the recapitulation. A better sense of overall formal balance is created when the temporal relationship between the themes is preserved in the recapitulation, but the second theme is adjusted to the level of the first.

Stravinsky's Octet disrupts this traditional balance. The second theme in this work never occurs at the level of the first theme. Rather, it retains its neighboring function in both exposition and recapitulation. It is the background double-neighbor figure that dictates the reversal of the order of the themes in the recapitulation. If Stravinsky wants to keep his first theme at its original tonal level, and if he wants a satisfying tonic ending, he must put the first theme in second place. The underlying centric relationships of the work dictate a change in the traditional form.

The reversal of the themes in the recapitulation makes the form retrograde-symmetrical (see Figure 5-I). A symmetry like this is antithetical to the dynamic of the traditional form. It imposes an almost static sense of formal deadlock. The form is circular—its ends are its beginnings—rather than propulsive and forward-moving. This sense of deadlock imposed by an underlying symmetry has its clear analogues in Stravinsky's harmonic language. Frequently in Stravinsky's music harmonic stasis resulting from the balancing of tonal centers against one another supplants the traditional propulsive movement from center to center.[8] By creating a large-scale formal symmetry, Stravinsky simultaneously responds to the demands of his musical material and subverts an important aesthetic element of the traditional form. The traditional formal outline remains largely in place, but its significance is called into question.

REMAKING THE PAST

TABLE 5-1

Exposition			Recapitulation		
First theme	Second theme	Development	First theme	Second theme	Coda
1–43	44–135	136–182	183–209	210–236	237–269

The Octet and the Symphony in C typify in many ways Stravinsky's relationship to the past and to his musical predecessors. His so-called neo-classicism has generally been regarded as a kind of extended homage to classical music. There is, however, as much defiance as reverence in these works. Stravinsky uses the sonata form as he uses other traditional style elements—to satirize, not to glorify, them. His use of sonata form is thus his supreme act of defiance. What better way to pursue his struggle against his predecessors than to remake the form that epitomizes their works? By leaving the traditional formal outline intact, Stravinsky makes his achievement all the more evident. He remakes the sonata from the inside and bends it to his own aesthetic and musical purposes.

Like Stravinsky, Bartók wrote important works that profoundly reinterpret the sonata form. His sonata-form works are fraught with a productive artistic tension between the traditional and the new.

The first movement of the Piano Sonata of 1926 is Bartók's first essay in sonata form.[9] Table 5-1 formally outlines this movement (in measures) and reveals how it follows the traditional plan. But Bartók, like Stravinsky, goes far beyond the mere use of a familiar thematic pattern. In the exposition the first and second theme areas are harmonically distinct. The accompanying harmonies in the first theme area, 3-3 (014) and 4-18 (0147) become, in inversion, the predominant harmonies of the second theme area. In this way, Bartók assures both continuity and contrast between the areas. To some extent the two theme areas are also distinguished by tonal center—the first theme is centered on E and the second theme begins on A, before moving through a succession of other centers. Centricity does not play a crucial form-defining role in this work, however, as it does in Stravinsky's Octet and Symphony in C. Rather, formal sections exist at harmonic plateaus, defined by the transpositional level of the principal pitch-class collections. This, of course, is similar to the traditional practice, although both the prevailing harmonies and the transpositional distances traversed depart in significant ways from common-practice norms.

Bartók's most radical reinterpretation of the traditional sonata takes place

EXAMPLE 5-13 First theme of Bartók, Piano Sonata (first movement). Piano
Sonata Copyright 1927 by Universal Edition, Copyright Renewed

in the recapitulation. There, the second theme makes an extraordinary attempt to break free of the gravitational pull of the first theme, shattering the boundaries of the form. This attempt is suppressed, but the victory of the first theme is equivocal. The traditional order of things is reimposed uneasily and insecurely.

The first theme begins strongly centered on E (see Example 5-13). Under an upper-voice arpeggiation from G-sharp2 through B2 (measures 1–6) and E4 (measures 7–13) to G-natural4 (measure 14), the accompaniment consists of an alternation of E-major triads with pitch-class set 3-3 (014), a set with a clearly audible neighboring function in this context. At the top of the arpeggiation in measure 14, the accompaniment changes to focus on a form of set-class 4-18 (0147), with pitch-class content E-sharp, G-sharp, C-sharp, and D (in registral order). This set is somewhat obscured at this point in the music but emerges clearly at analogous points later in the exposition and in the recapitulation. It defines the "tonic level" for this set-class. Virtually all of the harmonies in the first part of the exposition (measures 1–25) are drawn from a single octatonic collection: E, F, G, G-sharp, A-sharp, B, C-sharp, D.

In measure 26 the entire texture is transposed at T_5, the first of many transpositions in this work up or down by five. The principal upper-voice tone moves from G to C. The accompanying 4-18 moves from E-sharp–G-sharp–C-sharp–D to A-sharp–C-sharp–F-sharp–G. These two transposition levels of 4-18 are uniquely characteristic of the first theme. The same harmony will be intensively developed in the second theme area and in the development section, though always in inversion. The shift to T_5 also brings in a second octatonic collection (A, B-flat, C, C-sharp, D-sharp, E, F-sharp, G) and prepares the second theme, which is centered on A, five semitones above the opening E.

After an arresting hint in measures 36–37, the second theme proper begins in measure 44 (see Example 5-14). The centricity on A is unmistakable. The principal harmony is 3-3 (014) consisting of A, C, and C-sharp. In measure 46, and in many subsequent places, F-sharp is added to these, creating 4-18 (0147). Set-classes 3-3 and 4-18, which were accompanying harmonies in the first theme area, now dominate the texture. Furthermore, they are related by inversion, not transposition, to the forms found in the first theme area.

As the second theme area continues, these new forms of 3-3 and 4-18 are transposed in a highly significant way, through a sequence of ascending perfect fifths. This transpositional scheme is most apparent in the treatment of the initial material of the second theme. Example 5-15 shows the three principal occurrences of that material and its variants, first on A, then on E, and

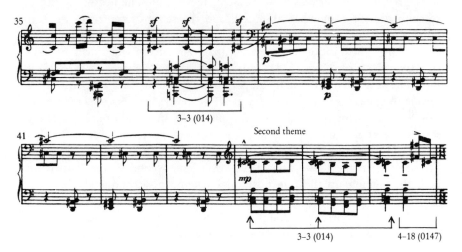

EXAMPLE 5-14   Second theme on A (with inverted forms of 3-3 and 4-18)

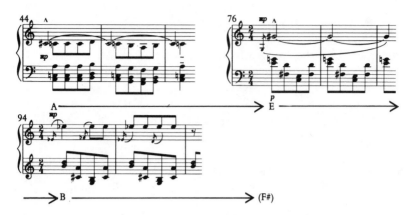

EXAMPLE 5-15   Second theme transposed by perfect fifth (T₇)

then on B. If the scheme continued, it would take the music to F-sharp, but instead the harmony is revoiced in measure 113, leading to material on E-flat that ends the exposition. The second theme thus spans a tritone from A (measures 44–53) to the concluding E-flat (measures 117–135). In the recapitulation that structural tritone will assist in diverting the second theme back to the level of the first theme. Such a diversion will be necessary because the second theme has set itself on a headlong course that could carry it indefinitely onward. The pattern of ascending fifths, set in motion in the exposition, will prove difficult to break. Interrupted at the end of the exposition, the pattern continues in the recapitulation where it threatens to rupture the boundaries of the sonata form.

The recapitulation of the first theme is uneventful. The beginning of the recapitulation is somewhat obscured, and the sense of centricity on E is downplayed, but the tonal level is unambiguously the same as that in the exposition. The motion in the accompaniment from one form of 4-18 (E-sharp, G-sharp, C-sharp, D) to its T_5 (A-sharp, C-sharp, F-sharp, G) is the same, as is the motion in the upper voice from G to C. The return of the second theme is extraordinarily dramatic, however, as is its violent suppression by first-theme material (see Example 5-16). In a traditional sonata the second theme in the recapitulation is adjusted to the tonal level of the first theme. The second theme thus accommodates the structural requirements of the first. In the Piano Sonata, however, the second theme returns on F-sharp, picking up the transpositional scheme of ascending fifths right where it left off in the exposition.[10] The second theme attempts to continue blithely on its course, as though the first theme required no concession. After F-sharp, it threatens to continue chugging along, upward by fifths, indefinitely.

This has powerful and potentially disruptive implications for the form as a

whole. The transpositional scheme cuts across the traditional formal boundaries. It confers upon the second theme a degree of structural autonomy that
is not normally possible within the confines of a closed form like the sonata.
This second theme insists on going its own way, and strong action is required to prevent it from doing so.

In measure 218, with the second theme fully underway, the first theme
enters in stretto, accompanied by a sforzando statement of its characteristic
form of 4-18 (E-sharp, G-sharp, C-sharp, D). The entries are a semitone
apart and, at the end of measure 219, the music reaches a kind of harmonic
deadlock on set-class 4-1 (0123). The second theme tries to resume its course

EXAMPLE 5-16   Recapitulation of the second theme (and its suppression by the
first)

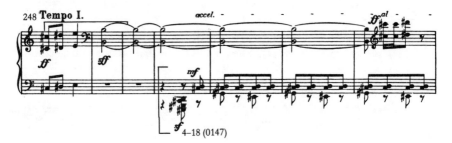

EXAMPLE 5-17   Second theme transposed to the level of the first

in measures 220–223 but again is cut off by stretto entries of the first theme. Again, these entries lead to harmonic deadlock, only now (measure 226), the material of the first theme emerges gradually through the repeated E's and the increasingly frequent statements of the familiar form of 3-3 (014) from measures 1–13.

The somewhat brutal triumph of the first theme is made clear in the coda, where a melodic figure taken from the second theme is transposed to the level of the first theme, framed by E and B (see Example 5-17). The melody has been transposed by a tritone, which was the interval of large-scale progression in the exposition of the second theme. Now, that same interval is used in the recapitulation to cut off the disruption threatened by the second theme. It forces the second theme to toe the line, to accommodate itself to the structural demands of the first theme. As the coda ends, the second theme is finally and irrevocably adjusted to the transpositional level of the first theme. It leaps between a central E and a low B, both of which characterized the first theme in the exposition. The accompaniment in the coda further ratifies the first theme's triumph. It consists almost exclusively of the two forms of 4-18 that dominated the first theme in both exposition and recapitulation.

Although the sonata form emerges intact, it does so only after a disruptive struggle, one with effects that linger until the end of the work and beyond. The musical forces that Bartók has set in motion can scarcely be contained by the sonata form. The first theme does eke out a victory, but one that feels strangely incomplete. The recapitulation itself does not resolve the underlying polarity, as would be the case in the traditional sonata.

Rather, any sense of resolution is deferred until the last possible moment, in the coda. Even there, the T_7 scheme of the second theme is not so much reconciled to the demands of the first theme as simply cut off in midstream. The scheme implies a continuation that extends beyond the boundaries of the work. This sonata form emerges from musical forces so strong they threaten to shatter the vessel that contains them.

—————

The first movement of Bartók's String Quartet No. 2 reconceives the sonata form in a somewhat different way. As in the Piano Sonata, the polarity that engenders the form is one of both harmonic content and transpositional level. Unlike that work, however, the polarity is resolved in favor not of the first theme but of the second. The thematic organization of this work, outlined in Table 5-2 (in measures), conforms closely to the traditional pattern. Bartók uses a new harmonic vocabulary and syntax to reanimate the old form, to reconstruct it from within.

String Quartet No. 2 uses two distinct groups of harmonies. The first group consists of harmonies that are subsets of the octatonic collection 8-28 (0134679T).[11] Of particular importance are the three symmetrical tetrachords that contain two tritones: 4-25 (0268), 4-28 (0369), and, above all, 4-9 (0167).[12] The second group consists of harmonies derived from the scalar hexachord 6-20 (014589).[13] The augmented triad, a prominent subset of this collection, is used frequently in this work with a conjunct semitone, to create the asymmetrical set-class 4-19 (0148).

In subset structure and in other formal properties, these two collections have interesting similarities and differences. Both are highly symmetrical and thus have few distinct forms. There are only three octatonic collections and only four 6-20's (see Table 5-3). Neither, of course, is diatonic, but both have surprising triadic resources (one can build major and minor triads at symmetrical nodes in each collection). At the same time, the collections are distinct in many ways. The octatonic collection is particularly rich in interval-classes 3 and 6. Interval-class 6 is the defining interval in the subsets Bartók derives from it. Set-class 6-20, by contrast, has few 3's and, most important, no tritones at all. The subsets that Bartók derives from it tend to feature the augmented triad, a set that is not available in the octatonic collection.

TABLE 5-2

Exposition				Recapitulation	
First theme	Transition	Second theme	Development	First theme	Second theme
1–19	19–31	32–69	70–116	117–140	141–180

TABLE 5-3

Octatonic								6-20 (014589)					
A	B♭	C	C♯	D♯	E	F♯	G	G♯	A	C	C♯	E	F
B♭	B	C♯	D	E	F	G	A♭	A	B♭	C♯	D	F	F♯
B	C	D	E♭	F	F♯	A♭	A	B♭	B	D	D♯	F♯	G
								B	C	D♯	E	G	G♯

Bartók employs both the contrast between these collections and their points of intersection to create a dramatic revision of the sonata form. In the first theme in the exposition, octatonic harmonies occur only fleetingly on the surface, controlled by a matrix of harmonies derived from 6-20 (014589). These 6-20–based harmonies completely control the second theme area in the exposition. In the recapitulation of the first theme, the octatonic harmonies, particularly 4-9 (0167), free themselves from their former subordination and permeate every aspect. In the recapitulation of the second theme, however, the first-theme harmonies are forced to submit. They lose their identity and get subsumed within harmonies derived from 6-20. By the end of the movement, despite some last-minute attempts to assert priority, the octatonic harmonies are entirely submerged.

The relationship between these two groups of harmonies thus articulates the sonata form, but with some unusual twists. Instead of sharp polarization, Bartok's exposition presents a subtle and somewhat ambiguous relationship. That relationship dramatically crystallizes and intensifies in the recapitulation. Ultimately, however, the first group of harmonies is forced to yield, to accommodate itself to the demands of the second group.

Example 5-18 contains the opening measures of the movement. Most of the harmonies and linear motions are derived from 6-20 (014589). The sets 4-19 (0148) and 3-4 (015) are particularly prominent, both locally and over larger spans. Neither is a subset of the octatonic collection. Both outer voices (first violin and cello) traverse forms of 4-19, the constituent pitches emphasized by duration, contour, and placement at the beginning or ending of a span. There are hints of the first group of harmonies, however, most significantly the statement in the first violin of 4-9 (0167) in measure 2. This motive is full of possibilities, but in its local context it is embedded in a large-scale statement of 4-19.

The pitch-class content of the large-scale 4-19 (0148) in the first violin is particularly important. It defines a transpositional level of 6-20 (A, B-flat, C-sharp, D, F, F-sharp) that will become the locus of activity in the second theme. The motive 4-9, then, is embedded in a structural network associ-

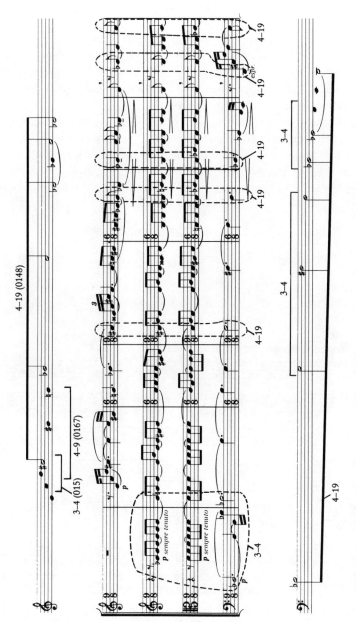

EXAMPLE 5-18   First theme of Bartók, String Quartet No. 2 (first movement).
String Quartet No. 2 Copyright 1920 by Universal Edition, Copyright Renewed

ated with the second theme. Its transformations during the first theme confirm this. With every recurrence, it appears less and less like 4-9 and more and more like 4-19. It tends to metamorphose into its contrary (see Example 5-19).

In the recapitulation, in contrast, this motive and other octatonic subsets entirely dominate the texture (see Example 5-20). The melody now consists of the same pitch-classes (G, G-sharp, C-sharp, D) as did that fleeting motive in measure 2. The accompaniment consists of 4-25 (0268), another symmetrical octatonic subset with two tritones.

The first theme does not remain at that transpositional level, however. At measure 123 the entire material is transposed at T_5 and then, at measure 127, at T_2.[14] The first theme concludes at this new transposition level with a unison statement of 4-9, now with the pitch-class content A, B-flat, D-sharp, E (see Example 5-21). This unison statement represents the most powerful,

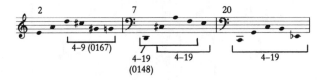

EXAMPLE 5-19 Transformation of a motive from 4-9 (0167) into 4-19 (0148)

EXAMPLE 5-20 Recapitulation of the first theme

REMAKING THE PAST

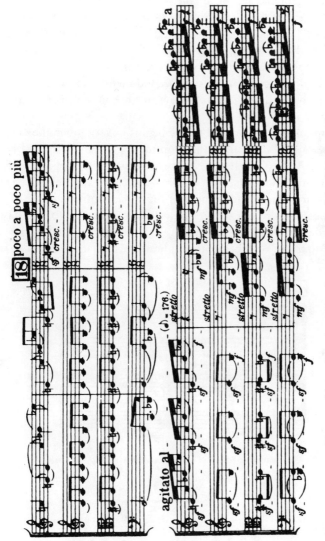

EXAMPLE 5-21 Transposition of 4–9 (0167) at the conclusion of the first theme in the recapitulation

intense expression of 4-9 in the entire movement. But in its transposition to a level where it contains an A and an E, the motive is preparing itself for its own demise. From this new level it is ultimately drawn into the harmonies of the second theme.

The beginning of the second theme in the exposition is drawn entirely from a single form of 6-20 (014589): A, B-flat, C-sharp, D, F, F-sharp (see Example 5-22). The one note from outside the collection, the G in measure 33, is easily heard as an appoggiatura. The collection features the augmented triad A–C-sharp–E-sharp and is centered on the bass note F-sharp. This F-sharp orientation is confirmed as the second theme composes-out a statement of 4-19, concluding back on F-sharp at the end of the exposition (see Example 5-23).

In the recapitulation the second theme begins in very much the same way but then, over a period of time, shifts up to a new transpositional level of 6-20: G-sharp, A, C, C-sharp, E, F. It is at this new transpositional level that the movement ends (see Example 5-24). The augmented triad A–C-sharp–F is prominent and comprises the three common tones between those two transpositions of 6-20. As indicated by arrows, 4-19 (0148) occurs with extraordinary frequency as a vertical harmony (the notes in the upper voices are assumed to reverberate throughout the final measure). The trans-

EXAMPLE 5-22   Beginning of the second theme in the exposition

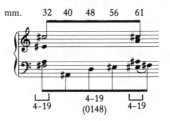

EXAMPLE 5-23   Schematic reduction of the second theme area

REMAKING THE PAST

EXAMPLE 5-24 End of the movement; arrows indicate forms of 4-19 (0148)

positional shift is associated with a shift of pitch center as well—the second
theme now focuses on A rather than F-sharp. Pitch-class A defines the registral extremes of the passage as well as its registral midpoint. The cello melody
also concentrates on A, reinforced by its upper-fifth E. The A-orientation of
these final measures, and the A–E melodic focus, strongly recall the transpositional shift of the first theme. That theme began the recapitulation at its
original transposition level (G, G-sharp, C-sharp, D), then shifted to A,
B-flat, D-sharp, E. That new pitch-class content, particularly the boundary
A–E, makes the first theme easier to assimilate within the second. When the
second theme reaches its new transpositional level toward the end of the
movement, it can easily reach out and swallow up the first.

It is in these concluding measures of the movement that the harmonies of the first theme, particularly 4-9 (0167), are forced finally to yield. The final statement of 4-9 occurs at the pickup to measure 171 at its original pitch-class level: G, G-sharp, C-sharp, D. The voice leading in the following measures resolves that sonority into the prevailing 6-20 of the ending. The first violin transfers its G-sharp up an octave (measures 172–173), where it resolves to A in measure 175. The second violin's D transfers and resolves in a similar fashion to C-sharp. The viola moves from G to F (measures 172–173) and then is retained as a common tone in measure 175. The cello is harder to trace. Its disjunct motions gradually settle on the notes of the A-minor triad, where it ends. This voice leading is summarized in Example 5-25. The final sonority of the piece (F, A, C-sharp, E) summarizes the final triumph of the second-theme harmonies even as it recalls the transposed 4-9 (A, B-flat, D-sharp, E) of the first theme.

As in the traditional sonata form, a harmonic polarity engenders the first movement of Bartók's String Quartet No. 2. But both the polarity itself and the way in which it gives rise to the movement are different from the traditional procedure. First, the harmonic polarity in Bartók is defined by harmonic contrast, not by competing tonal centers (as in Stravinsky) or key areas (as in the traditional arrangement). And this polarity, rather than being directly expressed in the exposition, is latent there. It gets clarified over the course of the development section and receives full expression in the recapitulation. Finally, at the end of the recapitulation, the polarity is resolved, but not in favor of the first theme as would be the case in the traditional form. Rather, the first-theme material that was latent in the exposition and strongly expressed in the recapitulation, finally gives way and becomes absorbed into the material of the second theme.

Bartók's sonata form arises, then, from the dramatic working out of an underlying polarity. In this sense Bartók has clearly captured the essential feature of the traditional sonata. At the same time, his revision of the form is profound. In the use of contrasting harmonies to define first and second themes, in the use of the recapitulation to crystallize the polarity before resolving it, and in the ultimate triumph of the second-theme harmonies, Bar-

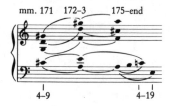

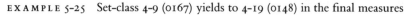

EXAMPLE 5-25   Set-class 4-9 (0167) yields to 4-19 (0148) in the final measures

tók has entirely reconceived the form. The form still emerges as the outward expression of underlying structural processes, but now those processes reflect Bartók's idiomatic compositional approach.

In his written comments Schoenberg takes an essentially nineteenth-century, thematic view of sonata form, very much in the tradition of Anton Reicha, Adolf Bernhard Marx, and Carl Czerny.

> This form . . . is essentially a ternary structure. Its main divisions are the EXPOSITION, ELABORATION and RECAPITULATION. It differs from other complex ternary forms in that the contrasting middle section (Elaboration) is devoted almost exclusively to the working out of the rich variety of thematic material "exposed" in the first division. Its greatest merit, which enabled it to hold a commanding position over a period of 150 years, is its extraordinary flexibility in accommodating the widest variety of musical ideas, long or short, many or few, active or passive, in almost any combination. The internal details may be subjected to almost any mutation without disturbing the aesthetic validity of the structure as a whole.[15]

This definition suggests that, for Schoenberg, the sonata was primarily a convenient way of articulating the proportions of a work through thematic contrast and associated changes of texture, articulation, and instrumentation. But in what is probably his clearest twelve-tone essay in sonata form, the first movement of his String Quartet No. 3, his reinterpretation extends to the most profound levels of harmonic organization as well. In this work he creates an authentic twelve-tone sonata form, one in which the formal outlines reflect the workings of twelve-tone syntax and, more accurately, Schoenberg's own conception of twelve-tone syntax.

Schoenberg's reinterpretation of sonata form in this string quartet depends above all on his concept of inversional symmetry and balance.[16] At the local level this principle provides a way of linking series forms and building up phrases and sections. At the highest level it brings about a thorough reinterpretation of the sonata form itself. In the traditional sonata the contrast between the first and second theme areas engenders the form. In Schoenberg's String Quartet No. 3 the form depends instead on the symmetrical balance of exposition and recapitulation around a central development section. To heighten this sense of formal balance, the order of the first and second themes is reversed in the recapitulation, as Figure 5-2 shows (the outline is presented in measures). In Schoenberg's conception the first theme in the exposition is balanced not against the second theme but against the first theme in the recapitulation. The second theme in the exposition is similarly balanced against the second theme in the recapitulation. This reinterpretation of the sonata form as an expression of inversional balance rather than dramatic polarity is Schoenberg's boldest stroke, one that preserves the the-

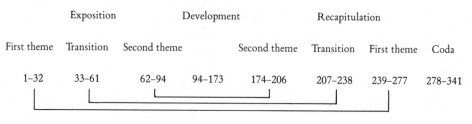

FIGURE 5-2

matic surface of a sonata form even as it undermines the traditional structural determinant of that form.

The basic musical idea for the piece involves an unvarying five-note figure followed by one of three possible continuations.[17] The resulting twelve-
note series contain the basic pitch material for the work. The three series are
shown in Table 5-4, in both letter and integer notation (G = 0). Throughout
this work a series form is usually paired with an inversionally related form.
This pairing creates a local sense of inversional balance around some axis of
inversion. For example, when the prime ordering of the first series, $P_o(1)$, is
paired with its inversion beginning on C, $I_5(1)$, a most common situation in
this piece, each note of the chromatic is balanced against some counterpart
(see Table 5-5). These pairings, and the inversional axis around which they
balance, can be clearly seen on the "inversional clock" shown in Figure 5-3.
The axis of inversion is A/B-flat–D-sharp/E; the other pitch-classes balance
symmetrically around it. As David Lewin has pointed out, "The 'balance' of
the total chromatic induced by the functioning of such an inversion was
treated by Schoenberg, throughout his career, as something quite analogous
to the balance induced by a tonal center."[18] For Schoenberg, the tonic in a
tonal work is a kind of fulcrum around which the other tones, harmonies,
and regions balance. In Schoenberg's twelve-tone music in general, and in

TABLE 5-4

Series:						Integer / Pitch-class						
1:	0	9	8	2	5	10	11	4	3	6	1	7
	G	E	D♯	A	C	F	F♯	B	B♭	C♯	A♭	D
2:	0	9	8	2	5	6	1	10	4	11	7	3
	G	E	D♯	A	C	C♯	A♭	F	B	F♯	D	B♭
3:	0	9	8	2	5	6	3	1	10	11	4	7
	G	E	D♯	A	C	C♯	B♭	A♭	F	F♯	B	D

REMAKING THE PAST

his String Quartet No. 3 in particular, the pitch-classes that define the axis of inversion have an important centric function.

The most frequently used axis of inversion in the work is the one shown in Figure 5-3. It is around this axis that the music begins and ends, and it figures prominently throughout. Series P_0 and I_5 are not the only pair that will produce this axis. Any inversionally related series whose transposition numbers sum to 5 (mod 12), like P_8–I_9, P_2–I_3, and so on, will do so as well.[19] I will call this Axis 5. Axis 5 is the most important axis of inversion in the work, but it is not the only one. The axes resulting from the sum 1 (G/A-flat–C-sharp/D) and from the sum 9 (B/C–F/F-sharp) play a crucial subordinate role. Significantly, these subordinate axes are symmetrical around the central axis (see Figure 5-4). These axes play a decisive role in shaping the large-scale harmonic organization of the work. They unify harmonic areas and guide the succession from area to area. They play the same role in Schoenberg's reinterpretation of sonata form that middleground and background tonal motions play in the traditional sonata form.

The first theme consists of five phrases, all but one of which contains two series statements. Table 5-6 summarizes the phrase structure and gives the inversional axes for the paired series forms. The first theme is highly unified motivically and texturally. More important, it is unified harmonically through its use of inversional axes. Axis 5 prevails in measures 1–18 where the basic five-note idea of P_0 is presented with each of its three aftersentences, and is then juxtaposed with I_5. Axis 9 controls measures 19–27,

TABLE 5-5

$P_0(1)$:	0	9	8	2	5	10	11	4	3	6	1	7
$I_5(1)$:	5	8	9	3	0	7	6	1	2	11	4	10

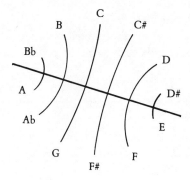

FIGURE 5-3

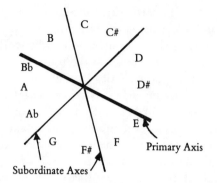

FIGURE 5-4

where P_0 is heard with I_9. In the final section of the first theme (measures 27–32), the cycle of axes continues with Axis 1, as I_5 is heard with P_8. The transition to the second theme, beginning in measure 33, leads the music back to Axis 5.

These axes are much more than a theoretical abstraction or a metaphor. They play a decisive and audible role in shaping the music. Example 5-26 contains the last three phrases of the exposition, featuring the motion through Axis 9 and Axis 1. The axial pitch-classes are strongly emphasized in the music. In the passage centering on Axis 9 (measures 19–27, comprising P_0, I_9, and P_0), F and G-flat are sustained throughout while B and C are strategically positioned, first at the beginning and then at the end of the staccato and cantabile five-note motives. The passage gives a palpable sense of balance on its inversional axis. In measure 27 the axis shifts to C-sharp/D–G/A-flat. Once again, these axial pitch-classes are strongly emphasized. The C-sharp and D are sustained throughout while the G and A-flat are strategically placed. The large-scale harmonic movement in this music is defined by the shift of axis. The return to the original axis (5), toward the end of the transition (measures 51–61), completes an interval cycle and closes off this large formal unit.

In a more abstract sense the inversional symmetry operates at the highest level. The central axis, Axis 5, is balanced symmetrically by motion above

TABLE 5-6

Measures:	1–12	13–18	19–24	25–26	27–32
Series:	$P_0(1)$, $P_0(2)$	$P_0(3)$, $I_5(3)$	$P_0(1)$, $I_9(1)$	$P_0(1)$	$I_5(1)$, $P_8(1)$
Axis:	5 (A/B♭–E♭/E)		9 (B/C–F/F♯)		1 (G/A♭–C♯/D)

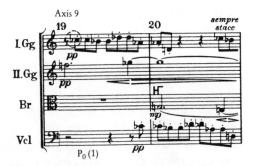

EXAMPLE 5-26 Motion in the first theme area through Axis 9 (F/F-sharp–B/C) and Axis 1 (C-sharp/D–G/A-flat) in Schoenberg, String Quartet No. 3 (first movement)

(to Axis 9) and motion below (to Axis 1). There is an unmistakable analogy here to the position of the tonic symmetrically between the dominant and the subdominant in the traditional Rameau-based tonal theory with which Schoenberg would have been familiar.[20] In Schoenberg's String Quartet No. 3, however, the harmonic balance is produced in purely twelve-tone terms.

The second theme contrasts with the first in many obvious ways (see Example 5-27). The melody in the first violin traces I_5 and then P_0, using the first series. As the second theme continues and concludes (not shown in the example), the melody states P_0 and I_5 using the third series. The accompaniment is cleverly devised to support these melodic statements. Every four or five beats, the four instruments together state a series form (these are indicated below the staff in Example 5-27). From each of these series, two notes (usually the sixth and seventh or eleventh and twelfth) are assigned to the first violin. The resulting melody in the first violin is thus the intersection of two musical dimensions. It merges with the accompanying parts to create many series forms, and it proceeds on its own to trace P_0 and I_5.[21]

The texture of the second theme contrasts clearly with that of the first, but the most prominent series forms, P_0 and I_5, remain the same. Even more important, the inversional axis, Axis 5, also remains the same. In this crucial sense there is no true polarity of first and second theme areas. In most circumstances this would be fatal to the sonata form, which traditionally springs from this basic polarity. But Schoenberg has shifted the structural issue here. The first and second themes contrast only mildly, while the true structure-generating polarity pits the exposition against the recapitulation. The first and second themes do not balance each other; rather, each balances its own repetition in the recapitulation. As a result, the exposition as a whole balances the recapitulation as a whole. Remarkably, this balance, like those of the smaller musical dimensions, occurs around Axis 5.

The recapitulation begins with the second theme (see Example 5-28). In comparison to its appearance in the exposition, the instrumentation is "inverted" (the melody has moved from the first violin to the cello), and the contours of both melody and accompaniment are generally reversed. Inversional balance defines the harmonic relations as well. In the exposition the melody described this succession: $I_5(1)–P_0(1)–P_0(3)–I_5(3)$. In the recapitulation the melody has been inverted around Axis 5, and the melodic succession is as follows: $P_0(1)–I_5(1)–I_5(3)–P_0(3)$. This large-scale inversional relationship extends to the accompanying series as well. Table 5-7 compares the accompanying series in the first phrase of the second theme in the exposition with those of the second theme as it occurs in the recapitulation. In virtually every case the transposition numbers of the corresponding series forms sum to 5. In other words, the series forms in the recapitulation are simply the

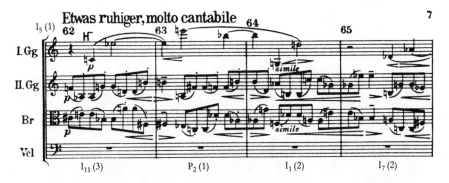

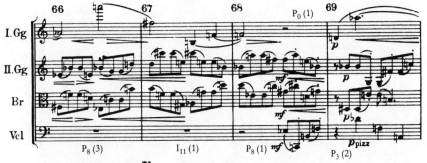

EXAMPLE 5-27   Second theme in the exposition

EXAMPLE 5-28 Second theme in the recapitulation—the inversion around Axis 5 of the second theme in the exposition

TABLE 5-7

Exposition (mm. 62–68):	$I_{11}(3) - P_2(1) - I_1(2) - I_7(2) - P_8(3) - I_{11}(1)$					
Recapitulation (mm. 174–180):	$P_6(3) - I_3(1) - P_4(2) - I_5(2) - I_9(3) - P_6(1)$					
Sums:	5	5	5	0	5	5

inversions of the corresponding series forms in the exposition around Axis 5 (A/B-flat–D-sharp/E). Axis 5 and, more generally, the concept of inversional balance thus govern both the small-scale musical successions and the structural relations of the work as a whole.

The recapitulation of the first theme (beginning in measure 239) involves a similar inversion around Axis 5. Each series form in the exposition is answered in the recapitulation by an inversionally related form whose transposition numbers sum to 5. Series P_0 is balanced by I_5 (and vice versa); I_9 by P_8 (and vice versa); and so on. The first theme in the recapitulation is greatly extended, so this precise balancing continues only through measure 260. At a deeper level, however, where the axes gradually move through an interval cycle, the balance is maintained. Where in the exposition the first theme cycled from Axis 5 through Axis 9 and Axis 1 before returning to Axis 5, the procedure is reversed in the recapitulation. There, the first theme cycles from Axis 5 through Axis 1 and Axis 9 before returning to Axis 5 (see Figure 5-5). The sense of inversional balance around a central axis defines the highest level of structure in this work.

The coda reaffirms both the central axis and the sense of inversional balance it induces. Example 5-29 shows the final measures of the movement.

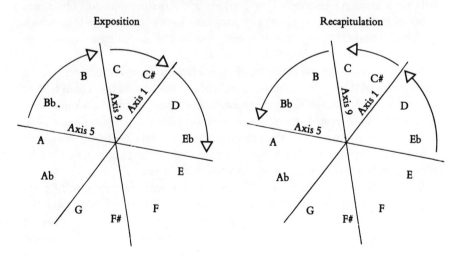

FIGURE 5-5

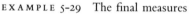

EXAMPLE 5-29   The final measures

The music traverses three pairs of series, all of which affirm Axis 5. The central pair, $P_8 + I_9$, lies between two statements of $P_0 + I_5$ (see Figure 5-6). As is usually the case in this movement, the sense of inversional pairing and balance is strongly reinforced by contour and instrumentation. The statement of P_0 in measures 334–335 is answered by a statement of I_5 in which the characteristic driving motive is both inverted in contour and transferred from the highest to the lowest instrument.

Within this strong affirmation of the central axis of the movement lie subtle hints of the subordinate axes, and thus of the symmetrical plan for the movement as a whole. The combination of series between, rather than within, the pairs, reveals a final suggestion of Axes 1 and 9 (see Figure 5-7). These measures summarize the principal structural idea of the movement: a central axis that both divides the chromatic into balancing pairs of pitch-classes and lies symmetrically between subordinate axes.

With such a powerful musical language, Schoenberg profoundly reinterprets the sonata form. The thematic surface of the work is reasonably conventional, with two contrasting themes, a section of relatively intense development (to be discussed in the following chapter), a modified recapitulation of the two themes, and a coda. Beneath this surface Schoenberg brings about a profound structural shift, through the revisionary strategy of symmetricization. The form becomes retrograde-symmetrical while the musical structure is charged with inversional symmetries. The sonata form remains the dramatic unfolding of an underlying conflict, only now the scene of the drama has moved. Whereas the conventional sonata form depends upon polarization of two key areas in the exposition, Schoenberg's sonata form depends upon inversional balance of exposition and recapitulation. Inversional balance pervades every level of musical structure. Individual phrases combine series forms that balance about a musically articulated axis. Larger sections cohere through focus on a succession of axes. The movement as a whole balances entire sections in a similar manner.

Some commentators have seen Schoenberg's use of traditional forms like the sonata as a sign of compositional weakness or failure of vision. Schoenberg would have been more successful, this argument goes, if he had found forms that arose spontaneously from the internal relations of his new musical language, rather than simply using the crutch of some familiar, traditional pattern. Pierre Boulez, the principal exponent of this view, refers to

a certain weakness in most of [Schoenberg's] twelve-tone works. The pre-classical and classical forms ruling most of his compositions were in no way historically connected with the twelve-tone discovery; the result is that a contradiction arises between the forms dictated by tonality and a language of which the laws of organization are still only dimly perceived. It is not only that this language finds no sanction in the forms used by Schoenberg, but something more negative: namely, that these forms rule out every possibility of organization implicit in the new material. The two worlds are incompatible, and he has tried to justify one by the other. This can hardly be called a valid procedure.[22]

Boulez misunderstands what Schoenberg has accomplished in String Quartet No. 3 and other similar pieces. In fact, Schoenberg uses a traditional form as a demonstration of the power of his musical language.[23] His use of sonata form signifies not a lack of compositional imagination or

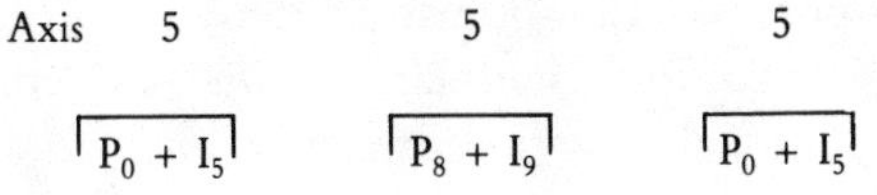

Axis   5   5   5

$\ulcorner P_0 + I_5 \urcorner$ $\ulcorner P_8 + I_9 \urcorner$ $\ulcorner P_0 + I_5 \urcorner$

FIGURE 5-6

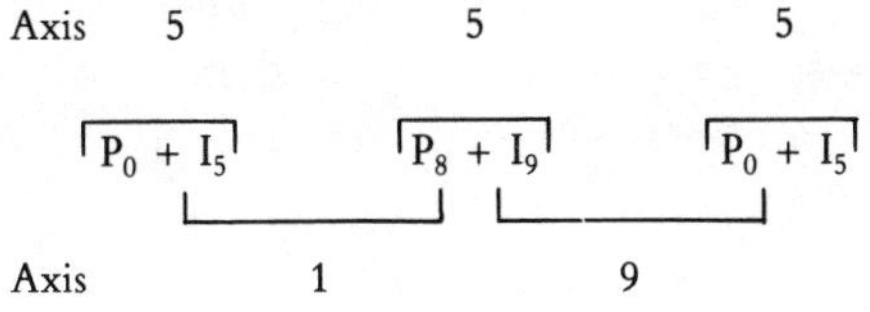

Axis   5   5   5

$\ulcorner P_0 + I_5 \urcorner$ $\ulcorner P_8 + I_9 \urcorner$ $\ulcorner P_0 + I_5 \urcorner$

Axis   1   9

FIGURE 5-7

structural integrity but rather an assertion of compositional strength with respect to common-practice norms. The twelve-tone principles of motivic association, set-class equivalence, aggregate completion, and, above all, inversional balance, are sufficient, as String Quartet No. 3 shows, to animate a variety of forms, including the sonata.

It is possible to write a work in sonata form that nonetheless ignores the central structural issues raised by the form, and many twentieth-century composers have done just this. The first scene of Act 2 of *Wozzeck,* for example, has been described by its composer as a "strict" sonata form.[24] The larger sections of the form are clearly delineated, both thematically and harmonically.[25] The larger structural issues—questions of polarity and reconciliation—are scarcely confronted, however. The recapitulation, rather than responding in some way to a polarity established in the exposition, merely repeats the exposition (although in a somewhat modified way). The music has a pattern of recurrences that conforms to the traditional sonata form. But beneath that pattern of recurrences the sonata form does not appear to implicate the deeper issues of musical structure and coherence. The formal outline rests quietly on the surface, no more than a generalized way of arranging themes and sections.

It is no longer possible in this century, however, to write a sonata form that arises organically, spontaneously, and seamlessly from the musical relationships. One hundred and twenty-five years after Mozart, Haydn, and Beethoven, and seventy-five years after Reicha, Marx, and Czerny, compositional innocence is inconceivable. Twentieth-century composers inevitably approach the sonata self-consciously and often, as we have seen, with malice aforethought. The most interesting twentieth-century sonatas are those that struggle most profoundly with the tradition, neither ignoring the structural implications of the form nor vainly attempting to regain a period of lost innocence, when the sonata form emerged organically from the musical language. Composers can adopt many different strategies in this struggle. They can immobilize the form with large-scale symmetries. They can subvert the form's traditional impetus toward reconciliation. They can set in motion musical forces that strain against the boundaries of the form. Although twentieth-century sonatas share no single common practice, therefore, they do share a revisionary impulse, a tendency to reshape the form in accordance with post-tonal concerns. They share also a deep and ineradicable sense of tension, of the traditional shape locked in the firm embrace of a new musical structure.

Six Emblematic Misreadings

Twentieth-century music exhibits both anxiety of style and anxiety of influence. Anxiety of style is manifested in the way composers misread salient aspects of an earlier style, as we saw in Chapters 4 and 5. Using triads and the sonata form, twentieth-century composers confront their predecessors by reinterpreting musical elements widely shared among works of the common-practice era. Anxiety of influence is more specific. It involves the reinterpretation of a single earlier work, as with the recompositions discussed in Chapter 3. In this chapter I return to the anxiety of influence with six analyses in which a twentieth-century work is paired with the significant predecessor that it revises.

As we have seen, the relationship between twentieth-century works and their significant predecessors is not necessarily an easy one. Direct, generous imitation is not possible across the stylistic and structural gulf that separates common-practice and twentieth-century music. Within a stylistically and structurally unified era, composers can imitate an earlier work without seriously compromising their own compositional norms. Brahms, for example, might imitate the sound or even specific structural features of music by Schubert, Beethoven, or Chopin in a relatively straightforward way.[1] In contrast, post-tonal composers cannot directly imitate tonal works without radically compromising their own characteristic style and structure. As a result, they must misread. An earlier work becomes enmeshed and transformed within a later one.

The more thorough the transformation, the more difficult it is to identify the predecessor. In the recompositions discussed in Chapter 3 the predecessor was unambiguous in each case. In the works to be discussed in this chapter, however, the earlier work leaves only a slight trace in its descendant. The trace may be a brief direct quotation, a similarity of texture and instrumentation, or a subtle motivic association. Usually, this effect hints at a deeper relationship between the two pieces, a relationship that is worked out beneath the musical surface.

The revisionary ratio Bloom calls *clinamen* describes this relationship in a general way. A clinamen "appears as a corrective movement in [the later] poem, which implies that the precursor poem went accurately up to a certain point, but then should have swerved, precisely in the direction that the new poem moves."[2] The later work thus incorporates certain elements of its precursor but then, at a certain point, takes those elements in a new direction. When a tonal motive is generalized into a pitch-class set, or when a peripheral element in the earlier work is centralized in the successor, a clinamen has taken place. Each of the six twentieth-century works to be discussed in this chapter involves a clinamen.

Clinamen, through the specific musical revisionary strategies by which it is worked out, frequently leads to what Bloom calls *apophrades*. As discussed in Chapter 3, apophrades describes the remarkable effect of a successful struggle on the part of the later work to resist the influence of a predecessor. When a work fully assimilates and transforms its predecessor, it can reorient our normal conceptions of chronology and influence: a sufficiently powerful new work can cause us to reinterpret the older one. In this sense, the new work influences the old one. The older work can even come to sound as though it is imitating its descendant, doing only partially what its descendant does fully. In the six paired analyses that follow, twentieth-century works seem to overthrow the tyranny of the past and even of time itself by revising their predecessors.

––––––––––

The second and central movement of Bartók's Piano Concerto No. 3 involves a misreading of the third and central movement from Beethoven's String Quartet in A Minor, Op. 132, "Heiliger Dankgesang eines Genesenen an die Gottheit" ("Hymn of Thanksgiving to the Deity from a Convalescent").[3] There are numerous superficial musical similarities and biographical affinities between these two works. On a deeper level there is a profound revisionary act of musical transformation. Bartók takes salient motives from Beethoven's quartet and misreads them as pitch-class sets. He then permeates the harmonic structure of his concerto with these sets, manipulating them in accordance with the norms of post-tonal practice.

Bartók began his Piano Concert No. 3 during a brief respite from the long illness that was to lead to his death before he could complete the final instrumentation of the work. The concerto represented for him the return of his creative powers after a long period of silence. It thus has a strong biographical affinity with Beethoven's hymn. The programmatic similarity be-

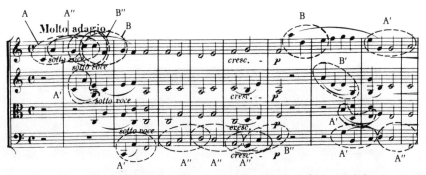

EXAMPLE 6-1 Beethoven's "Hymn of Thanksgiving" and its motivic structure (String Quartet in A Minor, Op. 132, third movement)

tween the pieces is underscored by Bartók's tempo indication for the middle movement of the concerto: adagio religioso.

The opening of Beethoven's hymn is shown in Example 6-1. The central feature of the music is the chorale in half-notes beginning in the second half of measure 2. The chorale, particularly with its Lydian flavor, is evidence of Beethoven's interest toward the end of his life in archaic forms.[4] Just as Bartók turned back toward Beethoven to find a model for expressing a profound religious sentiment, Beethoven turned back toward Renaissance and Baroque models. The phrases of the chorale (there are five of them in all) alternate with imitative interludes, which present the central motives of the work.[5] These are indicated in Example 6-1.

Beethoven uses two closely related three-note motives, labeled A and B. Motive A is an ascending major sixth followed by a descending major second, and motive B is a descending perfect fifth followed by an ascending major second. In addition to these direct statements, there are many motivic variants in the passage, marked A′ or B′. Some of these involve the octave displacement of one of the tones, some involve intervallic expansion or contraction, and some involve contour inversion. In addition, there are motives marked A″ and B″. These more remote motivic variants, which extend into the chorale itself, will be discussed in due course.

In Bartók's Piano Concerto there is a similar alternation of a slow chorale with imitative interludes. In the first section of the movement (measures 1–57), the solo piano states the chorale and the orchestra has the interludes. The opening of the movement, the first orchestral statement of the imitative material, is shown in Example 6-2. There is a striking resemblance to the imitative interludes of Beethoven's hymn. The instrumentation of the passages is similar because Bartók uses only an orchestral string quintet (plus clarinet). Both passages have an imitative texture and share the same order

EXAMPLE 6-2 Beethoven's motives generalized into pitch-class sets (Bartók, Piano Concerto No. 3, second movement); x = 3-7 (025), y = 3-9 (027)

of imitative entry, beginning with the first violin and working downward to the cello. Both passages are in 4 / 4 time with a regular quarter-note pulse. Both passages are very slow in tempo and very soft.

These superficial similarities set the stage for deeper structural links between the works. Beethoven's motives become the starting point for Bartók's revision of the passage. He begins with them and then swerves in a new direction to create the kind of set-class saturation that is typical of twentieth-century music. The crucial transformation involves generalizing Beethoven's motives into pitch-class sets. Motive A is a member of set-class 3-7 (025) and motive B is a member of set-class 3-9 (027). These set-classes permeate all dimensions of Bartók's music. Every note in the string parts through the beginning of measure 7 is part of a linear statement of one of these sets. Some of these linear statements reflect the original ordering that Bartók provides in measures 1 and 4 in the first violin—a descending minor third or perfect fourth followed by a descending major second. Others relate to those prototypes only by shared set-class membership. Bartók has taken Beethoven's motives and, by treating them as pitch-class sets, saturated his own music with them. He thus achieves a high degree of motivic density.

Even more striking, however, is Bartók's organization of the vertical dimension. In keeping with the twentieth-century concept of a unified musical space, Bartók deploys set-classes 3-7 (025) and 3-9 (027) vertically as well. Every beat between measure 4 and measure 6 (and frequently thereafter) presents a vertical statement of one of these set-classes. Beethoven's motivic organization unfolds within a tonal framework that requires a clear distinction between the melodic and harmonic dimensions. Motives may occur in a linear fashion, but the vertical organization must be triadic. Bartók, however, free of this constraint, is able to saturate the vertical dimension with the same set-classes that simultaneously define the melody. He has taken the principle of motivic association and development (already highly refined in Beethoven's music) and, by generalizing Beethoven's motives into pitch-class sets, radically intensified it.

Bartók's revision suggests a new hearing of Beethoven's hymn. Musical segments marked A″ in Example 6-1 can be regarded as variants of motive A only if they and motive A can be understood as representatives of the same pitch-class set, 3-7 (025). The same is true of the relationship between B and B″, both members of 3-9 (027). Bartók's rewriting of the passage provides us with the insight necessary to perceive these more remote motivic relationships. Beethoven's music influences Bartók's by providing motivic material and suggesting ways of working with that material. Simultaneously, Bartók's revision makes possible a new understanding of the precursor work. By compositionally misreading Beethoven's motives as pitch-class sets, Bartók invites us to do the same in our hearing.

The profound interconnection between the openings of the two movements initiates a more extended misreading. As the concerto continues, Bartók finds ways of using Beethoven's motives more persistently than Beethoven himself. Example 6-3 presents a sketch of the structural outer voices for the entire orchestral introduction, up to the entrance of the solo piano in measure 16. The lower voice describes a series of triadic harmonies, G–E–F–A–C, that is repeated once in measures 16–57 and again when the opening material returns in measures 89–121. The most heavily emphasized tones in this progression are G, F, and C. The structural bass line can thus be parsed, as in Example 6-3, to reveal a large-scale, embellished statement of 3-9 (027), derived from Beethoven's motive B. That bass line supports a structural upper voice that moves from an initial G, through a passing G-sharp to A, and then finally to C. That large-scale motion, G–A–C, describes a member of set-class 3-7 (025), derived from Beethoven's motive A. In this way, Beethoven's motives, generalized into pitch-class sets, help to shape the large-scale organization of Bartók's concerto.

EXAMPLE 6-3 Structural outer voices in the orchestral introduction

This kind of extended use of set-classes 3-7 (025) and 3-9 (027) becomes particularly pronounced in the contrasting middle section of the movement. The middle section begins with the music shown in Example 6-4. As the example makes clear, Bartók's music remains committed to Beethoven's motives even as the surface textures change dramatically. The cellos and trumpet state a framing interval A–E, which is filled in chromatically by the violin tremolos. More important, the piano states two balancing forms of 3-7 (A–B–D and B–D–E) that lie within the frame. The oboe and clarinet interject additional forms of 3-7 and 3-9.

The entire middle section of the movement (measures 58–88) is devoted to developing this material by transposing it to different pitch levels. At each level a framing perfect fifth is filled in by forms of 3-7 (025) and 3-9 (027). Example 6-5 shows the transpositional succession of those framing fifths. The structural bass as a whole moves A–E–D–G–F, framed by the D in measure 79 and the A in measure 58. Each three-note segment of that large-scale bass (A–E–D, E–D–G, and D–G–F) is a member of either 3-7 or 3-9. Hence, the large-scale progression of this music, like its immediate surface, moves within a framing fifth and fills that frame with statements of 3-7 and 3-9. Beethoven's motives have been generalized into pitch-class sets, and those sets are then used not only to saturate the new, post-tonal musical sur-

EXAMPLE 6-4 Motivic organization in the beginning of the middle section; x = 3-7 (025), y = 3-9 (027)

mm. 58 72 79 84 87

EXAMPLE 6-5   Successive transpositions of the opening material

face of Bartók's Piano Concerto No. 3, but also to define its deeper structural levels.

Bartók thus remains committed to Beethoven's motives in a way that Beethoven himself does not and cannot. Beethoven operates within tonal constraints that limit the scope of motivic development. Bartók, in determining all levels of musical structure with reference to Beethoven's generalized motives, offers a radical commentary. He depicts himself as one who does fully what Beethoven can do only partially, namely, to create an entire musical structure that grows from a motive.

When Berg wanted to express a deeply felt religious emotion, he, like Bartók (and Beethoven), turned to a four-part chorale. His Violin Concerto was composed as a memorial to Manon Gropius, the eighteen-year-old daughter of Alma Mahler and Walter Gropius. The work first makes a musical portrait of the girl, then describes the catastrophe of her death, an eventual acceptance of death, and a final transfiguration. In the section of the work that describes the acceptance of death, Berg incorporates J. S. Bach's harmonization of the chorale "Es ist genug." He does so partially for programmatic reasons: the text of the chorale describes acceptance and joy at God's final summons. Beyond the programmatic affinity lies a profound musical connection. The most striking melodic and harmonic events in Bach's setting, generalized into pitch-class sets, are embedded as segmental subsets within the twelve-tone series that underlies the entire concerto.

Example 6-6 shows the first phrase of the chorale in Bach's harmonization. The most striking features of the phrase are the melodic line that ascends in whole steps, the accented passing note on beat four of the first measure, and the end of the phrase on a dominant-seventh chord. One set-class is associated with each of these events, as Example 6-6 indicates.[6]

These tetrachords, particularly the one formed on the fourth beat of the first measure, would not be considered significant musical objects by traditional tonal theories. Rather, the D in the alto would be isolated from the progression and explained away as an accented passing note. But to give serious analytic attention to sonorities formed by nonharmonic tones is a procedure that Schoenberg, Berg's teacher, has urged. In the section of his *Theory of Harmony* discussed in Chapter 2, Schoenberg asserts categorically

EXAMPLE 6-6   First phrase of Bach's harmonization of "Es ist genug"

that any collection of notes sounding together may be construed as a significant harmonic unit and defends his assertion with an analysis of, among
other works, a Bach motet.[7] In this analysis he calls attention to vertical
sonorities that would traditionally be understood as by-products of linear
embellishment. Schoenberg makes explicit the potential relationship between such seemingly incidental sonorities in Bach and the central motivic
structures of his own music:

And granted that [Bach] could allow them only as passing tones because his ear
would not yet tolerate them if written freely—he did write them nevertheless, and
did more thereby than just nibble at the tree of knowledge. He followed his urge to
accommodate more complicated harmonies, wherever he thought he could do it
without danger to the intelligibility of the whole. But the essential thing, the urge to
write harsh harmonies, which I find identical with the urge to include more remote
overtones—this urge was there. He wrote them as passing phenomena so that we
can use them freely; he used a life-belt so that we learn to swim freely.[8]

As noted in Chapter 2, Schoenberg is engaged here in a misreading of
Bach. Schoenberg's own music makes use of "harsh harmonies" based on
the "more remote overtones." As a consequence, he reads into Bach the
same harmonic orientation. The derivation of twentieth-century harmonic
practices from the use of the "complicated," "harsh" harmonies of earlier
music, is a misreading that is compositionally realized by Berg in his Violin
Concerto, and not just in the last section but throughout.

The twelve-tone series for the Violin Concerto contains, as segmental
subsets, the three striking tetrachords from the Bach chorale (see Example
6-7). Set-class 4-19 (0148) occurs four times, 4-27 (0258) occurs twice, and
4-21 (0246) occurs a single time. Every note in the series is a member of at
least one of these subsets and some, like the F-sharp and A, are members of
as many as four. In other words, the series can be entirely understood in
terms of Bach's musical ideas, once those ideas have been generalized into
pitch-class sets.

This relationship is all the more remarkable in that Berg apparently did not become familiar with the chorale until the series, and more than half of the concerto, had already been written.[9] The relationship between the series and the chorale is an extraordinary, and for Berg an extraordinarily happy, coincidence. The series, composed independently, sounds as though it were constructed from the chorale and is thus ideally suited for a composition in which the chorale appears. Listening to the concerto, we recapitulate Berg's belated discovery of the chorale. During most of the concerto there is little hint of the relationship between the series and the chorale. A rich, varied musical surface springs from the series, concealing the music's deep associations with Bach. When the chorale finally appears explicitly in the final section, a strange reversal takes place. Bach harmonized the chorale long before Berg wrote his concerto. But as we listen to the concerto, the chorale seems to grow out of the series and its transformations, something the structure of the series itself makes possible. The chorale comes to sound like an outgrowth of Berg's serial composition. This reversal is the essence of Bloom's apophrades, wherein the predecessor comes to sound like an imitation of its descendant.

The compositional treatment of the chorale melody reinforces this sense of reversal. The form of the chorale melody—ABC ABC DD EE—permits a kind of antiphonal arrangement. The first three phrases, ABC, are heard first in a twelve-tone setting provided by Berg, then in Bach's original harmonization. Similarly, Berg's setting of the seventh and ninth phrases, D and E, are also followed by Bach's original harmonization of those melodies. In each case Bach's version is heard second and sounds like a commentary rather than a prototype.

At the first explicit appearance of the chorale melody in the solo violin, Berg provides two strands of accompaniment (see Example 6-8).[10] The middle strand states the second phrase of the chorale melody a perfect fifth lower, while the lowest strand of accompaniment states P_{11} of the series. At this transposition level, the final four notes are B-flat, C, D, and E—the same notes and in the same order as the first four notes of the chorale mel-

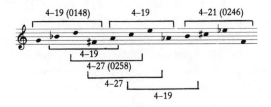

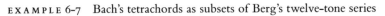

EXAMPLE 6-7   Bach's tetrachords as subsets of Berg's twelve-tone series

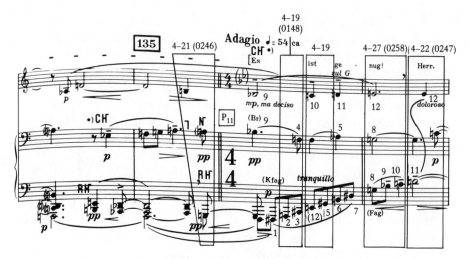

EXAMPLE 6-8   Berg's twelve-tone setting of "Es ist genug" (first phrase)

ody. The notes of the melody thus serve a dual function. In an implied tonal context, they are scale degrees $\hat{1}$, $\hat{2}$, $\hat{3}$, and $\sharp\hat{4}$ of B-flat major. When Bach's harmonization of this fragment is heard a few measures later, this implication will be realized. But in the context Berg provides, these tones are order positions 9, 10, 11, and 12 of P_{11} of the series. Berg reinterprets Bach's melody not by changing its pitches but by presenting it in a new context. The traditional function of its scale degrees is thus neutralized.

The integration of the chorale melody into the twelve-tone context is not confined simply to the linear order of the series. The melody also participates in vertical statements of the motivic tetrachords, as indicated in Example 6-8. These vertical harmonies are not segmental subsets of the series. Rather, they are composed of the interactions of three distinct musical strands: the chorale melody on top in the solo violin, the second phrase of the chorale melody a perfect fifth lower in the viola, and a linear statement of P_{11} in the contrabassoon. The second statement of 4–19 in measure 136 is particularly interesting, since it involves an alteration of the normal order of P_{11} (the fourth note of the series should be an F, not an E). The purpose of the alteration seems to have been precisely to create this vertical statement of 4–19. The final verticality in measure 137 is set-class 4–22 (0247). This is another musical idea that Berg gleaned from Bach's chorale harmonization. The last four notes of the chorale melody (F, D, C, B-flat) make up this set-class, which is also formed as a verticality at several points in Bach's harmonization of the later phrases. This set-class, like 4–19 (0148), 4–27 (0258), and 4–21 (0246), is a segmental subset of Berg's series (order positions 8–11). The chorale melody is thus thoroughly integrated into the musical texture, as part of both a linear statement of P_{11} and of several vertical statements of the series's segmental subsets. The irony that underpins this structure is that this series and these subsets can themselves be heard as derived from elements in Bach's chorale.

Berg's setting of the final phrase of the chorale involves a similar integration of the chorale melody within a twelve-tone framework (see Example 6-9). After presenting Bach's harmonization (measures 153–154), Berg ruminates on the same melodic phrase in a meditative coda. The melody for this phrase, comprising set-class 4-22 (0247), is harmonized in this coda primarily by the motivic tetrachords drawn from the first phrase of the chorale, 4-19 (0148), 4-21 (0246), and 4-27 (0258). Musical ideas derived from Bach are generalized into pitch-class sets, embedded within a twelve-tone series, and used to reinterpret their own musical source.

The relationship between the Bach chorale and the Berg concerto is subtle and complex. Insofar as the pitch structure of the concerto is determined by the structure of the twelve-tone series, it is determined also by the Bach chorale or, more accurately, by a misread version of the Bach chorale. In this sense, the chorale has a profound influence on the concerto, far beyond its actual quotation in the concluding section. At the same time, Berg's effect on Bach is equally profound. The twelve-tone context imposes a new meaning on the chorale, causing us to hear in it those motivic tetrachords. Berg invites us to understand Bach's music as Bartók did Beethoven's, not in the traditional terms of functional harmony and nonharmonic tones, but as a repository of pitch-class sets. Berg has misread Bach and, by quoting Bach

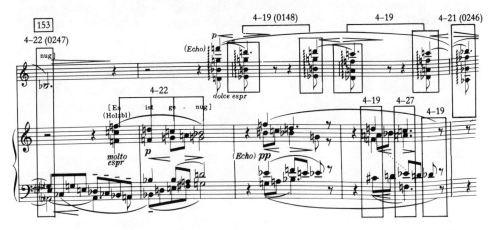

EXAMPLE 6-9   Berg's twelve-tone setting of "Es ist genug" (last phrase)

in the special twelve-tone context he provides, invites us to engage in the same misreading.

With its rich, tonic-obscuring chromaticism and tonal ambiguity, the Prelude to Wagner's *Tristan and Isolde* has come to epitomize late-romantic musical structure. It has been an extraordinarily influential piece—a magnet for analysis and a lightning rod for critical response to chromatic harmony. It is no exaggeration to say that, in some sense, every subsequent work, particularly in the generations immediately following Wagner, has had to come to terms with it. Despite the obvious dissimilarities (such as its twelve-tone structure and linear-contrapuntal surface), Berg's *Lyric Suite* is one work that is powerfully influenced by *Tristan*. It incorporates crucial structural features of *Tristan* and then swerves in a new direction. It does not imitate the style of *Tristan;* rather, it attempts, using the stylistic and structural norms of a later musical language, to revise a giant predecessor. What the Violin Concerto did with Bach's chorale, the *Lyric Suite* does with *Tristan*.

As with the Violin Concerto and "Es ist genug," the connection between the *Lyric Suite* and *Tristan* is, first of all, programmatic. The *Lyric Suite* describes events in Berg's life, specifically his unfulfilled love for Hanna Fuchs-Robettin.[11] Berg described the program in an annotated score that he gave her secretly, so that she alone might appreciate the extent to which the piece was for and about her. The principal motive of the piece, as these annotations make clear, is a cryptogram of the initials of Alban Berg and Hanna Fuchs-Robettin. These letters (H and B are the German nomenclature for B-natural and B-flat, respectively) comprise the motivic cell A, B-flat, B, and F, set-class 4-5 (0126). The myth of Tristan and Isolde is the epitome of unfulfilled romantic love in Western culture. Berg's secret program for the *Lyric Suite* is, in many ways, his personal version of the myth of Tristan and Isolde. He established a musical relationship to Wagner's *Tristan* in order to identify his love for Hanna Fuchs-Robettin with Tristan's for Isolde.

The last movement of the *Lyric Suite* is a thoroughly twelve-tone conception. All its significant harmonic and motivic structures can be readily accounted for with reference to two twelve-tone series. These are identified as Series A and Series B in Example 6-10. A musical relationship to *Tristan* is made explicit by a direct quotation of the opening measures of its Prelude. Berg himself pointed out that this quotation followed strict serial procedures. "The whole material of this movement, tonal included [triads, etc.], also the Tristan motive, results from strict observance of the 12-tone rows."[12] Berg's own derivation of the *Tristan* quotation from the basic sets of the *Lyric Suite* is shown in Example 6-11. This example follows Berg's own analysis provided in his pencil draft of the score.[13] I have translated his iden-

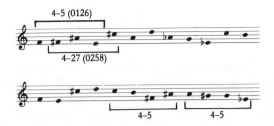

EXAMPLE 6-10 The series from Berg, *Lyric Suite* (Series A and Series B). *Lyric Suite* Copyright 1927 by Universal Edition, Copyright Renewed

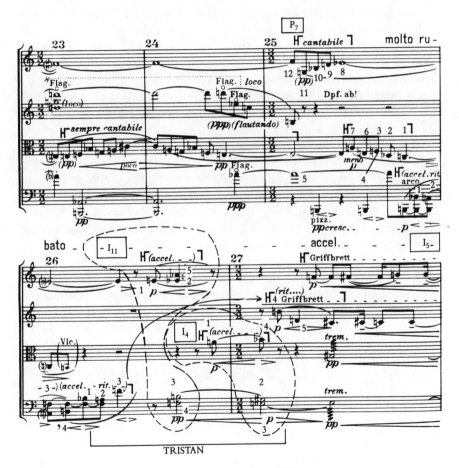

EXAMPLE 6-11 Serially derived quotation from *Tristan*

tifications of the series into the usual modern nomenclature (all forms relate to Series A).

The series forms crisscross in an elaborate twelve-tone texture from which the quotation of *Tristan* emerges. At the end of measure 25, I$_5$ brings in the beginning of the quotation with its second and third notes. It is then interrupted and begins again with the final note of the quotation, the B in the second violin in measure 27. The remainder of the quotation is produced by the first five notes of I$_{11}$ and the first four notes of I$_4$, both of which continue in measure 27. As in the Violin Concerto, the emergence of an earlier work amid a twelve-tone texture creates a strange, double shock. One is shocked first at the sudden appearance of passages by Bach and Wagner in works by Berg. One is even more shocked, however, at the extent to which the quoted material sounds as though it had been perfectly designed *by Berg* for this particular musical context. Berg seems to engender Bach and Wagner rather than follow them.

The quotation of this excerpt from *Tristan* is possible because musical ideas from *Tristan* are embedded within Berg's twelve-tone series. This embedding may not have been part of Berg's conscious compositional process, but it nonetheless underpins the connection between the two works. The set-class in order positions 2–5 of Series A, for example, is 4-27 (0258), as shown in Example 6-10. This makes possible the literal quotation of the Tristan chord, which is a representative of this set-class. The Tristan chord, generalized into its set-class, is embedded in a twelve-tone series. Over the course of the piece, this set-class is deployed in a variety of ways. In measure 26 it is voiced as the Tristan chord itself. The irony of the situation is familiar from the Violin Concerto. The Tristan chord, which is the original source of set-class 4-27 (0258), comes to be heard as merely one among many possible representations of that set-class.

Berg similarly generalizes other elements of the Prelude to *Tristan*. The first four notes of the cello melody that begins the Prelude, for example, ascend a minor sixth, then descend by semitone. This melodic fragment is a member of set-class 4-5 (0126) (see Example 6-12), which is, of course, the set-class of the Alban Berg–Hanna Fuchs-Robettin cryptogram (A, B-flat,

4–5 (0126)

EXAMPLE 6-12 The set-class of the Alban Berg–Hanna Fuchs-Robettin cryptogram in the beginning of *Tristan*

EXAMPLE 6-13 Wagner's motives and harmonies generalized into pitch–class sets;
x = 4-5 (0126), y = 4-27 (0258)

B, F), the central motive of the *Lyric Suite*.[14] The same set-class occurs as the
first tetrachord of Series A and as the second and third tetrachords of Series
B (see Example 6-10). Set-class 4-5 thus has a double meaning. It refers first
to Berg and Hanna Fuchs-Robettin, but also to their mythic counterparts,
Tristan and Isolde.

As with the set-class of the Tristan chord, 4-27 (0258), the set-class of the
opening cello melody, 4-5 (0126), is present in every statement of Series A
and Series B (see Example 6-13). In measures 39–43, for example, each of
the instruments presents a linear statement of either Series A or Series B.
Set-class 4-5 is stated thirteen times and set-class 4-27 five times in this pas-

sage. Of course, none of these occurrences shares the contour, rhythm, or pitch content of *Tristan:* the motives have been generalized to their present shapes.

The structure of the *Lyric Suite,* particularly its use of Series B in the last movement, has an even more intimate relationship to *Tristan.* The opening measures of the Prelude can be understood as a canon in inversion. The initial cello melody (A–F–E–D-sharp–D) is imitated in inversion by the line formed by the highest sounding notes beginning on the last eighth note of measure 1 (E–G-sharp–A–A-sharp–B), as Example 6-14 shows.[15] Furthermore, this melodic idea—a minor sixth followed by three half-steps in the opposite direction—is a pervasive figure throughout the Prelude to *Tristan.*[16] This figure forms set-class 5-5 (01237). Remarkably, the last ten notes of Berg's Series B consist of two inversionally related statements of the same set-class. The remaining two notes of Series B are F and E, the two bass notes of the first phrase in *Tristan.* This extraordinary relationship is shown in Example 6-15. The inversional canon from *Tristan* is thus embedded in one of the series for the *Lyric Suite.*

The misreading of *Tristan* in the *Lyric Suite* is similar to the misreading of Bach's chorale in the Violin Concerto. Striking melodic, harmonic, and motivic events in the earlier work are generalized into the set-classes they represent. Those set-classes combine to create a twelve-tone series. The series is deployed in a variety of ways in a new, twelve-tone work, following the norms of twelve-tone usage. The structure of the series, of course, makes possible the literal quotation of the source from which it was derived.

Through serial operations, Wagner's Tristan chord (generalized to set class 4-27), cello melody (generalized to set-class 4-5), and canonic subject (generalized to set-class 5-5) pervade Berg's composition. Clearly, *Tristan* exerts a pervasive and profound influence on the *Lyric Suite,* particularly its last movement. At the same time, the later piece suggests a new interpretation of the earlier one. The *Lyric Suite* calls attention to *Tristan*'s inner moti-

EXAMPLE 6-14 Inversional canon at the beginning of *Tristan*

EXAMPLE 6-15   Wagner's inversional canon embedded in Berg's twelve-tone series

vic structure, conceived in terms of set-classes, thus reflecting Berg's own compositional concerns.

Stravinsky's attitude toward nineteenth-century musical romanticism was somewhat different from Berg's. When Berg incorporated Wagner's music into the *Lyric Suite,* he incorporated also the sense of unrequited yearning associated with *Tristan's* harmony. When Stravinsky turned to nineteenth-century models, his principal concern, by contrast, was to empty his model of any emotional excess. His revisionary compositional strategies were directed toward an aesthetic reorientation.

In important ways, Stravinsky's Serenade in A may be understood has a response to Chopin's Ballade No. 2. The Ballade begins in F major (and is generally known as "The F-Major Ballade"), but it ends in A minor. It is one of only a small number of romantic-period works that begin and end in different keys. Most "dual-key" pieces involve relative keys, like Chopin's Scherzo, Op. 31, which begins in B-flat minor and ends in D-flat major. The second ballade is virtually unique in moving between keys that are not relative. Stravinsky must have found the Ballade's unusual tonal plan appealing in a number of ways. Its duality of key centers would have seemed congenial for a composer whose musical language relies so heavily on harmonic polarity. More specifically, the polarity of centers a major third apart, like the Ballade's F and A, was a reasonably common construct for Stravinsky—we have already seen it at work in the duality of C and E in his Symphony in C, a somewhat later work.

The opening passages of the two works reveal the beginning of the process of revision (see Example 6-16). The thematic resemblance between the passages is striking, particularly their shared use of a melodic figure that oscillates between A and F and that embellishes the A with an upper neighbor B-flat. Of course, Stravinsky's handling of the figure is somewhat different.

EXAMPLE 6-16A   The opening phrase of Chopin, Ballade No. 2

EXAMPLE 6-16B   The opening phrase of Stravinsky, Serenade in A (first movement)

Whereas Chopin's melody rocks gently and smoothly back and forth, Stravinsky's creates a sense of stasis and deadlock, punctuated by sharp breaks. Stravinsky's melody is hardly underway when it is interrupted by the long rest in measure 2. It then resumes its circumscribed movements only to end abruptly once more on the last eighth note of measure 5. Chopin's melody forms part of a continuous movement in the upper voice that spans from the principal melodic tone C (measures 1–5) downward by step through B-flat (last beat of measure 5), A (measures 6–8), and G (end of measure 8), to the goal F (measure 9). Stravinsky's melody acts as an isolated fragment; it participates in no larger continuity. What was smooth and gentle in the Chopin becomes something stark and abrupt in the Stravinsky.

The thematic link between the works sets the stage for a deeper revision that involves the central F–A duality of the Ballade. Stravinsky's principal revisionary strategy is compression: while the Ballade moves from F to A diachronically, as the work unfolds in time, the Serenade in A synchronically expresses the F–A duality and associated motivic and collectional clashes.

The first large section of the Ballade (measures 1–45) is securely in F major. It does, however, contain two A-minor episodes. The second of these (measures 33–37) is somewhat disquieting—it intrudes just at the moment a cadence on F major is expected—but both A-minor episodes function within large-scale arpeggiations of the F-major triad. The same is true of the much more extended A-minor passage that begins the second large section of the work (measures 46–81). The A minor asserts itself more vigorously in this section but is not confirmed by its own structural dominant. Rather, the goal of the section is E-flat (not E), which is subsumed into V of F. Once again, the A is part of a large-scale arpeggiation of the F-major harmony, although its autonomy is increasing.

In the return of the opening music (measures 82–139), F major is weakly reestablished and the A minor becomes increasingly assertive as a counterbalance. In the fourth large section (measures 140–167) we reach the point of no return. The A-minor harmony achieves its own structural dominant (measures 156–167) and asserts itself as the new tonic, a role that is confirmed in the concluding section of the work (measures 168–203). From the perspective of the end of the work, the initial F major appears as VI, and the tonal structure of the work as a whole is that of a large auxiliary cadence: VI–V–I.[17] One's experience of the work as it unfolds, however, is that of a progressive movement from F major, felt as a tonic, to A minor. More specifically, the work moves from F to A as tonal centers, from F–A–C to A–C–E as tonics, and from F major to A minor as referential diatonic collections.

Each of these motions is compressed by Stravinsky into a synchronous polarity. In the opening measures of the Serenade in A, A is clearly the pitch-class of priority: it is stated prominently in the outer voices throughout the passage. The harmonic context for the A, however, shifts between F–A–C and A–C–E. At the beginning of the passage, and on each of the strong beats from the opening to the beginning of measure 5, A is heard in the context of F–A–C, but the passage concludes on A–C–E. The centric polarity of Chopin's Ballade No. 2 is thus compressed within a single short passage. Indeed, tension between F major and A minor as simultaneous competing harmonic environments for the central pitch-class A pervades the entire movement.

The compression is even more radical at a number of crucial points in the work. On the last best of measure 5, for example, a four-note sonority, F–A–C–E, occurs. That sonority can be understood as a simultaneous statement of the competing triads F–A–C and A–C–E. The same sonority, with the same internal polarity occurs in measures 19 and 52 and several times in the final measures of the movement. Each of these marks an important point of articulation in the work as Chopin's gradual movement from F to A is compressed into a single sonority.[18]

The compression extends also to the referential collections. At the beginning of the Serenade in A, and throughout much of the first movement, the referential collection is a diatonic octad: A, B-flat, B, C, D, E, F, G. As is frequently the case in Stravinsky's use of this set-class, this octad can be thought of as resulting from two interpenetrating diatonic collections: A minor and F major.[19]

Stravinsky described pitch-class A as "an axis of sound": "I had a definite purpose in calling my composition *Serenade en LA*. The title does not refer to its tonality, but to the fact that I had made all the music revolve about an axis of sound which happened to be the LA."[20] The A lodges at the center of a continuous harmonic conflict that pervades the work and functions as a locus of musical tension. Is it a pitch-class center within a harmonic framework of A–C–E and the A-minor collection, or is it subordinate to F within a harmonic framework of F–A–C and the F-major collection? The piece offers no definitive response. Instead, the tension inherent within that ambiguity is a persistent feature, never to be resolved. When the movement ends, the A is left standing alone, still poised between the harmonic poles that shape the piece. What in Chopin's Ballade is felt as a definitive motion from one area to another is reinterpreted in Stravinsky's Serenade as a continuous, and unresolved, harmonic tension.

These compressions result in an aesthetic reorientation. Chopin's Ballade No. 2 is progressive and goal oriented. The music moves purposefully and smoothly from F major to A minor. Stravinsky's Serenade in A seizes that harmonic duality and, by compressing it, renders it static. The F and A, the F–A–C and A–C–E, the F-major and A-minor collections, now occur together and give the music a sense of deadlock, of motionlessness. The expressive content of the Ballade derives in large measure from its motion from F to A, with the A intruding more and more until the hegemony of the F is entirely and irrevocably overthrown. Through compression, Stravinsky strips the F–A duality of its traditional expressiveness. It becomes, instead, an emblem of Stravinsky's static diatonicism. The reorientation corresponds to what Bloom calls *kenosis*. As discussed in Chapter 3, this is a strategy for stripping an earlier work of expressive excess.[21] In a Bloomian kenosis, Stravinsky's interpretation of the F–A duality empties it of the sense of progress toward a goal. He makes it something static, motionless, austere. He thus invites us to hear Chopin's treatment of it as emotionally excessive by comparison.

Stravinsky's misreading extends also to the motivic organization of Chopin's Ballade. A stepwise connection between scale degrees $\hat{1}$ and $\hat{5}$ is a common feature of traditional music, but it occurs with unusual frequency in the Ballade and takes on a motivic charge. In the first phrase the motive occurs twice, descending by step at measures 4–5 and ascending in measures 8–9, slightly concealed within the alto voice. Later in the section (measures 41–45) the tonic F is confirmed by repeated motions from $\hat{1}$ to $\hat{5}$ and back in the bass.

The ultimate tonic, A, is also confirmed in this fashion later in the piece. When the structural dominant of A is finally attained in measure 156, it is approached by step from A (a chromatic passing note F-sharp is inserted within the descent), and the same descending motion A–G–F–E occurs many more times in the final section of the work. These stepwise motions, F–E–D–C and A–G–F–E, are reasonably important motivic elements in the Ballade, but they are not central to the large tonal plan of the work, and they are not used insistently enough, or at enough different structural levels, to be considered real structural determinants. Within the overall structure of the Ballade, they are secondary and subordinate.

In the Serenade in A, however, these tetrachords, and the set-class of which they are members—4-11 (0135)—are centralized: they move from the periphery of the predecessor work to the structural core of its strong descendant. Indeed, the large-scale organization of the Serenade composes-out the tetrachord A–G–F–E in both outer voices. Furthermore, those structural tones are often associated with surface statements of other members of the same set-class.

Like so many works by Stravinsky, the Serenade in A has a texture of relatively static, enclosed, and self-contained musical blocks. Each of these blocks tends to stabilize a central pitch-class. As the blocks succeed one another, the stabilized pitch-classes form a long-range path through the piece. Example 6-17 traces that path through the entire structural bass line of the

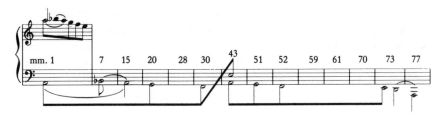

EXAMPLE 6-17   The structural bass line of the Serenade in A (first movement)

work. The bar lines in the example indicate clear breaks in the musical texture; each large measure contains a single textural block. In the upper voice of the first block, a structural A is embellished by an upper neighbor B-flat and followed by a small-scale descent through the tetrachord A–G–F–E. The bass line follows the same path but over a much larger span of time. In measures 7–14, B-flat2 is the most prominent bass pitch; it returns to A2 when the opening block repeats in measures 15–19. The large-scale neighboring motion A–B-flat–A is complete; now the descent begins. Pitch G2 is reached in measure 22—its arrival signaled by a change in figuration—and confirmed in the short block that comprises measures 28–29. In measure 39 F2 arrives after a long stepwise descent. At that point the contour reverses, moving back up to F3 in measure 42. From there the bass moves to E3 on the downbeat of measure 43 as a new block begins. Over the first forty-three measures, then, the bass begins on A and, after a large-scale upper neighbor B-flat, descends gradually along the A–G–F–E tetrachord to E.

The goal E, however, occurs in the wrong register and as an inner voice. Beneath it, a new structural A2 is introduced that begins another large-scale descent. The G2 of this second descent arrives in measure 49 and is confirmed in measure 51. In measure 52 the bass moves to F2, a tone that is repeated at the bottom of most of the arpeggiating figures that follow, usually on the downbeat of each measure. Finally, in measures 74–75, E2 replaces F2 at the bottom of the arpeggiations. At this point the A–G–F–E tetrachord has been spanned for a second time. Now, however, the bass pushes beyond E to D. This is so that, in the last two measures of the piece, the concluding A can be approached symmetrically, from D in the bass and E in the upper voice. Over the movement as a whole, then, the bass spans the central tetrachord twice.

In this way, Stravinsky seizes a surface motivic detail of Chopin's Ballade No. 2, a stepwise motion between scale degrees $\hat{1}$ and $\hat{5}$, and transforms it into the central structural determinant of a new work. As with the harmonic compressions discussed earlier, this motivic centralization involves an aesthetic reorientation. In Chopin's music coherence is assured by the smooth progression from harmony to harmony, organically linked by traditional voice leading. His stepwise motions from F down to C and from A down to E are commonplace linear progressions that smoothly span a triadic interval. Stravinsky's music, in contrast, has a texture of sharp breaks and sudden discontinuities. As a result, the creation of large-scale coherence becomes a central compositional problem. In his Serenade in A, Stravinsky finds a solution in his misreading of Chopin. He transforms Chopin's fourth-progressions into a large-scale musical path, linking together texturally disparate blocks. Hence, an emblem of organic coherence is transformed into an emblem of a different kind of coherence, one that emerges from a conflict between the tendency of the textural blocks toward isolation and the counter-vailing tendency of the larger work to subsume them.

Stravinsky's misreadings of eighteenth-century models do not involve so decided an aesthetic reorientation. Stravinsky's antiromantic sentiments are well known and received frequent musical expression. The relatively reserved ethos of musical classicism was always more congenial to him than the emotional extravagance of much late nineteenth-century music. Yet, Stravinsky's specific musical strategies for revision remain remarkably the same, regardless of the historical style of the predecessor.

In *The Rake's Progress* Stravinsky works with eighteenth-century operatic conventions, including the use of self-contained numbers (such as arias, duets, and trios), secco recitative with harpsichord accompaniment, small classical orchestra, and da capo forms. More specifically, traces of operas by Mozart are evident at various points. Stravinsky himself has said that "*The Rake* is deeply involved in *Così*,"[22] and Robert Craft has confirmed that connection.[23] Despite these assertions, it is *Don Giovanni,* more than *Così fan tutte,* that exerts a decisive influence on *The Rake's Progress.* As he did with Chopin, Stravinsky misreads Mozart through compression of disparate events into synchronous wholes and through centralization of telling details.

To understand the relationship between *The Rake's Progress* and *Don Giovanni,* one must first understand the relationship between the characters of the protagonists, Tom Rakewell and Don Giovanni. Tom Rakewell is a weak hero. His "progress" involves a descent into degeneracy and despair and then, at the last moment, a partial redemption. Tom shares with Don Giovanni a certain quality of "rakishness" and pleasure seeking, but Tom has none of Don Giovanni's strength of will, his resolution, his arrogant defiance of moral conventions, his cynical worldview. These qualities are more fully personified in the character of Nick Shadow. Shadow is Tom's "shadow" in the Jungian sense, the representative of the darker impulses within Tom's character.[24] Shadow is quite literally the projection of Tom's desires—each time Tom expresses a wish, Shadow appears. Tom is pulled in two directions, between Ann Truelove, who represents his feeble striving toward spiritual purity, and Nick Shadow, who represents his darker, more Don Giovanni–like impulses.

The parallel between Nick Shadow and Don Giovanni is most apparent in the scenes where each descends to Hell. In *Don Giovanni* the descent is followed immediately by a comic sextet that states a moral about how to avoid becoming a rake. In *The Rake's Progress,* because of the more ambiguous role of Tom Rakewell, further development is necessary. The dark side of

Tom has been purged by Nick Shadow's descent, but reconciliation with Ann Truelove is still required before this opera also can conclude with a comic ensemble that states a moral about how to avoid becoming a rake.

The final utterances of Don Giovanni and Shadow are strikingly similar, as both characters hurl defiance and mockery at heaven. Even the imagery they use is similar. The similarities are brought into sharp relief by the translation from the Italian by W. H. Auden and Chester Kallman, who were also (not coincidentally) the librettists for *The Rake's Progress.* Their translation emphasizes the idea of defying heaven and mocking God. When Don Giovanni tells the Commendatore, "Vanne lontan da me!" Auden and Kallman translate it as "God is a fairy tale." Similarly, when Don Giovanni refuses to repent and calls the Commendatore a "vecchio infatuato," Auden and Kallman propose, "I scorn him, I defy Him." Their translation also introduces the image of Hell as combining fire and ice. These ideas are directly recalled in Shadow's "I sink in ice and flame to lie, But Heaven's will I'll hate and till Eternity defy." The obvious dramatic parallels between the two scenes are intensified by the linguistic parallels Auden and Kallman have created.

Characterization, dramatic structure, and poetic language establish *Don Giovanni* as the significant predecessor for *The Rake's Progress,* particularly in the parallel scenes of descent to Hell. At the deepest levels of musical structure, the music for Shadow's descent (Act 3, Scene 2, Rehearsal 201–213) grapples with and recomposes the music from Don Giovanni's descent (Act 2, Finale, from the entrance of the Commendatore to the beginning of the concluding sextet).

Stravinsky's musical misreading focuses on certain striking harmonic events in *Don Giovanni.* The music of the final scene involves a good deal of chromatic motion and many diminished seventh chords, but it rarely wanders far from the tonic, D minor. The most remote harmonic area, B-flat minor, is suggested at the moment when the Commendatore first invites Don Giovanni to join him for supper (see Example 6-18). Throughout this passage F remains in the bass. In the overall structure of the scene, this note is part of a large-scale bass arpeggiation of the tonic D minor. Locally, however, the F is clearly the dominant of B-flat minor, simultaneously establishing that tonality and, by its persistence in the bass, preventing any definitive arrival there.[25] Stravinsky takes this most extreme musical moment and centralizes it as the basis for Nick Shadow's music.

Most obviously, Shadow's central harmony, B-flat minor, derives from this moment. This focus, however, does not involve traditional tonal harmony or voice leading. Rather, it involves the brute assertion of the B-flat–minor triad in the presence of other pitches and in juxtaposition with other triads. The climax of Shadow's scene is the dramatic intrusion of

EXAMPLE 6-18 Remote harmonic area, B-flat minor, and striking sonority, 4-18 (0147) (Mozart, *Don Giovanni,* Act 2, Finale)

E-natural into the B-flat–minor harmony at the moment that he causes Tom to become insane (see Example 6-19). The harmony formed at Shadow's climactic utterance, 4-18 (0147), is then repeated as he disappears.

This musical idea comes directly from the B-flat–minor section of *Don Giovanni.* There, too, the note E-natural intrudes dramatically (see Example 6-18), creating two occurrences of the same form of 4-18 used by Nick Shadow. In *Don Giovanni,* of course, this harmony is an incidental by-product of voice leading. In *The Rake's Progress* the voice-leading elements are compressed into a single harmony, and that harmony becomes central, not only at the moments shown in Example 6-19 but elsewhere in the scene

EXAMPLE 6-19 Nick Shadow's descent (Stravinsky, *The Rake's Progress,* Act 3, Scene 2)

as well. In fact, it is an important harmony throughout the opera. The first vocal phrase in the entire opera, Ann's "The woods are green," for example, is a member of the same set-class. Stravinsky has thus taken something incidental within *Don Giovanni*, a sonority created by voice leading within a remote harmonic digression, and generalized it into a set-class and made it central. In the process, he seems to turn Mozart inside out. The central structural determinants in Mozart, including the dominant-tonic relationship, become secondary, surface gestures in Stravinsky, while secondary aspects of *Don Giovanni* move to the structural center of *The Rake's Progress*.

The B-flat–minor section of *Don Giovanni* yields one additional significant relationship. During that section the vocal highpoint is Don Giovanni's reiterated D-flat. When the Commendatore interrupts him, the harmony is pushed abruptly onward and the vocal line reaches up to D-natural. This relationship between D-flat and D, delineated registrally in *Don Giovanni*, becomes the central motivic idea of Shadow's descent, expressed both on the musical surface and at the deeper levels of structure. It is Shadow's first vocal idea and permeates his music (see Example 6-20). In measures 6–7 this central motive is expanded vocally into a statement of set-class 4-18 (0147), and a transpositionally related form of the same set-class occurs simultaneously in the accompaniment. These statements, particularly the one in the accompaniment, prefigure Shadow's climactic ascent to E later in the scene. Again, we see Stravinsky's reinterpretive strategy: a musical idea from the model is given a new meaning in a new musical context.

Reinterpretation takes place also at the highest levels of musical structure. Both Don Giovanni's descent and Shadow's descent involve a shift from minor to major and, in both cases, the shift is mediated through contact with the G-minor harmony. The significance of the modal shift and the role of G minor is quite different in the two cases. In *Don Giovanni* the G-minor harmony comes in dramatically at the moment when the Commendatore commands Don Giovanni to offer his hand. It is introduced, of course, by its dominant, D major. This moment is strongly recalled at the end of the scene where the shift to I$^{\flat 3}$ (D major) occurs in association with IV$^{\flat 3}$ (G minor), a plagal relationship that controls the concluding measures of the scene.

In *The Rake's Progress* the motion from minor to major (in this case, B-flat minor to B-flat major) is also mediated by the G-minor harmony, which occurs strikingly at the beginning of the second section of Shadow's aria (Rehearsal 203). The large-scale tonal motion of Shadow's descent can be summarized as in Example 6-21. The scene begins with a stable B-flat–minor triad supporting D-flat as the upper voice. The most striking harmonic shift in the scene involves motion to the G-minor triad, supporting

EXAMPLE 6-20   Mozart's musical ideas transformed in Shadow's music

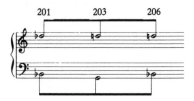

EXAMPLE 6-21   Large-scale tonal structure of Shadow's descent (rehearsal numbers shown)

D-natural in the upper voice. This involves the large-scale juxtaposition of D-flat and D-natural, a motivic idea borrowed from Mozart and here expressed at a high structural level. The conflict between D-flat and D-natural (and between B-flat minor and G minor) is resolved when, following Shadow's disappearance, the music shifts to B-flat major, which represents a synthesis of the two competing triads. It combines the B-flat orientation of the first triad with the D-natural upper voice of the second. The concluding B-flat major is thus won through a struggle between B-flat minor and G minor.

The situation is remarkably similar to the scene of Oedipus's enlightenment in *Oedipus Rex* (discussed in Chapter 4). There, the D-minor music of the Shepherd and Messenger supporting an upper-voice F-natural is juxtaposed with Oedipus's B-minor music supporting an upper-voice F-sharp. Their synthesis into an incomplete D-major harmony (D supporting F-sharp) is the musical expression of Oedipus's self-realization. This kind of thesis-antithesis-synthesis construction is reasonably typical of Stravinsky and is frequently worked out in just this way, with competition between tonal centers a minor third apart. Often, it involves the kind of modal shift described above. In *Don Giovanni* the G-minor harmony introduced the tonic major as part of the tonally constrained plagal relationship. In the music of Shadow's descent the G-minor harmony also brings about a modal shift, but now within an idiomatically Stravinskian framework.

Stravinsky's central misreading begins with salient harmonic events in *Don Giovanni*—the hint of B-flat minor, the intrusion of E-natural into that context, the shift from minor to major. In Stravinsky's hands these events blossom out in a new way, producing a music that acknowledges its roots in *Don Giovanni* even as it ironically distances itself from that precursor.

Schoenberg's revisionary approach is often quite similar to Stravinsky's. He finds ways of recreating in a new musical language the structural effects of his models. Like Stravinsky, he seizes upon telling details in his model and moves them to the center of a new musical structure. String Quartet No. 3, Op. 30, is one of his most explicitly backward-looking compositions. In many overt ways, this piece evokes the textures, timbres, phrasing, and—as we saw in Chapter 5—the forms of a nineteenth-century string quartet. Its most obvious antecedent is Schubert's String Quartet in A Minor, Op. 29, to which it bears so many surface resemblances.[26] Beneath the surface Schoenberg's quartet misreads Schubert's, reinterpreting both the phrase structure of its exposition and the large-scale harmonic organization of its development section.

The opening passages of the two works are similar in many respects, most obviously in their texture and instrumentation (see Example 6-22). Both passages begin with a repeated accompanimental figure and then, while the figure continues, introduce a lyrical melody in the first violin. Underlying these overt similarities of instrumentation and texture are more subtle correspondences, for example in the relationship between melody and accompaniment. Schubert balances a clear motivic resemblance between the melody and accompaniment with an equally clear delineation of their separate roles. Both parts use melodic arpeggiation while a distinction is maintained between them through register, instrumentation, and level of rhythmic activity. In Schoenberg's piece, similarly, there is clear motivic association between melody and accompaniment, but the association is produced within a twelve-tone framework. The set-class formed by the second, third, and fourth notes of the accompanying figure, for example, is found twice in the melody (see Example 6-23). At the same time, a clear distinction between the parts is maintained by their lack of pitch-class intersection: the melody and the cello part use only the seven pitch-classes excluded by the accompanimental figure. Schoenberg thus achieves similar effects—motivic association between melody and accompaniment—through extremely different means.

Schoenberg offers an equally forceful misreading of Schubert's phrase structure. In Schubert's quartet, following the initial accompanimental figure in measures 1–2, there are two four-measure phrases that together form a single eight-measure phrase. In general, phrase structure in tonal music is

EXAMPLE 6-22A The opening phrase of Schubert, String Quartet in A Minor, Op. 29

EXAMPLE 6-22B The opening phrase of Schoenberg, String Quartet No. 3, Op. 30

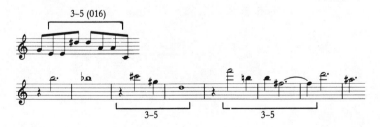

EXAMPLE 6-23 Melody and accompaniment distinguished by pitch–class content but linked by motivic structure

articulated by relatively self-contained voice-leading spans. A group of measures coheres as a phrase because it is unified by a single musical motion at some level of structure. In the Schubert, the first four-measure phrase consists of the establishment of scale degree $\hat{5}$ in the upper voice and a subsidiary descent of $\hat{3}-\hat{2}-\hat{1}$, which concludes as the phrase ends. The second four-measure phrase involves an ascending fourth-progression from an inner voice B back up to the initial E, arriving as the phrase ends. Harmonically, the first four-measure phrase prolongs I, the second prolongs V. The phrase structure of this music, like that of common-practice tonal music generally, is thus articulated by prolongational spans.

In the Schoenberg, the rhythmic organization and the texture suggest a similar division (following the initial accompanimental figure) into two four-measure phrases, and that phrase structure is confirmed by the idiomatic twelve-tone processes of the work.[27] The melodic line of the first four-measure phrase (measures 5–8) is shown in Example 6-24. The example illustrates two significant features of the phrase that lend it a sense of internal coherence. First, the first two notes of the melody are imitated, in inversion, by the cello at the end of the phrase, completing an aggregate. This interplay spans the phrase and causes it to be heard as a unit. Second, the last three notes of the phrase (the D in the violin and the E-sharp and F-sharp in the cello) state the same set-class, 3-3 (014), as the first three notes of the accompanying figure. This resemblance causes the phrase ending to stand out as a point of articulation.

The same two factors cause the second four-measure phrase to be similarly heard as a single unit. As Example 6-25 shows, the cello part again restates, in inversion, a motive from the melodic line (completing an aggregate) and, again, the last three notes of the phrase form set-class 3-3 (014). In place of common-practice norms of phrase construction, Schoenberg offers motivic imitation, pitch-class set equivalence, and aggregate completion.

In similar fashion, Schoenberg unifies the entire eight-measure span into a single musical unit. As Example 6-26 shows, the two four-measure units complement and balance each other. The second four-measure phrase begins by stating, with its dyads in reverse order, the same trichord-class with which the first phrase ended. This is also the same trichord-class, 3-5 (016),

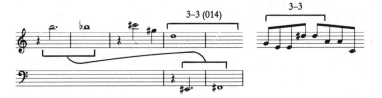

EXAMPLE 6-24 Four-measure phrase

EXAMPLE 6-25   Balancing four-measure phrase

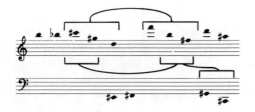

EXAMPLE 6-26   Eight-measure phrase consisting of two balanced four-measure phrases

as the second, third, and fourth pitches of the accompanimental figure—see Example 6-23. As a result, the two four-measure phrases form a single symmetrical unit, balancing around its central point. This kind of inversional balance is, as we saw in the previous chapter, the central structural feature of the work.

In addition, there are direct pitch associations that unify the eight measures: the melodic C-sharp–G-sharp in measure 7 is imitated in measure 10 and directly restated in inversion in the cello in measures 10–12. Taken together with the previous E-sharp–F-sharp in the cello, it forms set-class 4-14 (0237), one that also occurs as a linear segment of the basic series, forging an additional link between the two four-measure phrases.[28] The G-sharp–C-sharp is thus tightly embedded in this musical structure, its meaning constrained by the twelve-tone framework. At the same time, of course, it recalls the V–I cadential formula of traditional tonal music. This, as we have seen, is typical of Schoenberg's practice. He creates rich, coherent musical structures that, with parodistic effect, refer to the music of an earlier era. The phrase structures of the Schubert and Schoenberg quartets are thus similar but are articulated in entirely different ways. Schoenberg reproduces the four-plus-four phrasing of his model by using his own structural devices of aggregate completion and motivic association. He translates Schubert's music into his own idiom.

The similarity in the openings of the two works sets the stage for a deeper relationship between them, one that extends to the widest musical spans.

Schoenberg's own comments on Schubert's Quartet in A Minor point directly to this deeper relationship:

The richness of Schubert's harmony perhaps marks the actual transition to Wagnerian and post-Wagnerian composers' procedures. In a relatively short *Durchführung* of a String Quartet (!) he stays, for longer or shorter periods, in the following regions: **sd** [subdominant], **sm** [submediant], **m** [mediant], **sd** [subdominant], and **smsm** [submediant of the submediant] . . . The **smsm** region (ms. 150) seems more distant because of the somewhat roving modulations in the preceding measures, which define it as derived from **sm**. But an enharmonic change would make it tonic major's mediant ($d\flat = c\sharp$).[29]

For Schoenberg, then, the crucial motion within the development section is from the submediant, F, through the submediant of the submediant, D-flat (or C-sharp), and back to the tonic, A. Schoenberg thus identifies in Schubert's quartet a large-scale progression that traces an interval cycle of descending major thirds: F–D-flat (C-sharp)–A. As we saw in the previous chapter, the same intervallic cycle defines the principal motions in Schoenberg's quartet, where a central axis, which we called Axis 5, lies symmetrically between two subordinate axes, Axis 1 and Axis 9. The first theme describes a complete cycle through those three axes. The development section does so also, but on a larger scale.

The development section of Schoenberg's quartet begins in measure 94 with a juxtaposition of P_0 and I_5 (Axis 5). By measure 107, the first step in the large-scale progression is complete, as Axis 9 takes over (see Example 6-27). As is customary in this quartet, special treatment is given to the axial pitch-classes, particularly the F–F-sharp dyad, which is held invariant in the viola throughout the passage, right in the middle of the texture. Axis 9 remains in control through measure 135, the approximate midpoint of the development section.

As the development section moves toward its close, the focus shifts to Axis 1, although the axial pitch-classes are not as strongly emphasized. Any sense of centricity dissolves as the development ends and gives way to the recapitulation of the second theme, with its clear focus on Axis 5. The development section as a whole thus traces a complete interval cycle, beginning and ending on Axis 5, and moving by four semitones each time. The large-scale structures of Schubert's and Schoenberg's development sections are thus remarkably similar, although based on entirely different compositional systems.

The revisionary strategy here involves both marginalization and centralization. In Schubert's quartet, as in traditional sonata forms generally, the development section functions, at the deepest structural level, as a large-scale expansion of the dominant harmony. The tonic of the first theme leads

EXAMPLE 6-27   Arrival on Axis 9 (F/F-sharp–B/C)

through the mediant of the second theme to the dominant attained at the
end of the development (measures 165–166). That dominant, the structural
goal of the development, leads to the tonic of the recapitulation. The roving
modulations of the development section are thus ultimately under the control of the tonic-dominant axis. In Schoenberg's reinterpretation the tonic-
dominant relationship is marginalized—it appears in String Quartet No. 3
as only a vestigial surface detail, as we saw in the opening measures of the
work. At the same time, the modulatory path of Schubert's development

section, which in Schoenberg's view traces a cycle of descending major thirds, is centralized into the generating principle of an entire movement. The procedure is like Stravinsky's transfer of the B-flat–minor harmony from *Don Giovanni* to *The Rake's Progress,* but it operates at a deeper structural level and over a much wider musical span.

Schubert's texture, instrumentation, phrase structure, and even large-scale tonal motions have all been produced by Schoenberg in a new musical language. Schoenberg is not imitating Schubert nor is he being influenced by Schubert in the usual sense. Rather, he is misreading Schubert, endowing traditional elements with a new significance in a new musical context. Like the other five twentieth-century works discussed in this chapter, Schoenberg's quartet bespeaks an anxiety of influence. The later work bears a trace of the earlier one as a signal of their kinship but swerves in a new direction, engaging a variety of compositional strategies that are widely employed by twentieth-century composers. By misreading their predecessors in this way, twentieth-century composers simultaneously assert their links to the tradition and clear creative space for themselves.

CHAPTER 7

Middleground Misreadings

In twentieth-century music the past is remade at all levels of structure. When triads appear in a post-tonal setting, their reinterpretation takes place on the foreground level. The same kind of musical reinterpretation can also occur at the deeper levels of musical structure, the middleground and background.[1] In many twentieth-century works musical motions over large spans of time seem to follow traditional tonal patterns, like the descending perfect fifth. Usually, however, their customary meaning is effectively neutralized. They evoke traditional practices but derive a more potent meaning from the specific post-tonal context in which they occur. The reinterpretation of a traditional large-scale musical motion is a middleground misreading.

Post-tonal music has many ways of creating coherence at the deeper levels of structure, among the most important of which are establishing harmonic areas and composing-out motives. Harmonic areas can result from the transposition of a referential collection. Each distinct transpositional level constitutes a kind of harmonic plateau, providing pitch material for extended passages of music. Motion from plateau to plateau can define large-scale musical structure. When the referential collection contains all twelve pitch-classes, as in twelve-tone music, the creation of areas poses a problem, since transpositional levels cannot be distinguished on the basis of content. Combinatoriality, by associating series forms based on the content of their hexachords or other subsets, has provided a solution to this problem. The motion from area to area, however these areas are defined, sometimes mimics the procedures of traditional tonal music. When, for example, one area leads to another seven semitones lower, the traditional motion from dominant to tonic is inevitably recalled. Normally, however, that reference will be parodistic, not a concession to older imperatives but their subordination to new kinds of musical structure.

Large-scale motivic statements frequently provide coherence over large musical spans. The tones that make up a motive can be associated in a variety of ways, by register, timbre, metrical placement, dynamics, instrumentation, articulation, or shared value in any musical domain.[2] The associated tones may be temporally adjacent, creating foreground groupings, or more widely separated in time, creating a middleground composing-out. Sometimes, the path of the composing-out follows what appears to be a traditional tonal route, but this seeming adoption of tonal norms is usually a middleground misreading, the reinterpretation of traditional patterns at a deep structural level.

In Stravinsky's music the musical motions at the deeper structural levels frequently follow a motivic path that mimics traditional tonal patterns. The path is often determined by thematic association, by the successive transposition of some identifiable musical material. The principal melodic fragment of *Symphonies of Wind Instruments* is shown in Example 7-1 as it is harmonized toward the beginning of the work. The melody consists of one form of set-class 4-11 (0135), while the chord at the highpoint constitutes another, inversionally related to the first.

Later in the piece, the same melodic material comes back slightly varied. In its second occurrence (one measure after Rehearsal 27), the harmonization includes two forms of 4-11 (0135), as does the third occurrence, which immediately follows (see Example 7-2). In the first occurrence the bass begins and ends on F. In the second the bass begins and ends on E. In the third

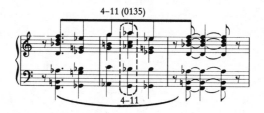

EXAMPLE 7-1 First statement of the principal melodic fragment (Stravinsky, *Symphonies of Wind Instruments*)

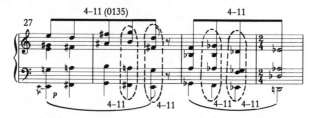

EXAMPLE 7-2 Second and third statements of the principal melodic fragment

EXAMPLE 7-3   Climactic and concluding arrivals on C (rehearsal numbers shown)

EXAMPLE 7-4   Middleground and background statements of 4-11 (0135) (rehearsal numbers shown)

the bass descends strongly to D. These three pitches (F, E, and D), widely separated in time but strongly associated thematically, are one pitch shy of creating a large-scale statement of 4-11, a set-class that permeates not only this melodic fragment but a great deal of the musical surface of the entire piece. The missing pitch, C, is attained at the two most important structural points in the piece, first at Rehearsal 54 (the dramatic climax of the piece) and finally in the last measure, as the bass note of the final chord.

At both arrival points the large-scale descent is recapitulated as a surface detail (see Example 7-3). At Rehearsal 54 the complete tetrachord, F–E–D–C, is presented in the bass, while at the end of the work, only the final three notes, E–D–C, lead to the final chord. The large-scale motions can be summarized as in Example 7-4.[3]

Although set-class 4-11 (0135) is a prominent linear subset of the diatonic collection (the first four notes of the major scale, for example), the actual music strips it of that association. The middleground and background descents in Example 7-4 may vestigially recall a descent through scale degrees $\hat{4}$, $\hat{3}$, $\hat{2}$, and $\hat{1}$ of the C-major scale, but they are more fully understood as composings-out of the central motive of this particular piece. In their stepwise descent, the background and middleground structures of this piece mimic the appearance of linear progressions from tonal music, but the resemblance is deceiving. Here again we see a phenomenon noted in the earlier chapters: the neutralization and reinterpretation of a once-familiar musical object.

In the opening of Stravinsky's Symphony in Three Movements (up to Rehearsal 29), the large-scale upper voice traces an ascending fifth from G to D. This motion takes place over a reasonably stable bass on G (see Example 7-5).[4] The motion thus has the appearance of a familiar initial ascent in tonal music in which the structural upper voice moves from the tonic scale degree to one of the more active scale degrees of the tonic triad, $\hat{3}$ or $\hat{5}$. In this piece, however, the path in the upper voice from G to D is determined by the motivic processes of the piece, not by the norms of tonal voice leading.

In between the initial G and the goal D, there are two intermediate goals, B-flat (at Rehearsal 7) and B (at one measure after Rehearsal 19). The path from G to D thus traces a statement of 4-17 (0347), consisting of two overlapping forms of 3-3 (014) (see Example 7-6). These sets, 3-3 and 4-17, pervade the surface of the music, both melodically and harmonically. At the moment that the goal D is finally attained and confirmed, for example, the larger motivic path, via B-flat and B, is recapitulated by brief restatements (see Example 7-7). The central motives are emphasized locally and simultaneously composed-out over a span of 107 measures. A large-scale motivic statement thus gives the appearance of a familiar tonal motion.

The two motions discussed so far—a linear progression through the in-

EXAMPLE 7-5 Middleground structure (after Salzer) (Stravinsky, Symphony in Three Movements). Symphony in Three Movements © Associated Music Publishers, Inc., New York, 1946, Assigned to Schott and Co. Ltd., London, 1946, © Renewed

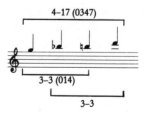

EXAMPLE 7-6 Large-scale upper voice reinterpreted as motivic composing-out

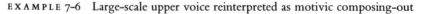

EXAMPLE 7-7   Arrival on D, with small-scale motivic restatements (winds only)

terval of a fourth and an initial melodic ascent through a fifth—are common elements in tonal music. Their reinterpretation involves a middleground misreading. The works to be discussed in the remainder of this chapter reinterpret bass motion by perfect fifth, the emblematic motion of tonal music. By evoking the functional relationship between tonic and dominant that lies at the nexus of the tonal system, these works misread the tonal system itself.

A portion of the second theme from the exposition section of the first movement of Bartók's Piano Sonata is shown in Example 7-8, with an analytical reduction. By register, metrical placement, duration, frequency of reiteration, and position within the passage, three sonorities have the greatest structural weight: the initial A–C–C-sharp, set-class 3-3 (014); the medial D–F–C-sharp, also set-class 3-3 and related by inversion; and the concluding return to A–C–C-sharp. The upper-voice C-sharp is sustained and harmonized by different forms of a single set-class.

A large-scale bass motion, A–D–A, spans the passage. Bass motion by fourth or fifth is the essential prolonging motion in tonal music, where it is integral to the structure of the triad. In the Bartók sonata, however, the principal sonority is not a triad but set-class 3-3 (014), a collection that con-

EXAMPLE 7-8A Reinterpretation of bass motion by perfect fifth (Bartók, Piano Sonata, first movement)

EXAMPLE 7-8B Analytical reduction, measures 44–53

REMAKING THE PAST

tains no fourths or fifths. As a result, the bass motion by fifth is not structurally integral. It does not arpeggiate or compose-out the initial 3-3. Rather, the 3-3 itself is inverted so as to keep the C-sharp a common tone in the melody. The bass motion by fifth is an incidental by-product of that process of inversion. It looks tonal but is more meaningfully explained in terms of the contextual associations of this individual piece.

The second part of the motion, the ascending fifth from D to A, is particularly important in this work. As discussed in Chapter 5, a long-range pattern of ascending fifths begins in the exposition on A, reaches all the way to F-sharp in the recapitulation, and threatens to go even farther before being squelched by the return of the first theme. Before this long-range pattern gets under way, the motion described above (A–D–A) takes place. The second theme starts on A and then, before beginning its pattern of ascending fifths, retreats momentarily to D, a case of *reculer pour mieux sauter*. The ascending fifth from D that brings us back to the starting point A is thus preliminary to, and predictive of, the long-range pattern. Motion by perfect fifth has traditional associations, but in this work that motion is highly determined by the specific musical context. The structural integrity of the work constrains the meaning of that traditional motion and brings about a middleground misreading.

The post-tonal literature contains progressions by fifth that even more strongly evoke the functional relationship between tonic and dominant. The passage from Stravinsky's Concerto for Two Pianos (third movement) shown in Example 7-9 seems to compose-out a motion, in C-sharp minor, from tonic to dominant (measure 4) and back (measure 6). But closer inspection shows the extent to which Stravinsky has embedded that motion within a musical framework that redefines it.

The passage quoted in Example 7-9 is from the third of four variations on the single-line theme shown in Example 7-10. The four-note head motive of the theme comprises set-class 4-10 (0235), which results from a passing note C-sharp within the structural 3-7 (025) defined by the first three notes of the theme. In the variations the theme is stated and embellished in reasonably forthright ways. In addition, the theme's influence, particularly that of its head motive with its structural 3-7, penetrates far beyond the melodic surface.

A first inkling of a profounder dimension in Stravinsky's variation technique occurs in measure 1 of variation 3. There the prevailing C-sharp–minor triad is embellished by a sonority that results from neighboring notes A and F× applied to the melodic tone G-sharp. That sonority is repeated and extended through measure 3. It forms set-class 3-7 (025), thus prefiguring the entrance of the theme. The head motive of the theme, starting on G-sharp and with free octave displacements, is stated in the left hand of piano 1

EXAMPLE 7-9 Reinterpretation of a seeming tonic–dominant–tonic progression (Stravinsky, Concerto for Two Pianos, third movement). Concerto for Two Pianos © B. Schott's Soehne, Mainz, 1936, © Renewed

EXAMPLE 7-9   (*Continued*)

EXAMPLE 7-10   Theme with its head motive analyzed

EXAMPLE 7-11   Concealed motivic statements

in measure 3. At that transposition level, the theme comprises a form of 4-10 (0235) that features the trichord E-sharp–G-sharp–A-sharp, a form of 3-7. The arrival on G-sharp at the end of the measure initiates a statement of a closely related tetrachord, 4-11 (0135), this time featuring the trichord G-sharp–A-sharp–C-sharp, another form of 3-7. The C-sharp is then transferred up an octave, where it descends through a form of 4-10, now featuring the trichord G-sharp–B–C-sharp, yet another form of 3-7, and one with important large-scale implications. These relationships, indicated by stems and beams in Example 7-9, are summarized in Example 7-11.

Set-class 3-7 (025) penetrates into the accompanying parts as well. When piano 2 finally starts to move, in measure 4, it describes a line in octaves that consists entirely of overlapping forms of 3-7, the first of which is G-sharp–B–C-sharp (see Example 7-12).

In light of this musical focus on set-class 3-7 (025), and particularly on small-scale uses of the trichord G-sharp–B–C-sharp, the large-scale organi-

EXAMPLE 7-12 Overlapping statements of 3-7 (025)

EXAMPLE 7-13 Middleground composing-out of 3-7 (025)

zation of the entire passage can now be fully understood. In between the structural G-sharp at the beginning of measure 4 and the return to C-sharp in measure 6 lies a significant B, in measure 5. This B redefines what had seemed a simple I–V–I pattern (see Example 7-13). The large-scale bass motion is now understood to consist of two overlapping statements of 3-7, both containing C-sharp, B, and G-sharp. The motion from C-sharp to G-sharp and back thus composes-out the central musical idea of the piece, even as it refers to a traditional tonal pattern. The motion recalls I–V–I but receives a more potent meaning from its motivic surroundings. The traditional pattern is thus reinterpreted in motivic and contextual terms.

A more extensive reinterpretation of the dominant-tonic relationship takes place in Schoenberg's Little Piano Piece, Op. 19, No. 2 (see Example 7-14). At its deeper structural levels, the piece alludes to the classical progression from dominant to tonic. It begins with G as its lowest sounding note within an ostinato figure, the interval G–B, that recurs throughout the piece. In the final measures the lowest part descends stepwise to C, arriving in the last measure. Motion from G to C is easily perceived. The problem is how to interpret that motion. It clearly hints at a progression from dominant to tonic, but if we follow that hint, and try to understand the piece in terms of traditional harmony and voice leading, we are led quickly to an analytical dead end.

Aside from the G–C descent itself, no aspect of the piece is amenable to a tonal-style approach, even a liberally modified one.[5] None of the individual harmonies in the piece can be satisfactorily described in terms of traditional harmonic functions; none gratefully receives a descriptive roman numeral. In the realm of voice leading, the traditional model of tonal prolongation also proves inappropriate. The G that occurs so persistently in measures 1–6 is associated with the concluding F–E–D–C through shared articulation, but it is not prolonged in the tonal sense.[6]

We can make better sense of the descent from G to C by relating it not to the normal procedures of earlier music but to the specific musical setting in which it occurs. The pitches in the descent derive their most potent meaning from the associations they create with the pitches around them, a small number of which are suggested in Example 7-14 above. The concluding C, for example, creates a number of important associations. It is part of the final sonority of the piece, the eight-note collection in the last measure. This is a form of set-class 8-19 (01245689), the complement of the central four-note set-class of the piece. Several occurrences of its complement, 4-19, are

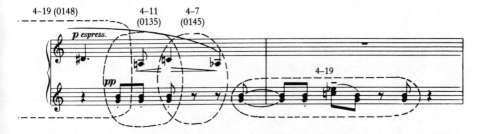

EXAMPLE 7-14 Descending perfect fifth embedded within a network of motivic associations (Schoenberg, Little Piano Piece, Op. 19, No. 2)

indicated. The final pair of thirds in the descent, D-flat–F to C–E, constitute another four-note set, 4-7 (0145), which occurs numerous times in this piece. The final portion of the descent, F–E–D–C, describes a form of set-class 4-11 (0135), another set with clear associations elsewhere in the piece. This final portion of the descent is doubled a major third above with a parallel form of 4-11.

The arrival on C is also contextually determined by the subtle inversional balance of the work. The ostinato G4–B4 that runs through the piece is the fulcrum for the entire musical structure. The first occurrence of 4-19 (0148), for example, is created by the combination of G4–B4 with D-sharp4–F-sharp4 (measures 1–2). A few beats later that harmony is balanced by an inversionally related form of the same set-class, created by combining G4–B4 with C5–E-flat5. A similar process of inversional balance produces the high B-flat5–D6 in the final measure. That measure contains two forms of 4-19. The lower one combines the central G4–B4 with E-flat5–F-sharp5. The upper one balances the lower, using E-flat5–F-sharp5 as a fulcrum. The B-flat5–D6 at the top of the upper 4-19 balances G4–B4 at the bottom of the lower 4-19. That high D6 recalls the same pitch in measure 2 and creates a kind of registral ceiling for the work (breached only briefly in measure 5). The D6 lies a perfect twelfth above the central G4. Balancing that D6 is the final bass note, C3, a perfect twelfth below the central G4. The note at the bottom of the texture, a kind of registral floor for the work (breached only in measure 6), thus balances the note at the top of the texture around a midpoint provided by the central note, G4. In this way, C3 is the culmination of a carefully worked out registral plan for the work as a whole.[7]

The large-scale motions of the piece, and particularly the concluding arrival on C in the bass, are thus enmeshed within a network of registral and motivic associations. The middleground motion of this piece may look like motion from dominant to tonic, but it does not function that way. Schoenberg has used his contextual resources to mimic a tonal procedure. We must not ignore the obvious tonal allusions in this and similar pieces. Rather, our task is to place those allusions in a theoretical framework within which we can make meaningful analytical assertions about them. If we take the tonal allusions as our point of departure, we will be powerless to describe the rich particularity of the individual piece. We will tend to view it as a distorted, unidiomatic tonal work. If, however, we take the musical context as our point of departure, and view the tonal allusions from the point of view of post-tonal structure, we will be able to hear a richer fabric of relationships. We will come to appreciate the power of this music simultaneously to create coherence and to comment ironically on the conventions of the past.[8]

The large-scale organization of Schoenberg's twelve-tone music frequently reflects his use of combinatorial areas. Most of Schoenberg's series are constructed so that their two hexachords are inversions of each other. Such a series is said to be "inversionally combinatorial." When this kind of series is inverted (at some transposition level), the second hexachord will have the same pitch-class content as the first hexachord of the original series (and therefore the first hexachord of the inversion will have the same content as the second hexachord of the original series). The series, the inversion that preserves hexachordal content, and the retrogrades of each of these constitute a twelve-tone area.[9] With Schoenberg's typical inversionally combinatorial series, there are twelve such areas, which can be designated A_0, A_1, $A_2 \ldots A_{11}$. If, for example, the series is combinatorial with I_5, A_0 will include P_0, R_0, I_5, and RI_5; A_1 will include P_1, R_1, I_6, and RI_6; and so on through A_{11}. These twelve areas correspond roughly to Schoenberg's concept of "regions" in tonal music and probably represent his attempt to recreate, in twelve-tone terms, the central tonal concept of modulation.[10] Like tonal regions, twelve-tone areas define large, self-contained harmonic plateaus. Although there are profound structural differences between a twelve-tone area and a tonal region (reflecting the differences between the twelve-tone and tonal systems), the analogy between the two is unmistakable and would certainly have been evident to Schoenberg. His twelve-tone works move from area to area just as tonal works move from region to region.

The motion from area to area can follow many different paths. The path usually has some association with the motivic surface of the music and occasionally mimics the large-scale motions of a tonal piece. His Piano Piece Op. 33a, for example, employs three distinct areas: A_0, A_2, and A_7. The first section of the piece (measures 1–23) uses exclusively the series forms from A_0 (P_0, I_5, and their retrogrades). The middle section of the piece (measures 23–32) moves through A_2 to a more heavily emphasized A_7. The final section of the piece returns to A_0. In this large-scale progression from a "tonic" area to an area a perfect fifth higher, Schoenberg is clearly imitating tonal motions, specifically the motion from I through II to V and back to I. But in Op. 33a, the motion to A_7 and back is so strongly motivated contextually that the tonal reference can only be ironic, a middleground misreading.

The opening measures establish the basic premises of the work, particularly a structural emphasis on the perfect fourth and perfect fifth (and combinations of these intervals) (see Example 7-15). In the first two measures P_0, divided into its three tetrachords, is paired with RI_5, the retrograde of its inversion starting a perfect fourth away, similarly divided into three tetrachords. The first chord and the sixth chord in measures 1–2 are both

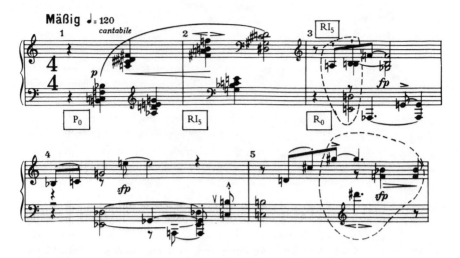

EXAMPLE 7-15 Combination of P_0, R_0, and RI_5 within A_0 (Schoenberg, Piano Piece Op. 33a)

members of the set-class 4-6 (0127), a collection that Schoenberg arranges registrally to feature a stack of three perfect fourths. The pairing of P_0 and I_5 continues in measures 3–5, where their retrogrades run against each other in a linear fashion. In this arrangement tetrachords are formed between the series forms by combining the six dyads of P_0 with the six dyads of I_5. The first and sixth of these between-series tetrachords, circled in Example 7-15, are members of 4-23 (0257), a set-class that can be thought of as a stack of perfect fourths or fifths. This set is prominent in this work, particularly at cadential points, and is strongly associated with the structure of the first tetrachord of the series, 4-6. It is particularly significant that the first trichord of the series is set-class 3-9 (027), a stack of three perfect fourths or fifths.

The structural and motivic use of perfect fourths and fifths, of stacks of perfect fourths and fifths, and, above all, of the trichord 3-9 (027), are what motivate the large-scale succession of areas: A_0–A_2–A_7–A_0. The first three pitch-classes of the series itself describe set-class 3-9 (027). The set of areas thus mirrors the initial set of pitch-classes.[11]

The moment where A_7 returns to A_0 is shown in Example 7-16. There is an obvious tonal allusion here. In tonal music the concluding return to the tonic region is normally preceded by the dominant region, just as here A_7 leads to A_0. In addition, Schoenberg has emphasized this sense of V leading to I by exposing the B-flat–E-flat movement in the bass.

Schoenberg thus alludes to tonal practice both on the musical surface and at the deepest level of structure, in the succession of twelve-tone areas. But tonal practice is only the object of an allusion; it is not a structural determinant. The relationships among A_0, A_2, and A_7 grow from the musical context, from a replication at the deepest structural level of a gesture from the musical surface. The idea of progression by perfect fifth emerges from the structure of the series, not from what Schenker poetically calls "the sacred triangle" of the tonic-dominant-tonic progression.[12] In composing a piece that moves A_0–A_2–A_7–A_0, Schoenberg hints at a traditional I–II–V–I har-

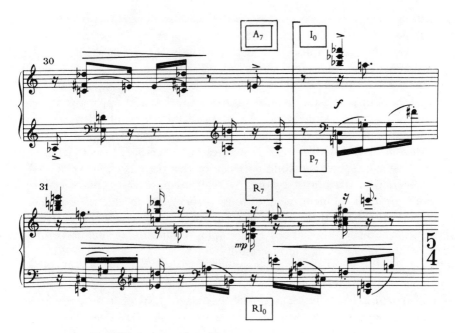

EXAMPLE 7-16   Transition from A_7 back to A_0

monic progression but simultaneously neutralizes that interpretation. He creates an allusion to tonality at the deepest level of musical structure without in any way compromising his own idiomatic compositional procedures.

———————

Allusions to traditional tonal music permeate the music of this century. Some are overt, in the form of direct quotations or references, while others are concealed beneath the surface. They penetrate all levels of structure. Their treatment ranges from delicate changes of orchestration and transformation of single sonorities to the reinterpretation of entire forms and piece-spanning motions. They are too numerous, too pervasive, too characteristic of twentieth-century music to be explained away as anomalies. They cannot be ignored. They demand systematic explanation.

At the same time, we must not make the mistake of assuming that the presence of these allusions requires us to engage the entire apparatus of tonal theory. To do so would result in analytical and critical blunders. First, it would obscure the coherence of the works in question. The tonal allusions exist side by side with musical structures that are clearly post-tonal in nature. We must shun a theoretical orientation that permits us to explain only one section or stratum of a work. Second, to approach twentieth-century works from the point of view of tonal theory is to devalue their achievement. If we admire these works, we will not want to view them as strange, deformed tonal compositions that employ traditional techniques grudgingly, incompletely, and unsuccessfully.

In this book tonal allusions have been neither ignored nor overvalued but placed in an analytical and critical context where they can be most richly understood. The analytical approach has taken post-tonal structure as its point of departure and made extensive use of pitch-class set theory and twelve-tone theory. These are our best analytical tools for the post-tonal repertoire, and they remain so even in the presence of apparent tonal formations. With them we may hope to incorporate both post-tonal and seeming tonal elements into a single analytical framework. Within this framework, we have seen that while the best twentieth-century works are certainly coherent, they are not necessarily organically so. Their coherence is won through a struggle in which old sonorities, old forms, even entire old compositions, are subsumed within a new musical structure.

The historical realities that confront twentieth-century music impinge on each composition. The larger musical culture is increasingly bifurcated between the traditional, canonic music of the eighteenth and nineteenth centuries and the new, post-tonal music of the twentieth. The two musics compete for access to an audience. The same split, and the same competition, can be felt within individual compositions. Traditional elements are incorporated and reinterpreted, but not effaced. Rather, the past remains a living, forceful presence.

Twentieth-century composers cannot escape their past—it presses in on them in too many ways. Their admiration for the tonal masterworks contributes to their anxiety about their ability to measure up. They are steeped in tradition, but fiercely assertive of their own originality. They wish to establish links to the tradition and simultaneously to assert themselves as its rightful heirs. In their desire to equal the achievement of their predecessors, they acknowledge the impossibility of writing in the old style—to do so would compromise their artistic integrity. They know that the lost Eden of the tonal common practice can never be regained in its original fullness. In this postlapsarian world, composition becomes a struggle for priority, a struggle to avoid being overwhelmed by a tradition that seems to gain in strength as it ages. That struggle, and the musical strategies composers use to pursue it, can be felt in a wide range of twentieth-century music. Despite dissimilarities of style, there is a clearly defined mainstream of musical modernism, shaped by common strategies of misreading. By transmuting received materials, composers can push their precursors aside and clear creative space for themselves. In doing so, they remake the past.

Notes

1. Toward a Theory of Musical Influence

1. For an extended and revealing study of the neoclassical-progressive dichotomy, see Scott Messing, *Neoclassicm in Music: From the Genesis of the Concept through the Schoenberg/Stravinsky Polemic* (Ann Arbor: UMI Research Press, 1988). Messing points out that critical interest in the dichotomy was intensified by nationalism (early polemicists saw neoclassicism as a way of resisting German musical hegemony) and embittered by the principal composers involved (see, for example, Schoenberg's nasty *Three Satires,* Op. 28, and numerous offhand remarks by Stravinsky cited by Messing). Many studies from the last twenty years have continued to insist on essential differences between the music of the neoclassicists (particularly Stravinsky) and the progressives (particularly Schoenberg). See, for example, Ernst Křenek, "Tradition in Perspective," *Perspectives of New Music* 1/1 (1962): 27–38, and Alan Lessem, "Schoenberg, Stravinsky, and Neo-Classicism: The Issues Reexamined," *Musical Quarterly* 68/4 (1982): 527–542.

2. Igor Stravinsky and Robert Craft, *Conversations with Igor Stravinsky* (Berkeley: University of California Press, 1980), p. 126. I should point out that there is doubt regarding Stravinsky's authorship of all the published documents that bear his name. All were essentially written for him by others. According to Richard Taruskin ("Russian Folk Melodies in *The Rite of Spring,*" *Journal of the American Musicological Society* 33/3, 1980: 502), the *Autobiography* "was largely ghostwritten by the Diaghilev acolyte Walter Nouvel." Robert Craft ("Roland-Manuel and the 'Poetics of Music,'" *Perspectives of New Music* 21/1–2, 1982–83: 487–505) has shown that the *Poetics* are only partially Stravinsky's. "Stravinsky wrote approximately 1,500 words for the *Poetics of Music,* but in verbal note-form: not a single sentence by him actually appears in the book of which he is the author. The 30,000-word text was written by Roland-Manuel, with assistance, in the lecture on Russian music, from Pierre Suvchinsky" (p. 487). There is as yet no definitive documentation, but it seems possible that Stravinsky's comments in the Stravinsky-Craft dialogues may contain a good deal of Craft.

Indeed, Craft has acknowledged his own active role in these dialogues as more than a mere interrogator. See Robert Craft, "On a Misunderstood Collaboration: Assisting Stravinsky," *Atlantic Monthly* (December 1982): 68–74. Stravinsky certainly approved the sentiments expressed in these documents, but the words should not be taken strictly as his.

3. Igor Stravinsky and Robert Craft, *Dialogues* (Berkeley: University of California Press, 1982), p. 129.

4. Peter Burkholder has eloquently expressed a similar view in a series of articles, the most important of which is "Museum Pieces," *Journal of Musicology* 2/2 (1983): 115–134. Burkholder argues that the unifying feature of twentieth-century music is not a shared style or structure but a shared preoccupation with the past. For Burkholder, twentieth-century music is essentially historicist in nature. He makes a similar argument in "Brahms and Twentieth-Century Classical Music," *19th-Century Music* 8/1 (1984): 75–83: "I wish to define 'modern music' as music written by composers obsessed with the musical past and with their place in music history, who seek to emulate the music of those we call the 'classical masters,' measuring the value of their own music by the standards of the past" (p. 76). In both articles Burkholder attempts to shift the focus of critical attention from questions of musical construction to the impact of the musical past on the shared musical, social, and intellectual concerns of twentieth-century composers, performers, and listeners.

5. The theory, developed by Milton Babbitt, David Lewin, and especially Allen Forte, has exerted a profound and pervasive influence on analytical studies of twentieth-century music. The basic outlines of this theory are now accessible through two sources: Allen Forte, *The Structure of Atonal Music* (New Haven: Yale University Press, 1973), and John Rahn, *Basic Atonal Theory* (New York: Longman, 1980). Important refinements and extensions of the theory may be found in David Lewin, *Generalized Musical Intervals and Transformations* (New Haven: Yale University Press, 1987), and Robert Morris, *Composition with Pitch-Classes* (New Haven: Yale University Press, 1987).

6. Rahn's comments on Stravinsky have a wider applicability: "Probably, satisfactory analyses of the preserial works of Stravinsky will, when they finally appear, employ theories that graft nontonal referential collections and unique Stravinskian transformation rules into a wildly Schenkerian-derived kind of theory of [pitch-class] set 'prolongation' in various pitch-structural and rhythmic-structural 'levels'" (*Basic Atonal Theory*, p. 79).

7. For an interesting and less optimistic view on this subject, see Robert Morgan, "Secret Languages: The Roots of Musical Modernism," *Critical Inquiry* 10/3 (1984): 442–461.

8. The discussion that follows is based on a series of articles by William Weber: "The Contemporaneity of Eighteenth-Century Musical Taste," *Musical Quarterly* 70/2 (1984): 175–194; "Mass Culture and the Reshaping of European Musical Taste, 1770–1870," *International Review of the Aesthetics and Sociology of Music* 8/1 (1977): 5–22; "Learned and General Musical Taste in Eighteenth-Century France," *Past & Present* 89 (1980): 58–85.

9. Mozart's teaching of composition is fully documented in *Thomas Attwoods*

Theorie- und Kompositionsstudien bei Mozart, ed. E. Hertzmann, C. Oldman, D. Heartz, and A. Mann, in Mozart: Neue Ausgabe sämtlicher Werke, supplement, section 30, vol. 1 (Kassel: Bärenreiter, 1965).

10. The term "burden of the past" and many of the concepts associated with it were developed first by Walter Jackson Bate in his study of eighteenth-century poetry and prose, *The Burden of the Past and the English Poet* (Cambridge, Mass.: Harvard University Press, 1970). Bate argues "that the remorseless deepening of self-consciousness, before the rich and intimidating legacy of the past, has become the greatest single problem that modern art (art, that is to say, since the later seventeenth century) has had to face, and that it will become increasingly so in the future" (p. 4). In fact, a sense of the past as a burden was not felt in music until the middle of the nineteenth century; since then it has intensified continuously and dramatically.

11. Stravinsky and Craft, *Conversations*, p. 21.

12. Igor Stravinsky and Robert Craft, *Memories and Commentaries* (Berkeley: University of California Press, 1981), p. 110.

13. Stravinsky and Craft, *Dialogues*, p. 47.

14. Ibid., p. 43.

15. Stravinsky and Craft, *Memories and Commentaries*, p. 158. Stravinsky's identification of *The Rake's Progress* with *Così* is not entirely persuasive. A more significant predecessor is *Don Giovanni* (see Chapter 6).

16. Stravinsky and Craft, *Memories and Commentaries*, p. 127.

17. Stravinsky and Craft, *Dialogues*, p. 30.

18. Remarks made by Milton Babbitt and Claudio Spies at a conference on the music of Stravinsky, Notre Dame University, November 1982.

19. Arnold Schoenberg, *Style and Idea*, ed. Leonard Stein, trans. Leo Black (New York: St. Martin's Press, 1975; reprint ed. Berkeley: University of California Press, 1984), "New Music: My Music," p. 104.

20. Schoenberg, *Style and Idea*, "How One Becomes Lonely," p. 53.

21. Anton Webern, *The Path to the New Music*, ed. Willi Reich, trans. Leo Black (Bryn Mawr, Pa.: Theodore Presser Company, 1963), p. 45.

22. Schoenberg, *Style and Idea*, "On Revient Toujours," p. 109.

23. Schoenberg, *Style and Idea*, "How One Becomes Lonely," p. 50.

24. Bloom's theory is set forth in a tetralogy of works: *The Anxiety of Influence: A Theory of Poetry* (Oxford: Oxford University Press, 1973), *A Map of Misreading* (Oxford: Oxford University Press, 1975), *Kaballah and Criticism* (New York: Continuum Publishing Company, 1983), and *Poetry and Repression: Revisionism from Blake to Stevens* (New Haven: Yale University Press, 1976). Bloom is neither the originator nor the sole exponent of this third theory of influence. Walter Jackson Bate, for example, has argued along similar lines. Bloom is, however, the most forceful advocate for this view, which has become principally identified with him. I have recently become aware that several other scholars are also currently engaged in incorporating Bloom's ideas into studies of music, particularly nineteenth-century music, and especially the music of Brahms. See Elaine Sisman, "Brahms's Slow Movements: Reinventing the 'Closed' Forms," in *Brahms Studies*, ed. George Bozarth (Oxford: Oxford University Press, 1990);

three unpublished papers by Kevin Korsyn, "Towards a New Poetics of Musical Influence," "Brahms, Chopin, and the Anxiety of Influence," and "Directional Tonality and Intertextuality: A Comparison of the Second Movement of Brahms's Quintet Opus 88 and Chopin's Ballade Opus 38"; and an unpublished paper by John Daverio, "Brahms, Mozart, and the Anxiety of Influence."

25. Roman Vlad, *Stravinsky,* trans. Frederick Fuller and Ann Fuller (London: Oxford University Press, 1967), pp. 3–4.

26. T. S. Eliot, "Tradition and the Individual Talent" (1919), in *Selected Essays* (New York: Harcourt, Brace, 1950), p. 4.

27. Ibid., pp. 3–4.

28. Ibid., pp. 6–7.

29. Leonard B. Meyer, "Innovation, Choice, and the History of Music," *Critical Inquiry* 9/3 (1983): 529.

30. Charles Rosen, "Influence: Plagiarism and Inspiration," *19th-Century Music* 4/2 (1980): 94.

31. Ibid., p. 88.

32. Bloom, *Kaballah and Criticism,* p. 106.

33. Bloom, *Poetry and Repression,* p. 2.

34. Bloom, *Anxiety of Influence,* p. 43.

35. Bloom, *Kaballah and Criticism,* p. 106.

36. Bloom, *Poetry and Repression,* p. 3.

37. Ibid., p. 25.

38. Bloom, *Anxiety of Influence,* p. 5.

39. Ibid., p. 30.

40. Bloom, *Kaballah and Criticism,* p. 121.

41. Bloom, *Map of Misreading,* p. 19. Wordsworth's formulation may be found in the Preface to *Lyrical Ballads* (1800).

42. Bloom, *Kaballah and Criticism,* p. 108.

43. Bloom, *Map of Misreading,* p. 199.

44. Ibid., p. 9.

45. Bloom, *Anxiety of Influence,* p. 30.

46. Bloom, *Map of Misreading,* p. 69.

47. Bloom, *Anxiety of Influence,* p. 12.

48. Bloom, *Map of Misreading,* p. 35.

49. Bloom's limitations have been pointed out before, particularly by feminist critics. See, for example, Sandra Gilbert and Susan Gubar, *The Madwoman in the Attic: The Woman Writer and the Nineteenth-Century Literary Imagination* (New Haven: Yale University Press, 1979), pp. 47–53. "Bloom's model of literary history is intensely (even exclusively) male, and necessarily patriarchal. For this reason it has seemed, and no doubt will continue to seem, offensively sexist to some feminist critics . . . [But] Western literary history *is* overwhelmingly male—or, more accurately, patriarchal—and Bloom analyzes and explains this fact, while other theorists have ignored it . . . Bloom's model of literary history is not a recommendation for but an analysis of the patriarchal poetics (and attendant anxieties) which underlie our culture's chief literary movements" (pp. 47–48).

50. Joseph Kerman, in "How We Got into Analysis, and How to Get Out," *Critical*

Inquiry 7/2 (1980): 311–331, offers a related critique of what he calls "the ideology of organicism." See also his *Contemplating Music: Challenges to Musicology* (Cambridge, Mass.: Harvard University Press, 1985), esp. pp. 64–90. For a lucid account of the philosophical and literary origins of organicism and its impact on music theory, see Ruth Solie, "The Living Work: Organicism and Musical Analysis," *19th-Century Music* 4/2 (1980): 147–156.

51. Arnold Whittall makes a similar point in "The Theorist's Sense of History: Concepts of Contemporaneity in Composition and Analysis," *Proceedings of the Royal Musical Association* 112/1 (1986–87): 1–20. He observes "that past and present may not always have been joined by bridges of transition: they may actually be, and need to be, in conflict" (p. 2). In describing works that juxtapose old and new elements, "the theorist needs to bring to the musical result . . . a sense of history both segmented and stratified, like the music itself: a sense of the deep divisions between particular periods of time. What it is time for, in this view, is for theorists to do more than nurture their concern with the ways in which a particular structural principle may apparently be painlessly transformed into something totally different. History—even the history of art—is also about lack of reconciliation, and the music theorist needs to be able to sense when this is so" (p. 14).

52. Bloom, *Anxiety of Influence*, p. 13.

53. Ibid., p. 7.

54. Bloom, *Map of Misreading*, p. 3.

55. Ibid., pp. 19–20.

2. Analytical Misreadings

1. There is a large and growing literature on this point. See, for example, Felix Salzer, *Structural Hearing: Tonal Coherence in Music* (New York: Dover, 1962); Felix Salzer, "Tonality in Early Medieval Polyphony: Toward a History of Tonality," *Music Forum* 1 (1967): 35–98; Saul Novack, "The Analysis of Pre-Baroque Music," *Aspects of Schenkerian Theory,* ed. David Beach (New Haven: Yale University Press, 1983), pp. 113–34; Saul Novack, "Fusion of Design and Tonal Order in Mass and Motet: Josquin Desprez and Heinrich Isaac," *Music Forum* 2 (1970): 187–263; George Perle, "Integrative Devices in the Music of Machaut," *Musical Quarterly* 34/2 (1948): 169–176; Irving Godt, "Motivic Integration in Josquin's Motets," *Journal of Music Theory* 21/2 (1977): 264–292; Joseph Strauss, "The Motivic Structure of Palestrina's Music," *In Theory Only* 7/4 (1983): 3–23.

2. In the discussion that follows, my understanding of the motivic organization of tonal music is rooted in that of Heinrich Schenker. He discusses motivic structure most fully in *Free Composition,* trans. and ed. Ernst Oster (New York: Longman, 1979), pp. 93–107. His work has been clarified and extended in a number of more recent studies, including Charles Burkhart, "Schenker's 'Motivic Parallelism,'" *Journal of Musical Theory* 22/2 (1978): 145–175, and John Rothgeb, "Thematic Content: A Schenkerian View," *Aspects of Schenkerian Theory,* ed. David Beach (New Haven: Yale University Press, 1983), pp. 39–60.

3. "All diminution must be secured firmly to the total work by means which are

precisely demonstrable and organically verified by the inner necessities of voice leading. The total work lives and moves in each diminution, even those of the lowest order. Not the smallest part exists without the whole. The establishment of an inner relationship to the whole is the principal problem not only in the creation of diminution out of background and middleground, but also even in its re-creation, where constant reference to middleground and background must be made" (Schenker, *Free Composition*, p. 98).

4. "[Concealed repetitions] were fully as effective as the simple repetitions; they, too, sprang only from the blood relationship of statement and variant almost beyond the composer's volition—but they remained concealed. Yet it was precisely those concealed repetitions which freed music from the narrowness of strict imitation and pointed the way to the widest spans and most distant goals; thus even very extended tonal structures could be based upon repetition!" (Schenker, *Free Composition*, p. 99).

5. Milton Babbitt, "Review of *Polyphonie: Revue musicale trimestrielle,* Quatrième Cahier, *Le Système dodécaphonique,*" *Journal of the American Musicological Society* 3/3 (1950): 265.

6. See, for example, a recent series of articles by Allen Forte: "Motivic Design and Structural Levels in the First Movement of Brahms's String Quartet in C Minor," *Musical Quarterly* 69/4 (1983): 471–502; "Motive and Rhythmic Contour in the Alto Rhapsody," *Journal of Music Theory* 27/2 (1983): 255–272; "Middleground Motives in the Adagietto of Mahler's Fifth Symphony," *19th-Century Music* 8/2 (1984): 153–163; "Liszt's Experimental Idiom and Music of the Early Twentieth Century," *19th-Century Music* 10/3 (1986): 209–228. In these articles Forte shows the growing importance of contextual motivic relations and their increasing independence from a tonal framework.

7. Forte, "Motivic Design and Structural Levels," p. 471.

8. Anton Webern, "Schönbergs Musik," in *Arnold Schoenberg* (Munich: Verlag R. Piper, 1912). Portions reprinted in *Schoenberg, Berg, Webern: The String Quartets, A Documentary Study,* ed. Ursula v. Rauchhaupt, trans. Eugene Hartzell (Hamburg: Deutsche Grammophon, 1971), p. 16.

9. Alban Berg, "Why Is Schoenberg's Music So Difficult to Understand?" from the special issue of *Musikblätter des Anbruch* honoring Schoenberg on his fiftieth birthday, September 13, 1924; reprinted in Willi Reich, *Alban Berg,* trans. Cornelius Cardew (New York: Vienna House, 1974), pp. 199–200.

10. Arnold Schoenberg, *Style and Idea,* ed. Leonard Stein, trans. Leo Black (New York: St. Martin's Press, 1975; reprint ed. Berkeley: University of California Press, 1984), "Composition with Twelve Tones (2)," p. 248.

11. Arnold Schoenberg, "Analysis of the Four Orchestral Songs, Opus 22," trans. Claudio Spies, *Perspectives of New Music* 3/2 (1965): 7.

12. Schoenberg, "Analysis of the Four Orchestral Songs," p. 17.

13. See, for example, William Benjamin, "Ideas of Order in Motivic Music," *Music Theory Spectrum* 1 (1979): 23–34, and Benjamin Boretz, "Meta-Variations: Studies in the Foundations of Musical Thought" (Ph.D. diss., Princeton University, 1970).

14. In this book pitch-class sets will be identified by both their name and, in parentheses, their prime form. The prime form is a representation of a set in the most condensed possible format. From the prime form it is easy to grasp the essential

intervallic features of a set. All sets with the same prime form are members of the same set-class. The name of a set consists of two hyphenated numbers: the first tells the number of pitch-classes in the set; the second tells the position of that set-class on a list of set-classes compiled by Allen Forte and now widely in use (see *The Structure of Atonal Music,* New Haven: Yale University Press, 1973, appendix 1). Set-class 3-4, for example, is the fourth set on Forte's list of three-note sets.

15. Transposition and inversion are the basic operations in this theoretical system. Both operations preserve interval content. Sets related by either transposition or inversion are members of the same set-class.

16. The analysis in Example 2-2 is based on Allen Forte, "The Magical Kaleidoscope: Schoenberg's First Atonal Masterwork, Opus 11, Number 1," *Journal of the Arnold Schoenberg Institute* 5/2 (1981): 127–168. See also Gary Wittlich, "Interval Set Structure in Schoenberg's Op. 11, No. 1," *Perspectives of New Music* 13/1 (1974): 41–55; and George Perle, *Serial Composition and Atonality,* 5th ed. (Berkeley: University of California Press, 1981), pp. 10–15.

17. Two sets that are not members of the same set-class (that is, not related by transposition or inversion) but that have the same interval content are said to be "Z-related."

18. Will Ogdon, "How Tonality Functions in Schoenberg's Opus 11, Number 1," *Journal of the Arnold Schoenberg Institute* 5/2 (1981): 169–181. Another analyst, William Benjamin, believes the passage is centered not on G, but on F-sharp! (Paper presented at the national conference of the Society for Music Theory, Philadelphia, 1984.)

19. For a thorough and devastating critique of the tonal approach to this piece, see Allen Forte, "Pitch-Class Set Analysis Today," *Music Analysis* 4/1–2 (1985): 42–46.

20. Ernst Křenek, *Studies in Counterpoint, Based on the Twelve-Tone Technique* (New York: G. Schirmer, 1940), pp. vii–viii.

21. Arnold Schoenberg, *Structural Functions of Harmony,* ed. Leonard Stein (New York: Norton, 1969), p. 193; bracketed material is Schoenberg's.

22. Anton Webern, *The Path to the New Music,* ed. Willi Reich, trans. Leo Black (Bryn Mawr, Pa.: Theodore Presser Company, 1963), p. 35.

23. Webern, *The Path to the New Music,* p. 40.

24. Schoenberg, *Style and Idea,* "Twelve-Tone Composition," p. 208.

25. This realization is reflected to some degree in most recent work on Stravinsky and Bartók, although the terminology varies from study to study. See, for example, Allen Forte, *The Harmonic Organization of the Rite of Spring* (New Haven: Yale University Press, 1978); Christopher Hasty, "On the Problem of Succession and Continuity in Twentieth-Century Music," *Music Theory Spectrum* 8 (1986): 58–74; Paul Wilson, "Atonality and Structure in Works of Béla Bartók's Middle Period" (Ph.D. diss., Yale University, 1982); George Perle, "Symmetrical Formations in the String Quartets of Béla Bartók," *Music Review* 16/4 (1955): 300–312; Elliott Antokoletz, *The Music of Béla Bartók: A Study of Tonality and Progression in Twentieth-Century Music* (Berkeley: University of California Press, 1984), esp. pp. 78–137, where he discusses "intervallic cells," the term he and Perle use for pitch-class sets.

26. Schoenberg himself never gave sustained explanations of either term, but the

hints in his writing and the power of his teaching have spawned a large body of literature devoted to explaining, extending, and applying his ideas. For a good review of this analytical tradition (and an excellent example of it), see Walter Frisch, *Brahms and the Principle of Developing Variation* (Berkeley: University of California Press, 1984).

27. Schoenberg, *Style and Idea,* "Linear Counterpoint," p. 290.

28. Schoenberg, "Der musikalische Gedanke und die Logik, Technik, und Kunst seiner Darstellung," cited in *Schoenberg's Gedanke Manuscripts: A Reconstruction and Edition,* ed. Patricia Carpenter and Severine Neff (New York: Columbia University Press, forthcoming); bracketed material is Schoenberg's.

29. Schoenberg, *Fundamentals of Musical Composition,* ed. Gerald Strang (New York: St. Martin's Press, 1967), p. 9.

30. Schoenberg, *Style and Idea,* "Brahms the Progressive," pp. 398–441.

31. Ibid., p. 430.

32. Ibid., p. 431.

33. Ibid., p. 435.

34. Schoenberg, *Fundamentals of Musical Composition,* p. 21.

35. Ibid., p. 25.

36. Ibid., p. 29.

37. Ibid., p. 58.

38. Ibid., p. 41 (example 45i).

39. Ibid., p. 27.

40. Schoenberg, *Theory of Harmony,* trans. Roy Carter (Berkeley: University of California Press, 1978), p. 315.

41. Ibid., p. 317. Some remarkable analytical consequences of this point of view are described in Joel Lester, "Simultaneity Structures and Harmonic Functions in Tonal Music," *In Theory Only* 5/5 (1981): 3–28. See also David Lewin's response, *In Theory Only* 5/8 (1981): 12–13.

42. As Allen Forte points out, "Surely from the standpoint of triadic tonality this reinterpretation is untenable. However, with respect to Schoenberg's own evolution, the new concept of musical space that this rejection of tradition implies is of the utmost importance, for, in the most general sense, it opens up the universe of pitch-class sets and detaches pitch organization from the harmonic-contrapuntal syntax of triadic tonality. It points directly to the unordered pitch field of the atonal composition and to the segmentation of that field in the complex ways that are characteristic of Schoenberg's atonal music. In short, Schoenberg was not saying anything about the music of triadic tonality—surely he understood the linear origin of Mozart's 'chord'—but was attempting to justify his own musical concepts which, of course, at that time (1910–11) had already been reified in a number of important works" (Forte, "Schoenberg's Creative Evolution: The Path to Atonality," *Musical Quarterly* 64/2, 1978: 150).

43. Schoenberg, "Problems of Harmony," trans. Adolph Weiss, *Modern Music* 11/4 (1934): 179; reprinted in *Perspectives of New Music* 11/2 (1973): 15.

44. Letter to Josef Rufer, April 8, 1950. Quoted in H. H. Stuckenschmidt, *Schoenberg: His Life, World, and Work,* trans. Humphrey Searle (New York: Schirmer, 1977), p. 510.

45. Schoenberg, *Style and Idea,* "Composing with Twelve Tones," pp. 220–222.

46. Milton Babbitt has made this point with great force: "Schoenberg cites Beetho-

ven's Opus 135 as a work adumbrating, in motival form, the operations of the twelve-tone system, while admitting that the motival transformation in Beethoven are not literal, because of the tonal functions they must fulfill. But this is the crux of the problem. For it is just this aspect of the predetermined boundary conditions of tonality, that completely differentiates it from the twelve-tone set and its transformations, which are themselves the fundamental boundary conditions. The tonal motive assumes functional meaning within a context, and becomes, in turn, a vehicle of movement within this context; the twelve-tone set, however, is the instigator of movement and defines the functional context. To equate a compositional element with a pre-compositional element is not only to confuse the nature of the systems, but to reduce the number of levels of musical meaning, and, as a result, to reduce the functional multiplicity of the individual note. It is unfortunate that in attempting to make of the twelve-tone system something more than it can be demonstrated to be, in historical terms, Schoenberg reduces it to something less than it can be demonstrated to be, in autonomous terms" ("Review of *Polyphonie*," pp. 264–265).

47. Webern, *The Path to the New Music*, p. 23.
48. Ibid., p. 25.
49. Ibid., p. 53.
50. Ibid., p. 35.
51. Hans Pfitzner, "Die neue Aesthetik der musikalischen Impotenz: Ein Verwesungssymptom?" (The New Aesthetic of Musical Impotence: A Symptom of Decay?).
52. Alban Berg, "The Musical Impotence of Hans Pfitnzer's 'New Aesthetic,'" from *Musikblätter des Anbruch*, no. 11–12 (June 1920); reprinted in Willi Reich, *Alban Berg*, pp. 210–211.
53. Ibid., p. 210.
54. Béla Bartók, "The Folk Songs of Hungary," in *Béla Bartók Essays*, ed. Benjamin Suchoff (New York: St. Martin's Press, 1976), p. 335.
55. Ibid., pp. 336–338.
56. Igor Stravinsky and Robert Craft, *Dialogues* (Berkeley: University of California Press, 1982), p. 101.
57. Igor Stravinsky and Robert Craft, *Expositions and Developments* (Berkeley: University of California Press, 1981), p. 64.
58. Stravinsky and Craft, *Dialogues*, p. 112.
59. Pieter van den Toorn, *The Music of Igor Stravinsky* (New Haven: Yale University Press, 1983), p. 429.
60. Stravinsky and Craft, *Dialogues*, p. 124.
61. Cited in *Milton Babbitt: Words about Music*, ed. Stephen Dembski and Joseph N. Straus (Madison: University of Wisconsin Press, 1987), p. 20.

3. Recompositions

1. Howard M. Brown, "Emulation, Competition, and Homage: Imitation and Theories of Imitation in the Renaissance," *Journal of the American Musicological Society* 35/1 (1982): 1–48.
2. For a discussion of the evolution of the term "parody" and the range of its application, see Lewis Lockwood, "On 'Parody' as Term and Concept in Sixteenth-

century Music," in *Aspects of Medieval and Renaissance Music: A Birthday Offering to Gustave Reese,* ed. Jan LaRue (New York: Norton, 1966), pp. 560–575.

3. The Mahler works are the least known of these. See Mosco Carner, "Mahler's Re-scoring of the Schumann Symphonies," in *Major and Minor* (New York: Holmes and Meier, 1980), pp. 71–84.

4. For related discussions of Schoenberg's orchestrations of Bach and Brahms, see Walter Frisch, *Brahms and the Principle of Developing Variation* (Berkeley: University of California Press, 1984), and Klaus Velten, *Schönbergs Instrumentationen Bachscher and Brahmsscher Werke als Dokumente seines Traditionsverständnisses* (Regensburg: Gustav Bosse, 1976).

5. My discussion of articulation and register is based on observations made by Claudio Spies in "The Organ Supplanted: A Case for Differentiations," *Perspectives of New Music* 11/2 (1973): 24–55. This article also contains perceptive discussions of the other Schoenberg orchestrations of Bach: "Komm, Gott" and the Prelude and Fugue in E-flat Major.

6. Arnold Schoenberg, "National Music," in Josef Rufer, *The Works of Arnold Schoenberg,* trans. Dika Newlin (New York: The Free Press of Glencoe, 1962), p. 147. For a slightly different translation of the passage, see Arnold Schoenberg, *Style and Idea,* ed. Leonard Stein, trans. Leo Black (New York: St. Martin's Press, 1975; reprint ed. Berkeley: University of California Press, 1984), p. 173.

7. Arnold Schoenberg, letter to Fritz Steidry, July 31, 1930, in Rufer, *The Works of Arnold Schoenberg,* p. 94.

8. Arnold Schoenberg, "Vortrag/12 T K/Princeton," trans. and ed. Claudio Spies, *Perspectives of New Music* 13/1 (1974): 123.

9. Lawrence Morton makes a similar point when he discusses *The Fairy's Kiss,* in part, as "criticism" of Tchaikovsky. See "Stravinsky and Tchaikovsky: *Le Baiser de la fée,*" in *Stravinsky: A New Appraisal of His Work,* ed. Paul Henry Lang (New York: Norton, 1963), pp. 47–60.

10. Igor Stravinsky, *An Autobiography* (New York: Norton, 1962), p. 146.

11. Igor Stravinsky and Robert Craft, *Dialogues* (Berkeley: University of California Press, 1982), p. 27.

12. Harold Bloom, *The Anxiety of Influence* (Oxford: Oxford University Press, 1973), p. 14.

13. Stravinsky believed that all of his source pieces were composed by Pergolesi, but fully eleven of the twenty-one arias and instrumental movements of *Pulcinella* are, in fact, by a variety of other eighteenth-century composers, most of whom are virtually unknown today. See Barry S. Brook, "Stravinsky's *Pulcinella:* The 'Pergolesi' Sources," in *Musiques, Signes, Images: Liber Amicorum François Lesure* (Geneva: Minkoff, 1988), pp. 41–66.

14. Stravinsky, *An Autobiography,* p. 81.

15. Most discussions of *Pulcinella* have taken the "triad-plus-wrong-note" approach. See, for example, Robert Moevs, "Mannerism and Stylistic Consistency in Stravinsky," *Perspectives of New Music* 9/2–10/1 (1971), where he discusses the theme of the gavotte as "a progression in A . . . in which every chord but the last contains a 7th or a 9th" (p. 95).

16. Igor Stravinsky and Robert Craft, *Expositions and Developments* (Berkeley: University of California Press, 1982), p. 113.

17. "[Stravinsky's] interruption of the composition of *Canticum Sacrum* to transcribe that cornerstone of canonic writing, Bach's *Chorale Variations,* can thus be understood in the light of his conception of the canon as a traditional manifestations of serialism" (Milton Babbitt, "Remarks on the Recent Stravinsky," *Perspectives of New Music* 2/2, 1964: 49).

18. Igor Stravinsky and Robert Craft, *Conversations with Igor Stravinsky* (Berkeley: University of California Press, 1980), p. 120.

19. One serious attempt to understand the motivic consequences of this fragmentation is Carl Dahlhaus, "Analytische Instrumentation: Bachs sechsstimmiges Ricercar in der Orchestrierung Anton Weberns," in *Bach Interpretationen: Walter Blankenburg zum 65. Geburstag* (Göttingen: Vanderhoeck and Ruprecht, 1969), pp. 197–206.

20. Complement-related set-classes have a similar distribution of intervals. The difference in the number of occurrences of each interval-class is equal to the difference in size of the sets (except for the tritone, where it will be half that difference). An eight-note set, for example, will have four more of each interval-class than its four-note complement (except the tritone, of which it will have two more). This intervallic similarity holds even if the two sets have notes in common, and are thus not literally complements of each other, so long as they are members of complement-related set-classes. For example, any member of set-class 4-7 and any member of set-class 8-7 will have a similar distribution of intervals.

21. This means of organization is remarkably similar to that of Schoenberg in his twelve-tone pieces. There, as Martha Hyde has shown ("The Roots of Form in Schoenberg's Sketches," *Journal of Music Theory* 24/1, 1980: 1–36), nonadjacent notes of a series are frequently associated musically (by register, instrumentation, or other means) to create set-classes that can also be found as segmental subsets of the series.

22. Anton Webern, letter to Hermann Scherchen, January 1, 1938, cited in Hans Moldenhauer and Rosaleen Moldenhauer, *Anton von Webern: A Chronicle of His Life and Work* (New York: Alfred Knopf, 1979), p. 444.

23. Anton Webern, letter to Arnold Schoenberg, June 17, 1931, cited in Moldernhauer and Moldenhauer, *Anton von Webern: A Chronicle,* p. 440.

24. Bloom, *The Anxiety of Influence,* p. 15.

25. Ibid., p. 141.

4. Triads

1. Here, as elsewhere, my understanding of tonal music is rooted in Schenker's.

2. See, for example, Dika Newlin, "Secret Tonality in Schoenberg's Piano Concerto," *Perspectives of New Music* 13/1 (1974): 137–39, and Will Ogdon, "How Tonality Functions in Schoenberg's Opus 11, Number 1," *Journal of the Arnold Schoenberg Institute* 5/2 (1981): 169–181.

3. Alban Berg, "Lecture on *Wozzeck,*" in Hans Redlich, *Alban Berg: The Man and His Music* (New York: Abelard-Schuman, 1957), p. 275. Redlich points out that Berg originally had planned to use the term *Nüchternheit* ("prosiness") rather than *Sachlichkeit* ("objectivity").

4. In George Perle's analysis, this harmony is identified as Cell D. His Cell A is

also a member of set-class 4-19 (0148). See *The Operas of Alban Berg,* vol. 1, *Wozzeck* (Berkeley: University of California Press, 1980), pp. 153–154, for a related discussion of the C-major chord and the passage in which it occurs.

5. Janet Schmalfeldt, *Berg's Wozzeck: Harmonic Language and Dramatic Design* (New Haven: Yale University Press, 1983).

6. For a discussion of Stravinsky's emerging solution to the problem of simultaneity in serial music, see Milton Babbitt, "Stravinsky's Verticals and Schoenberg's Diagonals: A Twist of Fate," in *Stravinsky Retrospectives,* ed. Ethan Haimo and Paul Johnson (Lincoln: University of Nebraska Press, 1987), pp. 15–35.

7. The exotic spelling of a familiar E-major triad as an F-flat–major triad has the effect notationally of slightly concealing the sonority's triadic identity. The last movement of *Requiem Canticles* contains a similar effect. There, the sustained notes in the first horn part slowly unfold an F-minor triad spelled as F–G-sharp–B-sharp.

8. Arnold Schoenberg, *Style and Idea,* ed. Leonard Stein, trans. Leo Black (New York: St. Martin's Press, 1975; reprint ed. Berkeley: University of California Press, 1984), "Composition with Twelve Tones," p. 219.

9. Arnold Schoenberg, letter to René Leibowitz, July 4, 1947, cited in *Arnold Schoenberg Letters,* ed. Erwin Stein, trans. E. Wilkins and E. Kaiser (London: Faber and Faber, 1964), p. 248.

10. See, for example, Mosco Carner, *Alban Berg: The Man and the Work,* 2d ed. (New York: Holmes and Meier, 1983), pp. 155–162. Carner refers to the concerto's "tilt toward the traditional major-minor system" (p. 156).

11. Arnold Schoenberg, *Style and Idea,* "Opinion or Insight?" p. 263.

12. Craig Ayrey describes a similar situation in Schoenberg's "Am Scheideweg," from *Three Satires,* Op. 28, where "the omnipresence of the potentially subversive triad" is "subverted by, and not permitted to dominate, its atonal surroundings." "Berg's 'Scheideweg': Analytical Issues in Op. 2/ii," *Music Analysis* 1/2 (1982): 194.

13. Pierre Boulez, "Schoenberg Is Dead," *The Score* 6 (1952): 21; reprinted (and retranslated) in *Notes of an Apprenticeship,* trans. Herbert Weinstock (New York: Alfred Knopf, 1968), p. 273.

14. On Stravinsky, see Arthur Berger, "Problems of Pitch Organization in Stravinsky," *Perspectives of New Music* 2/1 (1963): 11–42, and Pieter van den Toorn, *The Music of Igor Stravinsky* (New Haven: Yale University Press, 1983). On Bartók, see Elliott Antokoletz, *The Music of Béla Bartók: A Study of Tonality and Progression in Twentieth-Century Music* (Berkeley: University of California Press, 1984).

15. Olivier Messiaen, *The Technique of My Musical Language,* trans. J. Satterfield (Paris: Alphonse Leduc, 1956), pp. 58–63.

16. Pieter van den Toorn describes the major or minor triad as among "the principal between-block or between-reference connecting links in octatonic-diatonic interaction" (*The Music of Igor Stravinsky,* p. 319).

17. The concluding arrival on G–B–D gives at least a hint of a half-cadence, preparing the C-centered second and third movements of the work. Seeming dominant-tonic relationships are reasonably common in Stravinsky's music but are usually structurally vestigial. As van den Toorn observes, "The 'resolution' may

seem incidental to pitch organization generally, and hence assume [a] 'distinctly parenthetical' character . . . Consequently, notwithstanding its blatant non-octatonicism, its origin as a C-scale functional *progression,* the Stravinskian dominant-tonic transaction in neoclassical contexts is reckoned as instantiating yet another form of octatonic and diatonic C-scale interaction" (*The Music of Igor Stravinsky,* p. 332).

18. Wilfred Mellers describes it in just this way in "Stravinsky's Oedipus as Twentieth-Century Hero," in *Stravinsky: A New Appraisal of His Work,* ed. Paul Henry Lang (New York: Norton, 1963), p. 42.

19. Lawrence Morton describes this moment in similar terms: "If D-major is . . . the key of 'inner light,' then B-minor is the key of outer darkness, and their simultaneity, through ambiguity, is the single stroke with which Stravinsky portrays Oedipus illumined and Oedipus blind" ("Review of Eric Walter White, *Stravinsky: The Composer and his Works,*" *Musical Quarterly* 53/4, 1967: 591).

20. Vera Stravinsky and Robert Craft, *Stravinsky in Pictures and Documents* (New York: Simon and Schuster, 1978), p. 264.

21. Walter Piston, "A Reminiscence," *Perspectives of New Music* 9/2–10/1 (1971): 6–7. This chord occurs on p. 57 of the full score and is not the same as the D–F-sharp dyad discussed above.

22. One critic has described the ending of this piece as "in A-major/minor." Jim Samson, *Music in Transition: A study of Tonal Expansion and Atonality, 1900–1920* (New York: Norton, 1977), p. 164.

23. Allen Forte, "Sets and Nonsets in Schoenberg's Atonal Music," *Perspectives of New Music* 11/1 (1972): 43–64.

5. Sonata Forms

1. There is an extensive literature on sonata form. A few of the more important sources are: James Webster, "Sonata Form," in *The New Grove Dictionary of Music and Musicians,* ed. Stanley Sadie (London: Macmillan, 1980); William Newman, *The Sonata in the Classic Era* (Chapel Hill: University of North Carolina Press, 1963; 3d ed., New York: Norton, 1983); William Newman, *The Sonata since Beethoven* (New York: Norton, 1983); Charles Rosen, *Sonata Forms* (New York: Norton, 1980); and Leonard Ratner, *Classic Music: Expression, Form, and Style* (New York: Schirmer Books, 1980). The brief account that follows is based upon these sources, which are in general agreement on the principal points.

2. Edward Cone refers to this as "the tendency of the B to act as a dominant rather than as a leading tone"; see "The Uses of Convention: Stravinsky and His Models," in *Stravinsky: A New Appraisal of His Work,* ed. Paul Henry Lang (New York: Norton, 1963), p. 26.

3. The completion of a large-scale statement of a motive frequently articulates large formal divisions and cadential arrivals in Stravinsky's music. See Joseph N. Straus, "A Principle of Voice Leading in the Music of Stravinsky," *Music Theory Spectrum* 4 (1982): 106–124.

4. This scheme bears an interesting relation to those traditional sonatas in which the recapitulation begins on the subdominant. In such cases (Mozart, Piano Sonata in C-major, K. 545, is one example) the tonal motion in both exposition

and recapitulation rises a fifth, moving first from I to V and then from IV to I. In the case of the Octet, however, the defining interval is a minor second instead of a perfect fifth, and the order of the themes is reversed in the recapitulation.

5. All Octet examples are from the piano reduction prepared by Arthur Lourié.

6. Rosen lists several classical sonata forms that reverse the order of the themes in the recapitulation (*Sonata Forms*, p. 274). The first movement of Mozart's Piano Sonata in D Major, K. 311, is an additional instance.

7. Rosen, *Sonata Forms*, p. 275.

8. This is one of the central contentions of Pieter van den Toorn, *The Music of Igor Stravinsky* (New Haven: Yale University Press, 1983).

9. For a good general description of this work, see Laszlo Somfai, "Analytical Notes on Bartók's Piano Year of 1926," *Studia Musicologica* 26 (1984): 5–58.

10. The use of transpositional schemes and their potential for conflict with the sonata form are discussed in Paul Wilson, "Form and the Quality of Time in Bartók's Piano Sonata," paper presented at the national conference of the Society for Music Theory, Bloomington, Ind., 1986.

11. "T" stands for the integer 10 in this compact notational format.

12. Set-class 4-9 is referred to by Leo Treitler as "Cell Z" in "Harmonic Procedure in the *Fourth Quartet* of Béla Bartók," *Journal of Music Theory* 3/2 (1959): 292–298. Elliott Antokoletz argues that "Cell Z" both permeates the surface of Bartók's String Quartet No. 2 and establishes axes of symmetry that operate at deeper structural levels. See Antokoletz, *The Music of Béla Bartók: A Study of Tonality and Progression in Twentieth-Century Music* (Berkeley: University of California Press, 1984), pp. 93–103 and 149–155.

13. This scale is described by Ernö Lendvai as "model 1:3," after its semitone structure (*Béla Bartók: An Analysis of His Music*, London: Kahn and Averill, 1971).

14. Paul Wilson, "Review of *The Music of Béla Bartók: A Study of Tonality and Progression in Twentieth-Century Music* by Elliott Antokoletz," *Journal of Music Theory* 30/1 (1986): 116–118.

15. Arnold Schoenberg, *Fundamentals of Musical Composition,* ed. Gerald Strang (New York: St. Martin's Press, 1967), p. 200.

16. See David Lewin, "Inversional Balance as an Organizing Force in Schoenberg's Music and Thought," *Perspectives of New Music* 6/2 (1968): 1–21.

17. For a discussion of Schoenberg's sketches for this work, and their implications for its structure, see Martha Hyde, "The Roots of Form in Schoenberg's Sketches," *Journal of Music Theory* 24/1 (1980): 13–19.

18. Lewin, "Inversional Balance," p. 2.

19. If two series are related by inversion, for each element x in the first series there will be a corresponding inversionally related y in the second. The sum of $x + y$ is called an "index number." The inversional axis of the two series is $n/2 - n/2 + 6$, where n is the index number. See John Rahn, *Basic Atonal Theory* (New York: Longman, 1980), pp. 49–51 and 91–95. In the system of arithmetic modulo 12, for which "mod 12" is an abbreviation, any integer larger than 11 can be reduced to an integer from 0 to 11 inclusive by subtracting 12 or a multiple of 12.

20. Lewin makes this analogy in "Inversional Balance," pp. 2–4.

21. Hyde discusses the "multi-dimensional harmonic structure" of the second theme in "The Roots of Form," pp. 15–17.

22. Pierre Boulez, "Schoenberg Is Dead," *The Score* 6 (1952): 20; reprinted (and re-translated) in *Notes of an Apprenticeship*, trans. Herbert Weinstock (New York: Alfred A. Knopf, 1968), p. 272.

23. Martha Hyde has made this point in a series of articles. See, for example, "A Theory of Twelve-Tone Meter," *Music Theory Spectrum* 6 (1984): 14–51, where she shows that Schoenberg articulates meter, including traditional meters, by deploying harmonic units transpositionally or inversionally equivalent to set-classes that are segmental subsets of the row. Schoenberg's meters, she demonstrates, are not arbitrary references to earlier music but grow directly from Schoenberg's individual use of twelve-tone syntax.

24. Alban Berg, "Lecture on *Wozzeck*," in Hans Redlich, *Alban Berg: The Man and His Music* (New York: Abelard-Schuman, 1957), p. 274.

25. See Janet Schmalfeldt, *Berg's Wozzeck: Harmonic Language and Dramatic Design* (New Haven: Yale University Press, 1983), pp. 176–192, and George Perle, *The Operas of Alban Berg*, vol. 1, *Wozzeck* (Berkeley: University of California Press, 1980), pp. 145–155.

6. Six Emblematic Misreadings

1. Charles Rosen describes some of Brahms's imitations of earlier music in "Influence: Plagiarism and Inspiration," *19th-Century Music* 4/2 (1980): 87–100.

2. Harold Bloom, *The Anxiety of Influence* (Oxford: Oxford University Press, 1973), p. 14.

3. A relationship between these works has been pointed out many times. See, for example, Ferenc Bónis, "Quotations in Bartók's Music," *Studia Musicologica* 5 (1963): 355–382.

4. Sieghard Brandenburg, "The Historical Background to the 'Heiliger Dankgesang' in Beethoven's A-Minor Quartet, Op. 132," in *Beethoven Studies*, vol. 3, ed. Alan Tyson (Cambridge: Cambridge University Press, 1982), pp. 161–192.

5. This kind of alternation was a typical aspect of contemporary church-music practice; the interludes were normally improvised by the church organist (Ibid., pp. 185–190).

6. Strangely, Berg altered the chorale slightly in his setting of it, placing the alto passing note after the third beat rather than right on the fourth beat. Although that does not alter the set structure shown in Example 6-6—the D can still be associated with the chord on the fourth beat to create set-class 4-19 (0148)—it does make it more difficult to perceive.

7. Arnold Schoenberg, *Theory of Harmony*, trans. Roy Carter (Berkeley: University of California Press, 1978), pp. 327–328.

8. Ibid., p. 328.

9. In a letter to Schoenberg (August 28, 1935), Berg described the relationship between the series and the chorale as a coincidence (*The Berg-Schoenberg Correspondence*, ed. and trans. Juliane Brand, Christopher Hailey, and Donald Harris, New York: Norton, 1987, p. 466). This is confirmed by Louis Krasner, the violinist for whom the concerto was written: "The Concerto and its unique tone-row was thus, conclusively, not fashioned and composed out of the note-sequence of the Chorale . . . I can attest to the fact that Berg had already set down most of the

Concerto on paper before the ultimate Bach Chorale even came to his attention" ("The Origins of the Alban Berg *Violin Concerto*," in *Alban Berg Studien,* vol. 2, *Alban Berg Symposion Wien 1980, Tagungsbericht,* ed. Rudolf Klein, Vienna: Universal Edition, 1981, p. 108).

10. For an excellent and related study of Berg's setting of Bach's chorale, and of Berg's other uses of precomposed material, see Douglass Green, "Cantus Firmus Techniques in the Concertos and Operas of Alban Berg," in *Alban Berg Studien,* pp. 56–68. See also Arnold Whittall, "The Theorist's Sense of History: Concepts of Contemporaneity in Composition and Analysis," *Proceedings of the Royal Musical Association* 112/1 (1986–87): 1–20.

11. George Perle, "The Secret Program of the *Lyric Suite,*" *International Alban Berg Society Newsletter* 5 (1977): 4–12.

12. Alban Berg, "Nine Pages on the 'Lyric Suite for String Quartet,'" reprinted in *Schoenberg, Berg, Webern: The String Quartets, A Documentary Study,* ed. Ursula v. Rauchhaupt, trans. Eugene Hartzell (Hamburg: Deutsche Grammophon, 1971), p. 111; bracketed material is Berg's.

13. Douglass Green published an elegant transcription of Berg's sketch in his "Letter," *In Theory Only* 8/6 (1985): 4–5. His discussion of the entire movement may be found in "Berg's De Profundis: The Finale of the *Lyric Suite,*" *The International Alban Berg Society Newsletter* 5 (1977): 13–23.

14. Douglass Green was the first to point this out, in "Berg's De Profundis," pp. 19–20.

15. This inversional canon was the discovery of Milton Babbitt. It was discussed in print by Edward Cone in "Analysis Today," *Musical Quarterly* 46 (1960): 172–174 (reprinted in *Problems of Modern Music,* ed. Paul Henry Lang, New York: Norton, 1960, pp. 34–36), and again in "Yet Once More O Ye Laurels," *Perspectives of New Music* 14/2–15/1 (1976): 294–301.

16. Cone, "Yet Once More O Ye Laurels."

17. L. Poundie Burstein, "The Non-Tonic Opening in Classical and Romantic Music" (Ph.D. diss., City University of New York, 1988).

18. The same kind of compression in the final chord of the Symphony in C was described in Chapter 5. For a fuller discussion of tonal polarities embodied within a single sonority, see Joseph N. Straus, "Stravinsky's Tonal Axis," *Journal of Music Theory* 26/2 (1982): 261–290.

19. Paul Johnson has documented the use of the diatonic octad throughout much of Stravinsky's music. See "Cross-Collectional Techniques of Structure in Stravinsky's Centric Music," in *Stravinsky Retrospectives,* ed. Ethan Haimo and Paul Johnson (Lincoln: University of Nebraska Press, 1987), pp. 55–75.

20. Igor Stravinsky, *An Autobiography* (New York: Norton, 1962), p. 124.

21. Bloom, *The Anxiety of Influence,* p. 14.

22. Igor Stravinsky and Robert Craft, *Memories and Commentaries* (Berkeley: University of California Press, 1981), p. 158.

23. "While composing *The Rake's Progress* almost the only music [Stravinsky] would play on the piano and on his gramophone was *Così fan tutte*" (Robert Craft, "A Personal Preface," *The Score* 20, 1957: 11).

24. This idea was suggested by Leo Treitler in a lecture at Queens College, City University of New York, December 1986.

25. As Carl Schachter has observed, "the literature abounds with cases where a

chord functions locally as a V and, at the same time, has a different and more significant long-range function" ("Analysis by Key: Another Look at Modulation," *Music Analysis* 6/3, 1987: 298).

26. This resemblance has been noticed before. See Charles Rosen, *Arnold Schoenberg* (New York: Viking, 1975), pp. 88–89.

27. For a good discussion of the general issues in post-tonal phrase structure, see Christopher Hasty, "Phrase Formation in Post-Tonal Music," *Journal of Music Theory* 28/2 (1984): 167–190.

28. Martha Hyde, "The Roots of Form in Schoenberg's Sketches," *Journal of Music Theory* 24/1 (1980): 16.

29. Arnold Schoenberg, *Structural Functions of Harmony,* ed. Leonard Stein (New York: Norton, 1969), p. 156.

7. Middleground Misreadings

1. The terms "foreground," "middleground," and "background" are not used here in the strict, specific sense they have in Schenker's theory. Rather, they are used informally, to suggest a hierarchy of structural levels.

2. This terminology is from Christopher Hasty, "Segmentation and Process in Post-Tonal Music," *Music Theory Spectrum* 3 (1981): 54–73.

3. The background descent and the smaller middleground descent embedded within it are also confirmed by many other registral and thematic associations not discussed here. See Joseph N. Straus, "A Principle of Voice Leading in the Music of Stravinsky," *Music Theory Spectrum* 4 (1982): 107–112.

4. My Example 7-5 generally follows Felix Salzer's analytical sketch in *Structural Hearing: Tonal Coherence in Music* (New York: Dover, 1982), figure 472.

5. Roy Travis attempts such an approach in "Directed Motion in Schoenberg and Webern," *Perspectives of New Music* 4/2 (1966): 85–89.

6. For a critique of the prolongational model of voice leading applied to this work and to post-tonal music generally, see Joseph N. Straus, "The Problem of Prolongation in Post-Tonal Music," *Journal of Music Theory* 31/1 (1987): 1–22.

7. For a related discussion of registral symmetry in Schoenberg's Op. 19, No. 2, see Jonathan Dunsby and Arnold Whittall, *Music Analysis in Theory and Practice* (New Haven: Yale University Press, 1988), pp. 125–126.

8. Allen Forte makes related observations in "Tonality, Symbol, and Structural Levels in Berg's *Wozzeck,*" *Musical Quarterly* 71/4 (1985): 474–499.

9. The concept of twelve-tone areas is developed in studies by David Lewin. See "Inversional Balance as an Organizing Force in Schoenberg's Music and Thought," *Perspectives of New Music* 6/2 (1968): 1–21; "*Moses und Aron:* Some General Remarks and Analytic Notes for Act I, Scene I," *Perspectives of New Music* 6/1 (1967): 1–17; and "A Study of Hexachord Levels in Schoenberg's Violin Fantasy," *Perspectives of New Music* 6/1 (1967): 18–32.

10. Schoenberg describes his concept of tonal regions in *Structural Functions of Harmony,* ed. Leonard Stein (New York: Norton, 1969), pp. 15–34. Milton Babbitt draws an analogy between tonal regions and twelve-tone areas in *Milton Babbitt: Words about Music,* ed. Stephen Dembski and Joseph N. Straus (Madison: University of Wisconsin Press, 1987), p. 52.

11. A similar procedure informs the beginning of Schoenberg's Piano Concerto,

where the succession of areas exactly duplicates the succession of pitch-classes in the series: 0, 7, 11, 2, 1, 9, 3, 5, 10, 6, 8, 4. After 46 measures in A_o, the music makes its first large-scale move, to A_7. Schoenberg thus hints at traditional motion up a perfect fifth from tonic to dominant. In this piece, however, the motion has an overwhelmingly contextual meaning—it reflects the motion between adjacent pitch-classes in the original series, as does each successive motion from area to area. For a brief discussion of "sets of areas" and "cycles of areas," in both Schoenberg's Op. 33a and Piano Concerto, see William Rothstein, "Linear Structure in the Twelve-Tone System: An Analysis of Donald Martino's *Pianississimo,*" *Journal of Music Theory* 24/2 (1980): 129–166.

12. Heinrich Schenker, *Free Composition,* trans. and ed. Ernst Oster (New York: Longman, 1979), p. 15.

Index

Developing variation, 28

Eliot, T. S.: theory of literary influence, 10–11; and Harold Bloom, 13–14

Forte, Allen, 22, 188n5
Fragmentation: defined, 17; in Stravinsky's analytical outlook, 43; in Webern's orchestration of Bach, *Musical Offering,* 70–71
Fuchs-Robettin, Hanna, 144, 146–147

Gallo, Domenico, Trio Sonata No. 8, 58–60, 63
Generalization, 55, 134; defined, 17; in Schoenberg, Concerto for String Quartet, 54; in Stravinsky, *The Fairy's Kiss,* 55, 57–58; in Stravinsky, *Pulcinella,* 58, 62; in Bartók, Piano Concerto No. 3, 136–137, 138–139; in Berg, Violin Concerto, 139, 140; in Berg, *Lyric Suite,* 146–149; in Stravinsky, *The Rake's Progress,* 159
Glazunov, Alexander, 9
Gropius, Manon, 139
Gropius, Walter, 139
Grundgestalt, 26, 28, 39

Handel, Georg Friedrich, 44, 45, 63; Concerto Grosso Op. 6, No. 7, 48–54
Haydn, Joseph, 3, 4, 6, 96, 132

Influence, theories of: "as generosity," 9, 10–12, 14; "as anxiety," 9, 12–19; and Harold Bloom, 9, 12–19; "as immaturity," 9–10; and T. S. Eliot, 10–11; and Leonard Meyer, 11; and Charles Rosen, 11
Intertextuality, 16
Isaac, Heinrich, 4

Kallman, Chester, 156
Kenosis, 17, 57–58, 152–153
Křenek, Ernst, 26

Landini, Francesco, 4
Lewin, David, 122, 188n5
Liszt, Franz, 22, 44

Machaut, Guillaume de, 4, 8
Mahler, Alma, 139
Mahler, Gustav, 6, 22, 44
Marginalization: defined, 17; in Schoenberg's analyses, 30, 31, 37; in Schoenberg, String Quartet No. 3, 166–168
Marx, Adolf Bernhard, 121, 132
Mendelssohn, Felix, 48

Messiaen, Olivier, 87
Meyer, Leonard, 11
Misreading, 12, 14–15, 16–17, 27, 133; and motivicization, 21, 29; in Schoenberg's analysis of Mozart, Piano Sonata K. 331, 35–36; in Schoenberg's analysis of Mozart, Symphony in G Minor, 36; in Schoenberg's discussion of nonharmonic tones, 36, 140; in Berg's analysis of Schumann, "Traümerei," 40; in Bartók's relationship to the folk tradition, 42; in Schoenberg, Concerto for String Quartet, 48; in Schoenberg's orchestration of Bach, Chorale Prelude "Schmücke dich," 48; in Stravinsky, *The Fairy's Kiss,* 55; in Bartók, Piano Concerto No. 3, 134, 137; in Berg, Violin Concerto, 143; in Berg, *Lyric Suite,* 148; in Stravinsky, Serenade in A, 153; in Stravinsky, *The Rake's Progress,* 155, 156, 161; in Schoenberg, String Quartet No. 3, 161, 162, 168; at the middleground, 170, 173; in Bartók, Piano Sonata, 175; in Schoenberg, Piano Piece Op. 33a, 181
Motivicization, 21, 55; defined, 17; in Schoenberg's analyses of Brahms, 29, 31; in Webern's analytical outlook, 39; in Berg's analysis of Schumann, "Traümerei," 40; in Schoenberg's orchestration of Bach, Chorale Prelude "Schmücke dich," 47–48; in Stravinsky, *Pulcinella,* 58
Mozart, Wolfgang Amadeus, 4, 6, 8, 41, 96, 132, 155; *Così fan Tutte,* 5, 155, 189n15; *Don Giovanni,* 155–161, 168, 189n15; Piano Sonata K. 331, 35–36; Piano Sonata K. 545, 201n4; Symphony in G Minor, 36

Neoclassicism, 6; in relation to progressive music, 1–3, 187n1
Neutralization: defined, 17; in Stravinsky's analytical outlook, 43; in Schoenberg, Concerto for String Quartet, 52; in Stravinsky, *The Fairy's Kiss,* 55; in Stravinsky, *Pulcinella,* 58; in Berg, Violin Concerto, 81; in Schoenberg, "Verbundenheit," from Six Pieces for Male Chorus, 86; in Stravinsky, *Oedipus Rex,* 92; of triads, 95; in Berg, Violin Concerto, 142; of traditional patterns, 169; in Stravinsky, *Symphonies of Wind Instruments,* 172

Pergolesi, Giovanni Battista, 44, 58, 63, 70; *Il Flaminio,* 60–63
Pfitzner, Hans, 40
Pitch-class set theory, 3, 27, 184; in relation to motivic structure, 24

206   INDEX